THE POWER OF CASH

THE POWER
OF CASH

WHY USING PAPER MONEY IS
GOOD FOR YOU AND SOCIETY

JAY L. ZAGORSKY

WILEY

Published by John Wiley & Sons, Inc., Hoboken, New Jersey.
Published simultaneously in Canada.

For general information on our other products and services or for technical support, please contact our Customer Care Department within the United States at (800) 762-2974, outside the United States at (317) 572-3993 or fax (317) 572-4002.

Wiley also publishes its books in a variety of electronic formats. Some content that appears in print may not be available in electronic formats. For more information about Wiley products, visit our web site at www.wiley.com.

Library of Congress Cataloging-in-Publication Data is Available:

ISBN 9781394299911 (Cloth)
ISBN 9781394299928 (ePub)
ISBN 9781394299935 (ePDF)

Cover Design: Jon Boylan
Cover Images: © ONYXprj/Shutterstock, © DesignSensation/Getty Images
Author Photo: Courtesy of the Author

SKY10097974_020625

To Grandma Betty, who started
me on this path, and
to my wonderful wife, Kim,
who helped write down the journey

CONTENTS

CONTENTS

PREFACE

Thirty years ago most people used cash. Today, the world has turned away from cash and toward a variety of electronic payments, like credit cards, Venmo, and cryptocurrencies. Most young people don't even carry paper money. Although many see this movement as a wonderful trend, the digital shift has overlooked dark sides. Eliminating cash harms us in many ways. It causes us to spend more, reduces our privacy, and boosts prices we pay. It hits the poor especially hard by making them pay for bank services they cannot afford. It weakens our national defense by making us vulnerable to cyberattacks and natural disasters. It increases crime because criminals can target us from anywhere in the world.

Countless times technologists have presented the electronic future as utopia, but they have failed to comprehend technology's problems. This book sounds an alarm because once paper money, ATMs, and cash registers are gone it will cost billions to restore them. Cash is an essential tool, and this book shows why preserving it for the long run makes us all better off.

Cash's benefits are needed in every society from the most underdeveloped to the most technologically advanced. This book's goal is not to turn back the hands of time and revert to the days when all transactions were done with paper money. Instead, the goal is to present a large number of simple reasons why all of us should carry and use cash alongside electronic payments.

Proponents of a cashless society have spent huge sums of money convincing us to abandon paper money. In 2023 US financial institutions spent $1 billion advertising just credit cards on television, radio, and the internet. That doesn't include all the money spent sending credit card offers in the mail to people's homes; plastering credit card logos on shop doors, menus, and cash registers; and advertising other cashless payment methods like buy now, pay later; debit cards; or cryptocurrency. This advertising is incredibly effective. I am a business school professor who teaches a lot of very smart executives and MBA students and the vast majority tell me they never carry cash anymore.

Compared to the loud calls to eliminate paper money, the voices of people extolling the virtues of cash are mere whispers. But even whispers are powerful if true. Cash has many benefits, from ensuring national security to enabling the poor to function. My goal is simply to ensure that cash continues to coexist with electronic forms of payment because once cash is gone and we realize what is missing, it will be difficult and very expensive to bring back.

* * *

Why am I writing a book extolling the virtues of paper money? Have I always been a strong advocate for using cash? No, like most of society, I abandoned cash and used electronic methods of payments for a long time. I was seduced by the offer of "free" credit card rewards and did everything possible to maximize my reward points. Yes, I was that person who charged even trivial purchases, like buying a small candy bar.

What did I do with all those points? During one sabbatical from teaching, my wife and I flew three-quarters of the way around the world in business class just using reward points. Isn't that reason enough to abandon cash: the opportunity to travel for free to exotic places?

It's not, because nothing in life is free. Businesses exist to make money; when they offer something for "free," customers pay for it some other way. As I will show in this book, reward cards are seductive but when analyzed closely, they are actually reverse Robin Hoods – stealing from the financially unsophisticated, who are mainly poor, and giving to the financially sophisticated, who are often rich.

My conversion to being a cash advocate started in 2010 when the Boston Federal Reserve, part of the US's central bank, called and asked me to join a team of unpaid advisors helping to create a "Survey of Consumer Payment Choice." It is important to note that anything in this book is my own view and in no way represents positions of the Federal Reserve System.

In addition to their well-known task of setting interest rates, central banks send coins and paper money to and from local banks. To understand how much currency needs to keep circulating, the Federal Reserve wants to understand how consumers pay for purchases. They debated the best means of collecting data and wanted guidance on designing and fielding a survey. They recruited me because of my business school, survey, and wealth research expertise.

When I joined the Survey's board of advisors I didn't know much about how people used cash or trends in electronic payments. By the time the board of advisors was disbanded in 2018, I began to understand how simple actions like buying a small candy bar using a generous rewards credit card likely wiped out the store owner's profit, because of the high card processing fees incurred.

I began publishing my thoughts, primarily as short online articles. Then I was asked to review a book called *The Curse of Cash*, written by Kenneth Rogoff, the International Monetary Fund's chief economist. His book asked a simple question: has the time come for developed economies to eliminate most paper currency?

Rogoff believes cash has outlived its usefulness and should be regarded as a curse in modern economies. After reading his book and thinking about what I had learned while studying the Boston Federal Reserve's data, I came to the opposite conclusion. Cash is not a curse that should be eliminated; instead, cash has some problems, but also many advantages even in a digital economy.

As I studied the issue and became a full-fledged cash advocate I realized no book existed that laid out simply why cash is a powerful tool, so I began to write. Although I am an academic who specializes in business data, this book uses stories in every chapter to get many of the points across, rather than a massive number of graphs, charts, and details.

I learned about the power of telling stories from my grandmother Betty, who was a master storyteller. She also was a strong advocate for using cash. Grandma had an amazing brown wooden dresser in her bedroom. As a very small child I would stand on the chair next to this dresser and watch as she opened the top drawer. The left side had a large tray filled with shiny coins lined up in neat rows from pennies to large dollar coins. She would often take a few out. In the summer we would take these coins and walk down the block to a store called Spritzie's. Giving a few coins to the man behind the counter would result in lemon or watermelon slush: wonderful, shaved ice mixed with sugar and syrup. In cooler weather we would take the coins and walk a few blocks further to a store selling toys.

As a small child I was fascinated by that tray. By taking shiny coins out, treats and toys magically appeared in my life. More important, using coins showed me a basic financial lesson: the bigger the slush or toy purchase, the more money was needed. This simple concept is tougher to explain to children in today's cashless world.

I was also fascinated by some of the other walks Grandma and I took. Sometimes we would walk to places where Grandma could "pay the bills." I especially remember her paying the telephone bill. This seemed silly to my young mind because the phone was already in Grandma's home. On most walks when we used money we got something in return. On these walks we got nothing in return!

Grandma, and many members of her generation, were among the last people to function in a purely cash economy. They used cash for everything. Today, these stories sound cute and nostalgic. Many people have trouble imagining using just cash to make purchases. They have trouble because over my lifetime the world has changed rapidly from one based on paper currency to electronic forms. In some countries like Sweden and China, cash is rarely used. Did we lose something in the transition? The rest of this book argues both individuals and society did, with the goal of convincing you to use and hold cash more often. You don't have to go to Grandma Betty's extreme, but I am sure she would not mind.

Boston, Massachusetts, 2024

CHAPTER ONE

INTRODUCTION AND OVERVIEW

A sudden loud noise wakes you from a deep sleep. What was that? You reach for your bedside lamp but it won't turn on. Suddenly your bed is shaking. Earthquake! Your lamp dances across the bedside table and falls off, crashing on the floor. You clutch the sheets and wait for the quaking to stop. Then you slip out of bed and walk carefully to the bathroom to splash water on your face and wake up fully.

A dribble of water comes out of the faucet and then stops. Looking out the window you see your neighbor's house has a huge crack. Part of the roof is hanging over their front door. You pull on some clothes, thinking fast as you feel another tremor shake the floor. No electricity, no water, more quakes coming – you need to get out of here!

In the dark you quickly collect your phone, computer, wallet, and keys. What else do you need? You grab your medications, and some warmer clothes, just in case. Wishing for coffee, you grab some juice and leftover dinner from the refrigerator. You back your car out of the driveway, listening to the news on the radio. The earthquake destroyed the city near you and many roads are impassable. Which way should you go?

Two houses away you see your elderly neighbor waving frantically from her front steps. You roll down your window and ask how she is. Her house is badly damaged and she begs you to take her with you away from this dangerous place. You agree and she rolls a small suitcase to your car and climbs in.

You drive to the route recommended by the radio broadcast. Along both sides of the road you see fallen trees, cracked buildings, and dazed people. The streetlights and traffic lights are out but there aren't many cars of the road yet. You hope you can make it to the next city where your sister lives.

After driving for about an hour you need to get gasoline. Up ahead you see a service station and pull into the line of cars waiting for the pumps. Thank heavens they are still working! You leave your neighbor with the car and go in to the convenience store to buy some food and coffee. At the checkout you present your credit card only to be told, "Cash only. The phones are out and the credit card machine is down."

Shocked, you stumble back to the car to tell your neighbor you can't buy anything. Not even gasoline! She says, "I have cash. My daughter told me two weeks ago I should always have some for an emergency so I got some. And I think this qualifies as an emergency!"

Thank goodness you brought her along! You thought she would be a drain but here she is saving the day. You fill the gasoline tank and buy sandwiches, fruit, and bottled water, along with that coffee you need so badly. Now you can make it to your sister's house. What would you have done without cash?

You haven't used cash in months. You either use your phone for electronic payments, or tap a credit card on a keypad. But the earthquake has knocked out the telecommunications that electronic payments require.

So many people have, like you, shifted to relying on electronic payments. But when a huge hurricane, raging wildfire, towering tsunami, or colossal solar storm knocks out electricity or telecommunications, electronic payments don't work. When a hacker takes control of central computer systems, your credit cards, debit cards, and Bitcoin can no longer be accepted in payment for food, transportation, or services. That's when cash is a lifesaver. Cash works when your phone runs out of battery, or your phone falls out of your pocket into the toilet, which happens more often than you think. Cash even works when it's soaking wet. In today's electronic payment world having cash gives you resilience.[1]

SHIFT AWAY FROM CASH

The world has seen a dramatic change in just a few years in how people use and conceive of money. Until the end of the 1900s people primarily used coins and paper money. Then, beginning in the early 2000s, people started abandoning paper money and switching to electronic forms of payment like credit cards, debit cards, cryptocurrency, and mobile payments.

The switch is not happening at the same rate everywhere. It depends on which country you live in. Places like China and Sweden are currently almost entirely cashless. Sweden has abandoned paper money to such a large extent that the Swedish government passed legislation forcing banks to handle cash. China has so thoroughly adopted mobile payments that some tourists try to get a Chinese cell phone number to effectively pay for purchases when visiting the country.

Other places in the world have not abandoned cash. Japan is still a cash-dependent society, where making large purchases with paper money is normal. If you want to purchase a home or apartment in Argentina, most transactions are done in cash. However, because Argentina's economy and currency are unstable, most sellers want the funds in US paper money. Around the world many rural communities, often located far from banks, still primarily use cash for transactions.

The abandonment of cash is both generational and based on income. Older individuals who grew up using cash still use it at a much higher rate than younger people. Poor people are using cash more often than the rich.

Although the rush away from cash is happening at different speeds around the world, it is clear that paper money is being abandoned from all directions. Restaurants, stores, and even many types of transportation are steadily preventing customers from using cash. For example, airlines used to accept cash to purchase in-flight food and drink. Today no major airline accepts cash for in-flight purchases. Not only do airlines no longer accept cash to buy a snack while flying but also it is difficult to pay for a plane ticket with cash. Decades ago many airlines had ticket offices located in major cities that accepted cash. Today many of those offices are shut and customers are directed to buy a ticket on the internet using a debit or credit card.

WHY THE SHIFT?

The shift is happening because there are many powerful groups pushing to get rid of cash.

Credit card companies like Visa, Mastercard, and American Express; financial service companies like PayPal, Afterpay, and Klarna; and a host of smaller financial startups want you to use electronic payments instead of cash because they get a small cut of every purchase. Although the percentage each takes is not large, a small percentage times billions of purchases adds up to huge amounts of money.

Banks and stores want you to use electronic payments because they know people who use electronic payments overspend. Stores are in business to sell. Encouraging people to overspend is a simple way of boosting sales. Cash, for reasons discussed later in the book, restrains people's spending, and electronic payments do not. Banks encourage overspending because after overspending, people borrow money, on which banks make billions each year in interest payments.

Companies selling on the internet also don't want you to use cash. It is impossible to hand paper money through a computer or phone screen to them. Instead, getting your financial information like a credit card or bank account number is far more efficient for them. Giant internet retailers want the online shopping experience to be as fast and frictionless as possible. Storing your financial information in their database enables them to offer one-click shopping. This sounds wonderful, but heavy internet shoppers need to ask themselves – how often do packages show up and you don't remember what you ordered?

Last, governments and the world's central banks, which print and distribute paper money, are also encouraging the trend away from cash. Many government officials believe most cash is used by criminals to hide their activities. The idea that eliminating cash will boost tax receipts, reduce crime, and eliminate corruption is demolished later in this book, but not all public policy decisions are based on facts or data. Central bankers dislike paper money because it reduces their ability to control a country's macro economy.

KEY QUESTION – IS THE SHIFT GOOD?

The shift to electronic payments is wonderful for credit card companies, banks, high-tech companies, and governments. However, what is good for them is not necessarily good for either you or society. Every large-scale societal shift has both good and bad points. People and companies benefiting from electronic payments are trumpeting the positives and ignoring the negatives.

This book shows the overlooked power for individuals and society of continuing to use paper money. The book's goal is to puncture the fairy-tale world presented by the world's largest banks, high-tech companies, and governments by showing that keeping and using "old-fashioned" cash has many positive aspects, ranging from improving a country's self-defense to helping individuals spend less.

The book is needed for three reasons. First, because of immense profits many types of businesses have a strong incentive to convince you that using paper money is bad and electronic payments are good. Next time you take a flight, count how many ads there are for credit cards and other cash alternatives. There are giant billboards, leaflets in the plane's seat pockets, flight crew announcements, and even small ads snuck into places like napkins and baggage carts. Then try counting the number of ads trying to convince you to use paper money. There are none. No advertising is pushing back against this tidal wave of persuasion.

Second, people's financial literacy is low and falling. FINRA (Financial Industry Regulatory Authority), a US organization responsible for protecting investors, found the typical American could only answer half of its basic financial questions correctly, down from 60% a dozen years ago. Reduced knowledge combined with increasingly complex payment choices enables businesses to take advantage of consumers. Cash, with no bells, whistles, or fine print protects consumers better than any watchdog agency.[2]

The last and most important reason for this book is that humans overreact. We quickly declare revolutionary new things are better than the old. Often the old is discarded. However, over time the flaws and problems of the revolutionary new product or idea show up and people reconsider what they have lost.

One of the simplest examples is social media. When social media first started, people hailed it as a revolution whose use would enable people to reconnect; find new friends; deepen relationships; provide access to unfiltered, unbiased news; and boost democracy. Today social media is blamed for almost every type of social ill from alienation to bullying, the rise of hate speech, and fringe groups.

After the overreaction, the world often sees the value of older technologies. While writing this book I have been amazed at the resurgence in old technologies, like manual typewriters and even fountain pens. All were considered obsolete until recently. Now they are coming back. The revival is occurring because now consumers understand that although digital technologies have many advantages, they also have unexpected problems and faults.[3]

The problem with overreaction is that once the old methods are discarded it is very costly to bring them back. One of my favorite examples of an old technology experiencing a startling resurgence is vinyl records. Recording Industry Association of America (RIAA) figures show vinyl records were king of the recorded music industry until the end of the 1970s. Record sales plummeted in the 1980s, first with the advent of compact discs and then with portable MP3 players. The promise of these digital technologies led me to sell my top-of-the-line record player and an extensive record collection built up over decades. By 2005 new vinyl records were almost extinct with total sales of just $14 million.

However, since that low, US vinyl album sales have been rejuvenated as people recognize their benefits. In 2023, record sales were $1.4 billion, which is 100 times larger than sales about two decades earlier. I am now tempted to switch back to vinyl because today's digital music files just don't have the same dynamism and life of records. However, because all of my equipment and music is gone it will cost me a small fortune to rebuild.

It is the same with cash. If society stops using paper money then cash registers, ATMs, coin counting machines, safes, armored cars, and even many bank branches will disappear. Bringing them back will be very costly once people understand what is lost by eliminating cash. If society does not overreact and uses both electronic money and "old-fashioned" cash simultaneously then we can maintain the resiliency and benefits paper money provide.

Digital technologies promise a utopian future. The world's experience with digital money has shown it has advantages, like speed and convenience. However, with these benefits come a loss of privacy, higher costs, and a total reliance on a network of computers, telecommunications equipment, and electricity, among many other concerns.

Is cash perfect? No, but neither are electronic payments and money. Let me be clear, this book does *not* argue that we should abandon electronic money. I use credit cards at times, pay some bills online, and occasionally use my cell phone to send money. But I also use paper money.

The goal of this book is to convince you to not abandon cash. The book's message is simple: use cash as well as electronic money when making payments and saving. Doing this will provide many powerful benefits to both you and society.

THE SYNOPSIS: A DOZEN REASONS CASH IS POWERFUL

Life is busy. There is never enough time to do everything we want. Reading books is no exception. I personally read bits and pieces of nonfiction books and do not always read books from cover to cover. For those of you who also jump around when reading a book, here are my personal favorite dozen reasons why cash is powerful. There are far more than a dozen reasons in this book, but this is a quick synopsis and guide.

For those who read straight through, this book contains six parts. The first section lays out the facts and figures of the transition from using cash to a cashless society. The second part discusses why using cash benefits society, the third explains the benefits for individuals, and the fourth shows how cash helps the vulnerable. The fifth section explains why cash is not causing crime, but instead is a symptom of criminal activity. The sixth section explains how cash provides limits on government's control, and the conclusion provides some simple ideas for boosting cash use. For straight-through readers the following reasons provide a preview.

The Dozen Reasons Why Paper Money Is Powerful for You and Society

1. *Cash works all the time.* The cashless society is dependent on electricity, communications, and computers. For cashless transactions to work, the electrical grid must provide stable uninterrupted power, the telecommunication network must transfer all messages seamlessly, and computers and their data must be secure. When any one of these three parts is broken, cashless transactions do not happen, but cash still works. Chapter 4 details how cashless payments work and shows how cashless transactions depend on three fragile pieces of technology.

2. *Cash reduces problems caused by major natural disasters.* Mother Nature is hitting the world with increasingly frequent and costly catastrophes. Natural disasters are the very moment when people are most desperate to spend money. In the face of impending hurricanes, typhoons, fires, and earthquakes people are trying to flee or buy supplies. After a natural disaster many people are frantically spending money rebuilding their homes and lives. During and after natural disasters, cashless transactions work poorly or not at all. Paper money, however, does work because it does not need power, connections, or computers. Chapter 5 delves into the problems of cashless societies facing increasing natural disasters.

3. *Cash protects a country from external enemies.* War has been a concern for thousands of years. One common method when waging war is to soften up an enemy's population. In previous generations this was done with tactics like naval blockades, starving cities into submission, and bombarding military and civilian targets. In a cashless society a simpler and more effective method is to deny people access to their money and the ability to spend it. Destroying the ability to move electronic money around in a cashless society grinds an economy to a halt by making it impossible to buy food, pay for medical care, or use transportation. A current example is Russia's repeated bombing of Ukraine's electrical grid. No electricity in Ukraine makes cashless transactions impossible. By using cash, Ukraine is thwarting Russia's intentions. Chapter 6 looks into how cash boosts national defense.

4. *Cash protects society from rogue individuals and criminal groups.* It is not just enemy nations that sap a country's resilience. Hackers and criminals have broken into networks that run our banking, transportation, health, communication, and other crucial infrastructures. Because electronic payments are dependent on computer systems, threats that shut down or compromise the massive databases holding our financial data can cripple a country's economy. As an example of why shifting to a cashless society makes a nation more vulnerable, just imagine the following: your bank and all the other financial institutions where you keep money have all accounts locked by ransomware. You might have lots of money in those accounts. However, until all the financial institutions come back online, you are broke. How will you make purchases if you do not have cash? Chapter 6 has details.

5. *Cash helps people spend less money.* Cash helps control impulse spending because we experience a tiny amount of regret on giving up paper money. Tapping a card, waving a phone, or clicking on a

link does not feel like spending real money, so we spend more. Cash also provides a hard budget. When there is no more paper money in your pocket you are forced to stop spending. Cashless methods break this hard budget and enable more spending to happen. Businesses love this feature, which is why so many accept a variety of payments. Chapter 7 looks at spending in more detail.

6. *Cash gives you privacy.* Cash is an anonymous means of payment. The cashless society generates a large amount of data with every transaction. It is clear people don't want to be associated with illegal purchases. No one wants a permanent record of buying illegal drugs like heroin or spending money on prostitutes or escort services. However, spending privacy goes well beyond purchasing illegal products or services. Not everyone wants others to know they are using weight loss products, coloring their hair, or buying lottery tickets. Privacy is covered in Chapter 9.

7. *Cash reduces the price you pay.* Cash hides both what you bought and how much you paid, but every cashless transaction generates data. One of the most valuable aspects of this information is the ability to create custom ads and prices for each customer. Some customers are willing to pay more, but currently don't have to. Your buying patterns can enable businesses to charge you higher prices. Pricing is covered in Chapter 10.

8. *Cash helps the poor.* A cashless society marginalizes the poor and those who are unbanked. Not everyone in society has or can get an account at a bank or financial institution. Moving to a cashless society forces all people to get bank accounts. For the rich and middle class, bank accounts typically have no out-of-pocket cost. However, for the poor, bank accounts are expensive. Bank accounts with little money in them typically have an up-front monthly charge. The up-front charge, overdraft, and other fees make banking costly for poor people and those living paycheck to paycheck.

As one advocate told me, "the fees charged to my poor clients are predatory." Chapter 11 focuses on the problems the poor have in the cashless society.

9. *Cash enables charity.* How often have you been asked for "spare change" or "can you help us with a small donation?" With cash if you are feeling charitable you pull some money from your pocket and continue on your way. In a cashless society making small donations and helping the poorest of the poor is difficult. Without cash what are you going to do: send money via PayPal, Venmo, or some other instant payment program? The person or group asking for change might not have a phone or an account. Charity is talked about in more detail in Chapter 11.

10. *Cash makes the lives of immigrants and tourists easier.* Immigrants and foreign tourists don't have local financial connections. For them it is easier to do things in cash than using the cashless system. Both groups often face language barriers. Electronic transactions come with a host of things that must be read, understood, and signed. With cash you only need to recognize a few commonly used digits. Making it easy for people to pay for lodging, food, and entertainment without excess fees and surcharges boosts local economies. Chapter 12 discusses paper money, immigrants, refugees, and tourism.

11. *Cash prevents governments from controlling protestors, minorities, and opposition groups.* A cashless society gives governments the power to shut down dissent quickly. Shutting off access to cashless payments and financial accounts is a simple way of restraining protests or punishing groups and individuals. You think this only happens in dictatorships or in countries most people cannot find on a map? In Canada truck drivers protested government policies by driving their tractor trailers slowly around Parliament while honking their horns for days. The government crushed the

demonstrations by shutting off the drivers' access to their money, which meant no food, gas, or ability to post bail for the protestors. With cash the truckers could have continued to dissent. Chapter 17 has other examples of government control.

12. *Cash ensures central bankers do not have unfettered ability to wreak economic havoc on the vulnerable.* For most of history people who saved money were paid interest and people who borrowed money owed interest. Saving was rewarded and borrowing was punished. Based on these rules in preparation for old age, many people saved money during their working years and lived off the interest and principal in retirement. Electronic money has turned this entire system on its head by allowing central banks to push interest rates below zero. Negative interest rates were common in Europe from 2014 to 2022 and also in Japan for many years. Negative rates punish anyone who saves money because a negative rate means savers have a portion of their money confiscated every month. Borrowers who get negative interest loans are rewarded for spending. Central bankers use negative rates to spur spending. However, what is good for a central banker is not good for the many elderly people who are concerned that spending too much today will leave them destitute tomorrow. Cash puts a brake on central bank policies, because taking paper money out of banks prevents central bankers from pushing interest rates much below zero. Chapter 17 goes into detail about negative interest rate problems.

CONCLUSION

Although I've identified my top dozen reasons, I always urge my business school students to give customers a bit more than expected. The bakery industry codified this by giving customers a "baker's dozen," which is

13 items instead of 12. Following that model, my 13th reason is *cash is fun to hold and use.*

At the beginning of my academic career I was very poor. Because of that experience, today I get a thrill out of holding a wad of cash and using it to make purchases. Holding these bills in my hand is fun because they are a concrete signal I have money and can now afford to buy things.

Beyond cash being fun, it provides clearer feedback on how well or poorly you are doing financially than is available in a cashless world. Many of us have no clue how rich or poor we really are. I wrote a series of research papers comparing people's perceptions of their wealth with reality. The findings were dramatic; the vast number of people underestimated their financial situation and the average person believed they only had about 62¢ for every $1 of wealth they actually held. One reason for the underestimation is for many people their paycheck, bank account, or retirement savings are just numbers that exist as a string of zeros and ones in some remote digital database. Having and using paper money makes your financial situation real instead of abstract.[4]

Many pundits have predicted the demise of cash. Hopefully, these 13 reasons, plus all the others in this book, will convince you of the power cash has over electronic forms of money. When you are convinced, join me in using paper money more frequently in your personal and business life. This will ensure cash does not become a thing of the past but, like vinyl records, enjoys a resurgence as an important method of paying and saving around the world.

SECTION I

IS CASH DISAPPEARING?

T he next two chapters look at data on how fast paper money is disappearing from society. Chapter 2 investigates trends in cash use for payments and Chapter 3 investigates cash use for savings.

Chapter 2 shows that although cash was once king for making purchases, it has been dethroned. The shift from cash to electronic payments was accelerated during the COVID epidemic, when people did not want to touch money. Chapter 3 shows something rather startling. Cash is not disappearing! Instead, the amount of paper currency in circulation has exploded.

Together, these two chapters point out that people are switching from using cash to buy things to holding it in case of emergencies. This presents a major conundrum. If no one uses cash for daily purchases, businesses lose the ability to handle it so when an emergency happens, no business accepts paper money.

CHAPTER TWO

IS CASH DISAPPEARING?

THE CASE
OF SPENDING

I'm sure you have seen pronouncements that cash is dead, or predictions that cash will become obsolete. Are these statements accurate?[1]

Although you might know many people who have stopped carrying cash, is it really on the way out? The first step to solving any problem is to quantify it. There is an old expression: "You cannot fix what you cannot measure."

How can we measure if cash is disappearing? We can track the percentage of people using cash over time. People use paper money for two primary reasons: to spend it and to save it. This chapter looks at the data to see how cash is faring in the fight over what methods people use to spend their money, and Chapter 3 focuses on savings.[2]

A national US survey highlights the dramatic shift away from using paper money for spending. It asked people if they were holding any cash.

In 2015 about one-fifth (17.1%) said they were not carrying any paper money. By 2022 the figure was over one-third (34.6%). In less than a decade the percentage of people walking around without any paper money doubled! If people don't carry cash they cannot experience any of its benefits.[3]

Before jumping into more numbers, let me tell you a couple of quick stories highlighting this transformation. When alternatives to cash, like credit cards, first started there very stringent rules about who got cards. Neil Armstrong was the first man to walk on the moon. For this feat he became internationally famous, got one of New York City's largest ticker tape parades, and received medals from 17 countries. Five years after his historic feat he applied for a Diners Club card, one of the first national credit cards. Armstrong was rejected because he didn't have enough income.

After walking on the moon Armstrong quit the space program and became a relatively low-paid professor at the University of Cincinnati. A half-century ago, immense fame did not help get him a credit card. The Armstrong family actually got the last laugh in this story. After Neil's death the family auctioned off his memorabilia and a collector paid $30 thousand for just the credit card rejection letter.[4]

While a half-century ago getting approved to use a cash alternative was tough, today it is trivial. After my father-in-law died, his mailing address was changed to my home. Five years after his death we continued to receive credit card offers in his name. Hopefully, banks investigate if a dead man decides to accept their "preapproved" offers, but other types of electronic payments do not. Cryptocurrencies attracted early interest because they were completely anonymous. When they first appeared, no name, address, or other identifying information was needed to buy or sell them.

The increasing ease of obtaining alternatives to cash is one reason why paper money is disappearing in daily transactions around the world. For those people who don't like numbers, feel free to skip to the conclusion of this chapter. For the rest, let's first take a look at which countries use cash the most and least. Then we will dive into who is still using cash and why it is important.

CASH USE AROUND THE WORLD

The fight over cash is happening all across the world, but the results of each battle vary widely. In some countries, like Sweden and China, the fight is over and the anti-cash forces have won. In other places, like Japan, pro-cash forces still have the upper hand.

Data showing which countries are the most and least dependent on cash are tracked by the Bank for International Settlements (BIS). The BIS, headquartered in Switzerland, is the world's bank for central banks. BIS has been tracking data on the shift from cash to cashless payments for years. One of their key indicators is the amount of cash in circulation as a percentage of GDP.[5]

We can use this ratio as a proxy representing cash demand. Countries that use a lot of cash to run their economy have a high percentage value, and cashless economies have a low percentage value.[6]

Figure 2.1 graphs the ratio of cash in circulation as a percentage of GDP for some of the world's major economies. The heavy cash-using countries are on the figure's left side. The more cashless societies are on the right.

Japan, at almost one-quarter (23%), is the most cash-intensive country, followed by India. The least cash-intensive country is Sweden at about 1% (1.3%), followed by the United Kingdom.

The United States, at about 10% (9.7%), is in the middle of the graph. Comparing the most to the least cash-intensive shows Japan uses about

Figure 2.1   Cash in circulation as a percentage of GDP: 2020.

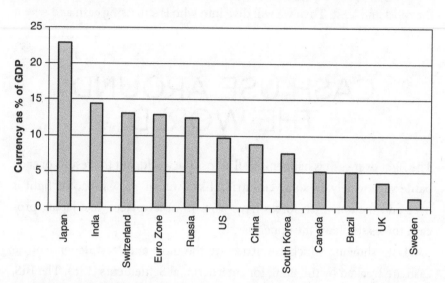

18 times as much cash as Sweden to run its economy. The United States, in the middle of the pack, uses about seven times as much cash as Sweden.

WHY DO SOME PLACES USE CASH MORE THAN OTHERS?

There is no simple explanation why people in some countries love cash and others do not. One example of dramatic differences is seen comparing two European neighbors, the Netherlands and Germany. Cash is widely used in Germany, but not in the Netherlands. The two countries share a long common border, both use the euro as currency, and quite a few people in the Netherlands speak German. There is, however, a clear divide in cultural attitudes toward the preferred payment method.

Dutch friends tell me, "We hate cash and Germans love it." This succinctly summarizes the cultural differences. However, for those interested in specific numbers, both country's central banks ran comparable surveys tracking cash use. In 2021 only 4% of Germans did not carry any cash.[7] When Germans were asked their preferred method of payment, roughly 30% said they liked paying with cash. The Germans don't lack access to electronic methods. Ninety-nine percent of Germans said they had a debit card, over half of all Germans stated they had a credit card, and about 30% stated they held multiple cards. Germans are fully able to use electronic payments, but many do not like to use them.

In that same year the Dutch national bank surveyed its population about cash use and found 24% stated, "No, I don't usually carry banknotes."[8] Six times as many Dutch people did not carry cash as Germans. It is not only people in the Netherlands who do not like cash but also businesses. The Dutch central bank commissions annual surveys to track business acceptance. The most recent survey found over half of all parking garages and lots, a third of all cinemas, and a quarter of pharmacies did not take cash. The pharmacy figure is the most disturbing because it means people who need medicine and only have cash in the Netherlands might not get the drugs they need.

No specific underlying reason for this split has currently been pinpointed. What is not driving the differences is either cell phone or internet penetration, which makes it easy to perform mobile banking and payments. Cell phone penetration in Germany is actually higher than it is in the Netherlands, and the two countries have roughly similar internet use rates.[9]

Government rules and regulations are a possible reason why people in some countries use or do not use cash. El Salvador is a small Central American country whose official paper currency is the US dollar. The country's president, however, is trying to wean the country off US paper money to reduce Washington's influence on the El Salvadorian economy.

To wean the country, in summer 2021 El Salvador declared the cryptocurrency Bitcoin as legal tender for all transactions. To boost cryptocurrency use, the government created its own app and gave away free cryptocurrency to any citizen who downloaded the program.[10]

After three years, El Salvador's policies clearly favoring electronic payments over cash have had no impact. A recent news article states, "To date, most Salvadorans ignore Bitcoin. They worry about the cryptocurrency's volatility in a cash-based economy where many live hand-to-mouth."[11]

Figure 2.1 shows stark differences in cash use between countries. Although the reasons for these differences are not yet clear, these differences ensure there are many more countries that will have battles between cash and electronic payments.

TRENDS IN PAPER MONEY USE

What is happening over time in paper money use? Let's first look at a low-cash-use country, the United Kingdom. The British Retail Consortium is a trade group that tracks the type of payments made in everything from the smallest shops to the largest stores across the UK. In 2015 the Consortium found almost half (47.2%) of people paying retailers used paper money to make a purchase. By 2022 the figure was down to one-fifth (18.8%). In less than a decade the use of cash by British retail customers was more than cut in half! As Chapter 10 points out, this denies UK businesses the lower costs of handling cash, which boosts prices for consumers.

People in the United States, a country that falls in the middle of the spectrum in Figure 2.1, are also steadily shifting away from paying using paper money. In the United States, a Federal Reserve's survey shows the percentage of payments done using cash is steadily declining. In 2015 the typical person made about one-third of their transactions in cash. By 2022 the number had fallen in half to just over 17%.[12]

Not only is the number of cash transactions decreasing but the average amount spent when using cash is also falling. In October 2015, the typical US adult made $470 worth of cash payments per month, after adjusting for inflation. However, by 2022, just eight years later, the amount spent had fallen by about half, to $238.

The drop in cash spending is not due to a reduction in overall spending. In 2015 the survey found the typical adult spent $4,500 during October after adjusting for inflation. By 2022 spending was over $5,000. Over this eight-year period, overall spending rose while the amount spent using cash dropped, showing cash use is falling out of favor.

WHO IS LEADING THE US SHIFT?

Not surprisingly, the young are leading the charge away from cash. The young are the least likely to report having any paper money on their person. In 2015, when the survey was first started, one out of every four people between the ages of 18 and 34 held no cash. Among older people the answer was very different. Among people over the age of 55 at that time more than 90% of people said they were holding cash.

Although older people are more likely to carry cash than younger, all age groups are moving away from cash. However, the young are moving the fastest. From 2015 to 2022, a span of just eight years, the group aged 18–34 went from one out every four people not having cash to almost one out of every two people. The trend of not holding cash extended even to the oldest group. In 2015 about 10% did not carry any cash, but by 2022 it had risen to one-quarter.

I see these trends in my own family. My grandmother Betty, to whom this book is dedicated, used only cash throughout her long life. Credit cards, debit cards, and even checks were not things she used or cared about. However, cash is not as beloved by the younger generations. I once owed a few $100 to my youngest child. To pay the debt I tried to hand over some cash only to be asked for an electronic transfer instead. However, attitudes are flexible. After reading various drafts of this book, that same child became a cash convert and now uses paper money frequently.

What do these age differences mean? If a country needs to revert to cash, like during a natural disaster, the young have the least experience and ability to make the transition.

* * *

The falling demand for cash is seen in other types of data beyond querying individuals. The US Federal Reserve runs a payments study every three years that asks banks how often people used their ATMs and the amount of money withdrawn. Table 2.1 shows ATM visits peaked in 2009, when about six billion withdrawals happened. Six billion means on average every person in the United States made almost 20 withdrawals a year. A dozen years later, in 2021 the number of withdrawals fell by over one-third to 3.7 billion withdrawals, or about 11 withdrawals a year.[13]

Table 2.1   US ATM Usage

Year	Number withdrawals in billions	Average amount withdrawn	Total withdrawn in billions
2006	5.9	$100	$580
2009	6.0	$108	$650
2012	5.8	$118	$690
2015	5.2	$146	$760
2018	5.1	$156	$800
2021	3.7	$198	$730

The middle column of Table 2.1 shows that although the number of withdrawals fell, the average amount taken out steadily rose. In 2021 the average withdrawal was almost $200 ($198), double the amount ($100) taken out 15 years earlier in 2006.[14]

The right-hand column of Table 2.1 shows the total impact. Even though people are withdrawing more money, the reduction in ATM visits has resulted in a falling demand for cash, with total money withdrawn from ATMs peaking about 2018.

The number of physical ATMs peaked in 2019 at close to a half-million machines, but has fallen since then. Plummeting withdrawals and a falling number of machines are a problem because in modern society ATMs are the primary place people obtain cash when banks are closed. Maintaining an ATM is expensive for banks because they need to be periodically filled with paper money, plus they need servicing, cleaning, and security. When ATMs are not used, banks take them out of service.[15]

What do all the numbers in this section tell us? Society is seeing a reduction in the number of places to get cash. If we want to ensure cash availability, society needs to keep ATMs in service!

IS CASH STILL USED FOR SMALL PAYMENTS?

Coins annoy many people. I have a number of students who refuse to use paper money because it means getting small amounts of change back that they are forced to carry. Other people do not like coins because they are upset the US government loses money minting low-value change. Today, each 1¢ coin costs the government about 3¢ to make, and each 5¢ coin costs about 10¢ to mint.

Although coin haters are vocal, the key question is not how loud people clamor but whether the silent majority are still using small denomination coins and cash. An unlikely source of information shows how much people are actively using pocket change – the Transportation Security Administration (TSA). Yes, the same people who screen US airport flyers at checkpoints can answer if people are still using coins because each year the TSA provides a detailed report showing how much money is left behind at checkpoints. A decreasing amount of change left behind means fewer people have coins in their pockets, and a steady or increasing amount would show people are still carrying coins.[16]

TSA records show people left behind half a million dollars in 2012. By 2023 the figure doubled to almost $1 million. However, these raw figures need two adjustments to accurately track trends in coins lost. First, the numbers need to be adjusted for inflation, because prices have risen over time. Second, there needs to be an adjustment for the number of people flying, which also increased over time.

Adjusting for both inflation and the number of people screened shows almost no difference in the amount of money lost. In 2012 about $1.10 in coins was lost for every 1,000 people screened. In 2023 about one penny more, or $1.11, was lost per 1,000 people. This suggests coins are still being kept and used for making small payments.

CONCLUSION

I watch how people pay. It seems no matter where I am in the world, fewer people are using cash when checking out of brick-and-mortar stores, paying for meals in restaurants, or using public transportation. Farmers' markets, pop-up shops, and even street vendors are now able to accept electronic payments. Credit cards, debit cards, smartphone apps, cryptocurrency, and other means of electronic payments all are replacing paper money.

This reduction in cash use makes words describing purchases seem archaic. In the United States people talk about paying at the "cash register," but few people use cash once there. Another term for paying is to "check out." However, paper check use has plummeted around the world and some major retailers are refusing to accept checks in the "check-out" line.[17]

Although cash use is falling, there is a big advantage for merchants when customers make purchases using paper money: businesses are paid in full. With electronic payments there is no guaranteed assurance of full payment because customers can dispute bills, resulting in the merchant getting partial or no money long after the purchase is made.

For example, many tow truck companies want only cash after hauling away an illegally parked car. Many states have laws requiring tow truck companies to accept credit cards. However, because many people dispute the tow truck charge after they get their vehicle back, some tow truck companies don't advertise they accept electronic payments. Other tow companies make it difficult to use electronic payments by mandating these payments are only accepted back at the tow company's office but not out on the road.

Beyond knowing you will be paid in full, another advantage of cash payments is instant settlement. This means paper money can be used immediately to pay workers, buy supplies, or start earning interest on the money. With electronic payments, businesses often wait days to be paid. Plus, when reputable businesses coexist with con artists, scam artists, and fraudsters there is always the chance a business is never paid if the non-cash method turns out to be fraudulent.

For example, recently someone in my family had a set of beautiful bookcases they no longer needed. They put the bookcases up for sale on the internet. A buyer quickly agreed to pay full price for the bookcases and arranged for them to be picked up immediately. Unfortunately, the check paying for the bookcases was a fake. Both the buyer and the bookcases disappeared long before the bank notification. Using cash would have prevented this theft.

Even with these advantages, cash is slowing disappearing as a way of spending money. Chapter 3 looks at savings and using data that track how much paper money is in circulation. This is an important indicator for how much paper money is being held in reserve. The results in Chapter 3 surprised me the first time I examined them and showed me an unexpected victory for pro-cash advocates.

CHAPTER THREE

IS CASH DISAPPEARING?

THE CASE OF SAVINGS

C hapter 2 made it clear that people around the world are shifting away from making purchases in cash and are using electronic methods for spending instead. But is cash really disappearing? Many people hold on to paper money for savings, protection during emergencies, and other reasons.

For people who think cash is dead – a bygone relic of yesterday – this chapter contains a big surprise. Starting in the mid-1980s, the amount of paper money in circulation in the world began increasing dramatically. This increase is not caused by inflation or by changes in the world's population. Adjusting for both of these factors still shows dramatic increases. As the next section shows, there is now three times as much currency per person in the United States as there was 40 years ago, even after adjusting for inflation.

What does this mean? Eliminating paper money when making purchases but holding increasing amounts for savings and protection during emergencies leads to a major problem. Paper money is not useful in an emergency if when an emergency happens no one is able to accept it as a means of payment.

TRENDS IN PAPER MONEY HOLDINGS

Governments around the world track how much money they release to the public. When central banks release paper money to the public they call it "currency in circulation." The amount circulating is tracked carefully by every country because this currency, along with government bonds and other borrowings, are important parts of a nation's financial liabilities.

With the world quickly switching to electronic means of payment, you might expect the amount of currency in circulation to be falling. If everyone is using less cash then there must be less cash being held throughout society, right? In fact, the opposite is true.

A careful analysis requires two major adjustments to show people are saving more cash. Just looking at the amount of currency in circulation presents a distorted picture because the world's population is growing rapidly. Somewhere about 1975 the world had 4 billion people. Today, there are 8 billion. More people mean more cash is needed to support that bigger population.

Let's imagine a country has 40 million people now and 25 years ago it had 20 million. If each person wants to hold the same amount of cash today as they did a quarter-century earlier, the government needs to print and release twice the amount of cash simply because the population has grown.

The second distortion is caused by inflation. Let's imagine the average person spent $5 in cash on lunch 25 years ago. Let's also imagine the country has experienced inflation over the years and by today all prices have doubled. This means lunch now costs $10. Because of inflation each person needs to be holding twice as much currency to purchase lunch today as they held a quarter-century ago.

These examples show the need to adjust the amount of currency in circulation for both price and population changes. Figure 3.1 does both adjustments for the United States and shows since the end of World War I the inflation-adjusted amount of cash per person has risen dramatically over time. From slightly less than $1,000 in the early 1900s to about $7,000 today.[1]

The amount of money held peaked in 2021, during the height of the COIVD-19 pandemic, when fear of the disease was rampant. After the COVID pandemic ended, the amount of money held fell back. Nevertheless, by 2024 there was about $7,000 of paper currency for every person living in the US. This is roughly nine times more than at the end of World War I and three times more than held in the mid-1980s.

Figure 3.1   Cash per person in the United States.

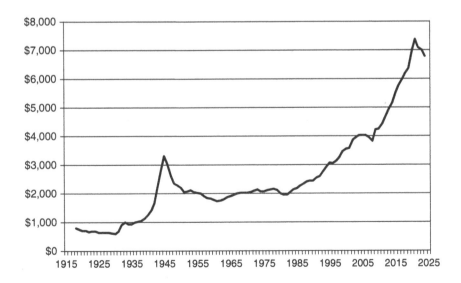

The figure shows a surprising trend. Since the mid-2010s, a time when fewer people were using cash for transactions, the amount of paper money per person expanded rapidly.

As an advocate for paper money the most frequent question I get is, "how much cash should a person hold for emergencies?" Using the graph's information plus annual income data provides a rough answer: about one month of expenses. This might not be the right figure for you or your family, but before deciding read the chapters on natural disasters (Chapter 5) and national defense (Chapter 6).[2]

Is it true people in the United States have so much cash? Some researchers have wondered if all this American cash is simply flowing overseas. One way to check is to track employment in the armored car industry because if more cash is used or hoarded inside the country then more people are needed to transport paper money to banks and ATMs. If less cash is needed or cash is only used outside the United States then armored car employment should fall over time.[3]

Data from the Census Bureau "County Business Patterns" survey show armored car employment did fall from 1998 to 2007. However, beginning in 2008, while the world experienced a severe financial crash and general unemployment soared, armored car employment experienced a resurgence. It continued rising until 2020; when the COVID lockdowns reduced people's need for cash and employment fell. The rise in armored car employment suggests the jump in US paper money is not just due to overseas demand.[4]

OTHER COUNTRIES

The amount of US currency per person has increased dramatically. Are the same trends happening in other countries? The answer is an unqualified yes. At a time when the entire world is steadily shifting toward electronic transactions, the amount of paper currency per person is exploding.

The top line of Table 3.1 shows in the year 2000 how much currency existed per person in five locations: United States, Euro zone, Japan, United Kingdom, and Switzerland. These five places were chosen because at the turn of this century these five currencies dominated world foreign exchange markets. Similar to Figure 3.1, the figures are adjusted for inflation and population changes.[5]

The second and third lines of the table show the change over 20 years. The previously shown rapid growth of US currency is not an outlier. Instead, the US's almost doubling of currency per person is actually in the middle of the pack.

The bottom line of Table 3.1 shows the most growth was seen in the euro, which grew 175%, more than doubling. The second highest growth happened in the Japanese yen, which doubled per person. The Swiss franc, a stable currency considered a safe haven, saw a 75% increase. The smallest growth occurred in the British pound, which increased by about 50%. Overall, all five of the world's major currencies experienced dramatic growth in paper money.[6]

What about other countries? Could the explosive growth in major currencies be caused by people in fast-growing economies like China or India holding not only US dollars but also other major currencies like the euro, yen, pound, and franc? Table 3.2 shows the amount of currency per person in inflation-adjusted terms for the BRICS, or Brazil, Russia, India, China,

Table 3.1   Currency per Person for the Five Most Frequently Traded Currencies

Year	US dollar	Euro	Japanese yen	UK pound	Swiss franc
Amount in 2000	$ 3,558	€ 1,669	¥ 4,86,479	£ 777	Fr. 4,950
Amount in 2023	$ 6,993	€ 4,597	¥ 1,009,278	£ 1,174	Fr. 8,663
Percentage change	97%	175%	107%	51%	75%

Table 3.2 Amount of Currency per Person in BRICS

Year	Brazil real	Russian ruble	India rupee	Chinese RMB	South African rand
Amount in 2000	R$ 545	17,869 ₽	₹ 7,317	¥ 1,805	R 1,734
Amount in 2023	R$ 1,544	1,20,825 ₽	₹ 23,073	¥ 7,465	R 2,323
Percentage change	184%	576%	215%	314%	34%

and South Africa. This economic block of five countries covers over 40% of the world's population, almost one-third of the world's land area, and the five countries are an important part of the world's economy.

Table 3.2 shows even more growth in their own paper money than found in Table 3.1. In the US, cash per person roughly doubled during the Table 3.1 time frame, which ranks near the bottom of Table 3.2.

The number of Russian rubles per person has increased by almost 600% (576%), even after adjusting for inflation and population changes. The Chinese RMB has increased by over 300% (314%) and the Brazilian real by almost 200% (184%) per person, even after accounting for inflation.

The dramatic increase in Indian rupees (215%) is surprising given the Indian government in 2016 banned the two highest-denomination bills, the 500 and 1,000 rupee notes. This banning resulted in some Indians losing their savings because they had paper cash that no longer could be spent.

The only country whose amount of currency per person did not increase more than the United States was South Africa. South Africa still saw a one-third (34%) increase.

There are far more than ten countries in the world. However, those highlighted in Tables 3.1 and 3.2 comprise a major portion of the world's wealth, income, output, land, and population. All ten show the same fact: the amount of paper money circulating has dramatically grown in the world, even after adjusting for population and inflation.

THE CHANGING MIX

Not only are people holding more cash around the world but the way they are holding paper money has also changed. People are increasingly holding just the largest denominations. Small bills are going out of fashion. This desire by the public for larger denominations flies in the face of decisions like by the European central bank to eliminate its highest-denomination bill, the €500 note.

In 2000, about two-thirds (67%) of all US currency was composed of $100 bills. A bit over two decades later, hundreds comprised over 80% of all currency in circulation. In simple terms the mix of US bills in circulation is shifting toward the largest denomination bill, the $100.

A similar trend is seen in the euro. The most popular euro note is the €50. In 2002 the €50 note comprised one-quarter of all notes in circulation. By 2020 it comprised about half of all euros circulating. This growth came at the expense of the €5, €10, and €20 notes, which have all shrunk in use.

Unlike US currency, the very largest euro notes, the €200 and €500, are not very popular. The market share of €500s rose for only the first few years after its introduction. Since 2009 the €500 has steadily fallen out of favor. The reason for this is clear. In 2018 the European central bank stopped issuing these notes and has been removing them from circulation. Although the notes are valid, the removal has caused public confusion over whether the notes are still accepted as legal tender.

WHAT IT MEANS

This shift from people using cash for transactions to holding cash for savings reasons will cause a major problem. When paper money is no longer used for transactions it becomes less useful or even useless for all other purposes.

Let's imagine you store around a $1,000 under your mattress, just in case a massive disaster happens. As a later chapter will point out, sometimes natural disasters shut off the power for a long time. For example, in 2017 Hurricane Maria hit Puerto Rico and power was shut off to large parts of the island for months.

If all companies switch to cashless methods of payments, they are not equipped to handle cash transactions. Then when you take out the money you stuffed under the mattress, the merchants have no means of accepting it as a means of payment.

However, the problem runs even deeper. Banks are closing branches even as the US population has grown. Since peaking in 2009 the United States has lost over 10,000 bank branches. Banks are removing ATMs. Fewer bank branches with a rising population mean banks are moving customers away from using physical locations. The banks' goal is to get customers to do as many transactions as possible using their computer or apps running on customers' phones.

Let's assume this trend accelerates and imagine a cashless society. When there is a need to break out the cash and spend it, the banking system has no way to give customers cash. It has no way to take cash from customers. In simple terms the ability to recycle cash is broken and this leads to an economic standstill when electronic payments break down.

A glimpse of this future was seen during the beginning of the COVID pandemic. In the first few months little was known about the disease. Many people thought that COVID could be transferred by germs on surfaces. Government officials incorrectly told people one way to prevent getting COVID was to wash items. People washed their groceries, sprayed their mail with bleach, and ran to the other side of the street when a stranger approached. In addition, officials told people to stay home and minimize the amount of time they spent outside. This led people to stop using coins because many feared touching coins transmitted COVID.

Coins became in very short supply, because they stopped circulating. The US Mint tried making millions of new ones but could not keep up with the demand from people who still wanted to use them.

The result was that people who tried to use cash, but did not have the exact payment, were either discouraged or overcharged because stores could not give change. This caused problems in many industries that were not equipped to handle electronic payments. Vending machines, laundry machines, and parking meters run on coins. Without coins circulating, simple acts like washing clothes became quite difficult for people who didn't own their own washer and dryer.

Laundry and other machines that use coins can be converted to cashless methods of payment. Many laundry machines in large buildings now have the ability to accept swipe and tap cards instead of coins. However, it is not cost-effective to convert every laundry machine to cashless methods, nor can every machine, like those in deep basements, reach the phone network.

COVID showed the disruptions that happened when coins stopped circulating. Imagine the disruption if paper money stops circulating and electronic payment systems go down.

CONCLUSION

I want to end the chapter with a personal story about what happens when you hold a large amount of cash and it becomes impossible to use it for transactions. I visited Greece in the mid-1980s, a time when the country had very strict currency controls. It was illegal to exchange foreign money in the country except at a bank.

Countries often implement these kinds of policies because it gives them a chance to impose a hidden tax on all foreign exchange transactions. The tax is hidden because the official rate is much worse than the free market rate. Currency controls primarily tax tourists and locals who buy imported items instead of locally produced products.

I arrived in Greece for a 10-day visit and exchanged US dollars without a problem into Greek drachmas, which was the country's currency prior to the euro. I had a wonderful time seeing the famous ruins, like the Parthenon, cycling through picturesque towns, and eating great food. My last day in Greece was in the middle of the week. I was staying in Athens and had already purchased a boat ticket to another country. I woke up and paid my hotel bill, which emptied my wallet of Greek money. Two days earlier I had dropped off most of my clothes at a nearby laundromat. The day of my departure I planned on stopping by a bank to get some money to pay the cleaners and then head down to the port for a leisurely lunch.

I was surprised to find the streets empty, many shops closed, and not a single bank open, all in the middle of the week. It was May 1, International Workers' Day, commonly called May Day. The streets were soon filled with tens of thousands of Greeks marching and chanting slogans. Luckily, the cleaner that had my neatly pressed clothes was still open. However, although my wallet was full of US currency, I had no Greek money.

The owner explained that if she took US paper dollars in payment she could be arrested for violating the currency controls. Plus, as a small business she could not afford to take credit cards. She took pity on me and gave my clean clothes back for free and even handed me a subway token to get me down to the port. I was a rich man with a full wallet. However, because the shop owner could not accept the type of paper money I had I was unable to pay my debt.

To this day I am confused on what was the right thing to do. Paying the shop owner in dollars was a crime. Not paying her was stealing. Before leaving the shop I surreptitiously slipped more than what I owed in US dollars under a vase near the cash register when the shop owner wasn't looking. Hopefully, the currency police didn't catch her.

The amount of paper money per person has been dramatically increasing over time in most of the world's major currencies. At the same time the use of paper money for transactions has been decreasing. If these trends continue paper money's usefulness will disappear. As I experienced long ago in Greece, money cannot be held for emergencies if during an emergency no one can or is able to accept it as a means of payment.

The next chapters show a wide variety of reasons for using cash for transactions ranging from boosting national defense to making a person better off financially. Convincing you and everyone else to use cash more often in stores, restaurants, transport, and other places will ensure paper money regains its status as an effective backup in times of trouble.

SECTION II

CASH PROVIDES SOCIETY WITH RESILIENCE

The next three chapters explain how keeping paper money around and continuing to use it provides resilience for society. Resilience is the ability to withstand and recover quickly from shocks, problems, and unanticipated circumstances. These three chapters explain why paper money ensures the economy can continue to function when electronic payments do not work.

Chapter 4 explains how electronic payments work. The key idea of this chapter is that a cashless society stands on three legs: a continuous and stable supply of electricity, communication networks working all the time, and secure computers. Unfortunately, even in advanced countries during the best of times power outages and fluctuations occur, communication networks fail, and computers are hacked. The failure of any one of these three legs means an inability to pay or move money electronically. In poorer countries, which often have unreliable electrical grids, communication equipment, and less secure computers, there is even more chance of electronic payments failing.

Chapter 5 looks at the problems when Mother Nature releases her fury on the world. The number of billion-dollar natural disasters is steadily growing over time as the world's weather becomes more extreme. Hurricanes, typhoons, firestorms, earthquakes, and a host of other disasters destroy electrical grids, take down communication networks, and wipe out computer servers rendering electronic payments impossible. Continuing to use paper money is a simple way to ensure people and businesses operate during and after a major natural disaster.

Chapter 6 examines why keeping cash around is important for national defense. One of the simplest methods of degrading an enemy's ability and will to fight is to take down their electrical grid, communications networks, and computers. Preventing people from using electronic payments ensures your enemies cannot buy food, purchase transportation, or pay for medical care. This saps the morale and helps grind an economy to a halt. However, using cash ensures purchases in war times are still possible.

However, for cash to be the fail-safe for running an economy that is attacked by an enemy or a natural disaster, it must already be in circulation. Eliminating cash in day-to-day transactions and having the government stockpile cash as a backup for release during an emergency will not work. Banks and ATMs depend on the same electrical, communication, and computer networks to give out cash as are used to make electronic payments. When any of these networks go down either accidently or for malicious reasons, people will be unable to get cash. Even if individuals have cash on hand, it is crucial that businesses know how to accept cash, and have enough cash to make change, or people will not be able to make purchases even when they have paper money. National security depends on our continuing to use cash regularly.

CHAPTER FOUR

HOW DO CASHLESS PAYMENTS WORK?

The cashless society is like a stool that rests on three legs: electricity, communications, and computers. When any one of the three legs breaks cashless payments do not work. Each leg is assumed to be strong and sturdy, but they are actually relatively fragile.

The fragility is becoming more obvious. For example, in summer 2024 a relatively unknown American cybersecurity company called CrowdStrike sent out a faulty software update. The update crashed millions of computers, shutting down large numbers of the world's banks, airlines, hospitals, and government agencies. Flights were canceled, surgeries postponed, and people without cash could not make purchases. One small software change resulted in worldwide chaos.

To understand the weakness of electronic payments we first need to understand how payments work. Let's imagine a customer wants to make a $50 purchase. The customer can make the purchase using paper money or using an electronic payment.

If a customer hands over paper money to the store owner to complete the purchase, this is a three-step process. There are three steps because in modern life neither customers nor businesses keep huge amounts of cash around. Instead, both often keep excess money in banks, which is safer, more convenient, and even earns some interest rather than storing cash in a mattress.

The first step is for the customer to get cash, typically by stopping at a bank or ATM to withdraw cash before making the purchase. The second step is when the customer hands over the money. The last step happens, typically at the end of the day, when the business deposits any extra cash they don't need back at a bank. Although this cash transaction takes three steps, what is important is that time is not a critical component. The customer could get cash out of the bank one moment before entering the store or weeks earlier. The store owner could immediately deposit the money or keep the cash on hand for a long time.

What happens if a customer decides to use a credit card, debit card, or mobile payment? From the customer's perspective all they do is one step. They pull out a phone or card and either swipe, tap, or hand it to the store's employee to complete the purchase. There was no need to go to the bank ahead of time. The money is either directly removed from their account if they use a debit card or their credit card balance increases. Simple! This is why so many people love credit cards, debit cards, and mobile payments.

The store owner's experience is also simpler. They see their bank balance increase. But the owner's balance doesn't go up by 100% of the purchase. To give customers the ability to pay with these electronic payments, the merchant pays fees. The fees typically are in two parts: a fixed base charge and then a percentage of the transaction total. Most owners are willing to part with some of the money made on the transaction because giving a customer the ability to charge or debit purchases typically boosts that customer's spending. Plus, many merchants recapture some of these fees by boosting prices.

On the surface the credit or debit transaction appears much simpler, but it is not. Although the cash transaction takes three steps, behind the scenes most credit transactions take 13 steps. Debit transactions take a few less steps than credit, but they are still much more complex than cash.

Figure 4.1 shows all 13 steps involved in a credit card transaction, where solid lines show how information is passed and dotted lines show money transferred. Beyond the number and types of steps being more complex than cash transactions, computers and electronic messaging are an important part of the story because time becomes a critical component.[1]

The number of steps balloons because there are a lot more parties involved and a lot more risk. When a customer pulls out $50 in cash, the store owner is assured the customer has enough money to pay for the

Figure 4.1 Steps in making a credit card purchase.

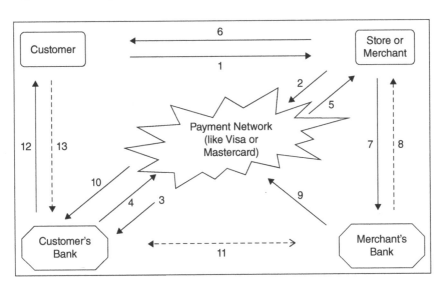

purchase. When a customer pulls out a credit or debit card, the owner has no idea if the customer has enough money to pay. Plus, the owner doesn't know if the card is actually the customer's. It might have been stolen.

Because Figure 4.1 is a bit confusing, let's break it down into parts. In the top left corner is the customer who wants to make a purchase from a store or merchant. The first arrow, labeled 1, is when the customer tells the merchant they want to pay using a credit card. This step takes many different forms. Sometimes the customer hands over a card. Customers can also swipe, tap, or just be in close proximity to a register. In making a purchase on the internet a person might type in their credit card number or use a number stored in an online wallet. Whatever the method, the first step is to initiate the transaction.

In step 2 the merchant contacts one of the major payment networks like Visa, Mastercard, or Discover. When credit cards first came out the merchant would pick up the telephone and call. Today, the merchant's computer sends an electronic message to the network telling the customer's account number and amount being purchased. The payment network then forwards that message in step 3 to the customer's bank. The bank checks to see if the account is still valid to make sure the card is not stolen and then checks if the customer can charge the amount requested.

In step 4, the customer's bank returns a message to the payment network telling them if the transaction was approved or denied. Then in step 5 the payment network passes on that message to the store owner. If the message was an approval another eight steps follow. If the message was a denial, well, there is that awkward moment many have either experienced or seen when someone's credit card is refused and they are not able to buy what they want. When a denial happens, either the process starts again with a different card or the transaction is abandoned.

Step 6 is when the customer or cardholder accepts liability. In the earliest days of credit cards people used to sign physical slips of paper. Over time this switched to people scribbling their signature, usually illegibly on a computer pad. Today customers are simply asked to press a yes or no button to confirm the transaction.

At this point the transaction is authorized. The next set of steps move money from the customer to the store or merchant. In step 7 the merchant tells their bank how much was charged and how much money they billed consumers. The amount is sometimes different than in step 2. For example, some restaurants send the amount of the bill in step 2, but in step 7 send the bill plus the tip.

The merchant's bank in step 8 then puts this money in the merchant's account after subtracting the bank's cut for credit card fees. The merchant's bank now needs to recover from the customer the money it has put into the merchant's account. It starts this process off in step 9. The merchant's bank sends a message to the payment network. In step 10 the payment network forwards the message to the customer's bank. Because huge numbers of charges occur each day, the merchant's bank and the customer's bank don't send individual payments back and forth.

Instead, at the end of each day all the charges are totaled up and the two banks determine how much they need to pay each other. The settlement, which is step 11, then goes over a different payment network such as the Fedwire, which is a secure method run by the US Federal Reserve for moving money between banks.

The last two steps are 12 and 13. In these two steps the customer's bank first tells the customer about the charge. Then the bank either directly takes money out of the customer's account or issues the customer a statement, which is either paid in full or paid over time.

There are two important things to take away from this figure. First, there are a lot of steps involved in electronic transactions. However, not all electronic transactions are this complex. For example, charges made with American Express cards are simpler because American Express both runs the network and acts as the merchant's and customer's bank.[2] Debit cards are also simpler especially if the customer and merchant use the same bank.

However, the more important idea is that all these complex steps demand electricity, computers, and communications. When electrical, computer, or communication networks are shut down or offline this complex set of steps grinds to a halt.

Some people have suggested that in the event of a problem, merchants and banks could go back in time to the original days of credit cards when the entire process was done with paper copies. Unfortunately, the present volume of electronic transactions make it impossible to revert to this older system.

Today over 120 billion credit and debit transactions are completed in the United States each year. Let's imagine rolling back time and doing each credit card transaction using paper copies, like when Diners Club, the first mass payment card, started out. Imagine each transaction takes 15 minutes, to fill in the charge slips, sign them, have the bank check and retype the values into the bank's computers, and do the other manual processing steps that happened at the dawn of electronic payments. At 15 minutes per charge almost one in every ten US workers would need to be devoted full-time to just handle the paperwork from credit and debit cards!

Financial institutions have spent massive amounts of money ensuring the steps moving electronic money around the system are safe, secure, and reliable. However, communication, electrical, and computer disruptions happen frequently in the modern world. The next sections of this chapter look at these disruptions, any of which prevent electronic payments from working.

COMMUNICATION DISRUPTIONS

Many people use their phone for all aspects of their lives. I have numerous students who proudly state they never carry cash and do everything from their phone. In response I remind them that cell phones don't work all the time or even everywhere. When your cell phone does not work, for whatever reasons, mobile payments are not possible. Governments sometimes shut off communications during times of civil unrest, which is discussed in more detail later in Chapter 17. However, even in calm times communications are disrupted.

How often has your phone shut off because it ran out of power? I am pretty good about charging my phone, but sometimes it is heavily used and runs out of power unexpectedly. Occasionally, I think my phone is recharging, but the phone is actually not. A dead phone eliminates any possibility of mobile payments.

Even when your phone is completely charged there is still a chance mobile payments will not work. Cell networks don't operate everywhere. I enjoy outdoor activities, but am constantly frustrated by coverage dead zones when traveling to rural areas. These dead spots are sometimes operator specific. My phone will have no coverage, but phones on a different carrier's network continue to work. A few years ago I traveled through Idaho and Montana. I met and saw lots of people talking on their cell phones. However, my phone company didn't cover large parts of these states, even though their chief competitor did.

It is not just in rural or wilderness areas. Urban areas also have dead zones that have no service. Signals are sometimes blocked in cities by other buildings or cannot penetrate basements or tunnels. There are even times in urban areas when there are so many other people using their phones that cell towers reach their maximum capacity and refuse to connect phones.

I was reminded of urban communication dead zones recently when going out to dinner with a dozen friends. The restaurant was in a popular downtown location and had great food. At the end of the meal the waiter stated unfortunately he was unable to split the bill a dozen ways. One person volunteered to pay the restaurant and collect money from everyone else. I pulled out some cash and handed it to the volunteer banker. The rest of the group all tried cashless payment methods to reimburse the banker.

This turned out to be a frustrating exercise because the dining room was a cellphone dead zone and the restaurant's Wi-Fi was locked. Most of my friends ended up wandering outside in a rainy, dark, cold night to connect their phones.

Last, communication is disrupted or lacking for people who have trouble paying their bills. About 2% of poor US households do not have a phone. Even if someone does have a phone, financial difficulties result in service being shut off. Without a phone a person has no ability to make mobile payments.[3]

My point is not to bash phone companies. They do a wonderful job enabling us to communicate. However, mobile payments, which are based on cell phones, don't work all the time. Unlike the problems with mobile payments, cash works in places that do not have cell signals, works in dead zones, works when a phone is out of power, and even works when someone cannot afford to pay for a phone.

ELECTRICITY DISRUPTIONS – UNDERSTANDING POWER GRIDS

Electrical disruption is just as important as communication problems. When the power goes down so does the ability to make cashless payments. Yes, some companies and a few individuals have backup generators to keep electricity flowing when the power stops. Others have battery backups to keep machines running during disruptions. I typed this book on computers, all protected by battery backups. However, all of these sources of backup power are temporary. None keep the power flowing forever. When the power finally goes out, so does the ability to do electronic payments.

The United States is susceptible to widespread electrical disruption because electricity flows over only three power grids, which are massive sets of wires that move power thousands of miles. The Eastern Interconnection grid covers most of North America east of the Rockies. The Western Interconnection covers most of the area west of the Rockies. The state of Texas is the third, with its own separate power grid.

Power grids are enormous because bigger grids provide three benefits over smaller grids. Larger grids are more reliable, financially cheaper to run, and are able to better use a mixture of power sources. Let's examine each of these three benefits in more detail.

First, larger grids are more reliable. Grids are like boats being rowed by people. Imagine a grid powered by two similar sized plants. This is like a small boat with two people, one rowing on each side. If one power plant goes down, either the entire grid fails or half of the customers need to stop using electricity. It is the same with a small boat. If one rower stops rowing, the boat stops moving forward and only spins in circles. Now let's increase the size of the grid, adding more customers and power plants. If the grid is powered by 100 plants and one fails, the others can pick up the slack. If there are 50 rowers on each side of a large boat and one person cannot row, the boat continues moving straight through the water with only a minor correction needed to adjust for the imbalance.

Second, larger grids are financially cheaper to run. The price of electricity is constantly changing. During peak demand, like during a heatwave, electricity is extremely expensive. During slack demand, like the middle of the night, electricity is cheap. In a large grid with more power sources, there is more competition, which results in lower prices for all when the most efficient power plants are used first and the least efficient are used only during peak demand. Continuing with the boat analogy, if there is only one person who can row you across the water to your destination, the price is going to be high. If many rowers are competing to ferry a passenger, the competition will drive prices down.

Third, larger grids are better at using a mixture of power sources. Modern grids use a wide variety of methods to generate power, like coal, oil, gas, wind, nuclear, and solar. Renewables like wind and solar are very efficient at generating power, but only at certain times of the day, like when the sun is shining. Having a large grid means people waking up in the west when it is dark can still power their morning using solar energy generated thousands of miles away to the east, where the sun has already risen.

However, although increases in size provide technical and monetary benefits, they increase the risk of catastrophic economic failure. When even one of the three US grids fails it causes disruption to millions of people and shuts down a significant portion of the overall economy.

NUMBER OF ELECTRICITY DISRUPTIONS

To give you an idea of the fragility of the power supply this section summarizes some US data sources that track electrical outages. Although the coverage and definitions are not consistent, the data show a similar pattern.

First, the United States experiences many power outages each year. The vast majority of these are local and brief. Second, every year there is at least one major event that leaves many people and businesses in the United States without electricity for an extended period of time. During these blackouts electronic payments do not work, but paper money does.

One source of data is the Eaton Corporation's annual "Blackout Report." Eaton is a major supplier of power backup systems to businesses. Publishing the "Blackout Report" helped boost sales of backup systems by providing facts about how often and why blackouts occur. The reports also highlight amusing ways these blackouts occur, such as bulls knocking over power lines and squirrels accidently connecting two cables and inadvertently forming a circuit.[4]

Averaging all of their reports shows in a typical year the United States experiences over 3,300 blackouts. The typical blackout affects a bit less than 9,000 people, which shows that most outages are local. The typical blackout lasts a bit more than two hours, which shows the vast majority are brief. Losing two hours of work or sales in one neighborhood or city is an inconvenience and not economically crippling to society. Data in the Eaton reports suggest no pressing need for cash as an electronic payment backup.

However, the Eaton reports that show most power outages are short and local provide only a partial picture of electrical outages. There is a second source of outage data from the Energy Information Administration (EIA) that tracks massive blackouts. These data show a very different picture of electrical outages, one where cash is extremely important to have on hand.

The EIA is a division of the US Department of Energy. The EIA expects whenever an electricity provider experiences a blackout or other disruptions like a prolonged drop in voltage, they will file an official report with the government. The EIA releases these reports publicly making it is easy to see how long a blackout lasted, the number of customers affected, and the amount of power lost.[5]

The EIA reports show at least one massive blackout every year that affects hundreds of thousands if not millions of people for long periods of time. From 2012 to June 2021, the EIA has 33 reports where the blackout lasted more than one week. Many of these blackouts were headline news stories that are soon forgotten by most people, for example, the Great Texas Freeze of 2021 when two million customers lost power for almost two weeks or when severe thunderstorms, called *derechos*, struck the Mid-Atlantic and Midwest in 2012 resulting in ten million customers being without power for two to eight days.

Massive blackouts are also experienced outside the US. Two of the world's biggest were not caused by natural disasters, but instead by maintenance issues that spiraled out of control. In 2012 India experienced a blackout that shut the power off to roughly 650 million people for two days. In 2019 the South American countries of Argentina, Paraguay, and Uruguay suffered a blackout in which 50 million were without power for a day.

Although most blackouts are short, each year there are a small number that involve widespread, long-term disruption. The more society relies on electricity and electronic means of payments, the more significant the impact of these events when the power fails.

CASH IS ENVIRONMENTALLY FRIENDLY

Before leaving the topic of electricity it is useful to point out another paper money advantage. Cash uses less energy. Printing a banknote takes electricity, but once it is put in circulation it does not take extra electricity to use. Bitcoin transactions take an enormous amount of energy to process, and so does each credit and debit card transaction.[6]

Once a banknote is used a dozen times, it uses less electricity than card payments. The more a banknote is used after this point, the more energy is saved. Given the lifespan of a $1 bill is almost 7 years and a $100 bill lasts almost 23 years and bills change hands more than once a year over their lifespan, paper money is the green choice.[7]

COMPUTER SECURITY

The third important part needed to make electronic payments is computers. People and businesses need to know that computers are secure.

Unfortunately, malware, spyware, denial of service attacks, and a variety of other malicious issues plague computers. Thieves, organized crime, and other nefarious actors are trying to break into and corrupt any computer they can. These bad actors especially attack computers associated with financial institutions for the same reason Willie Sutton, a famous robber, stole from banks: "That is where the money is."

One example of the disruption caused by computer hacks happened to the Chinese banking giant, Industrial and Commercial Bank of China, or ICBC. The newspaper headline "How a Hack Shook Wall Street's Multitrillion-Dollar Foundations" encapsulates the importance computers have in electronic payments. ICBC's New York City branch office participates in the US Treasury bill repurchase agreement marketplace, nicknamed the *repo market*. Every working day billions of dollars and billions of Treasury bills flow electronically through the system.[8]

Hackers injected ransomware into ICBC's computers. The ransomware locked up ICBC's systems and told the bank that unless a large ransom was paid, their computers would remain offline. A week and a half after the hack the same newspaper article stated "ICBC isn't fully back up-and-running, but its trades have been processed" manually. If a bank that is important to the financial system's foundations can be taken offline for more than ten days can individuals, stores, and restaurants that depend on electronic payments ensure their computers are safe all the time?

Because electronic payments depend on secure computers, the US Treasury has required since August 2018 that banks and other financial institutions report cyberattacks that pose a threat to financial stability. The Financial Crimes Enforcement Network (FinCEN) collects data on cyberattacks on forms called *Suspicious Activity Reports*. Table 4.1 shows the number of cyberattacks in thousands against banks, other financial institutions, and their customers starting in 2019, which is the first full year of data.[9]

Table 4.1 Reported Cyberattacks Against US Financial Institutions and Customers

Suspicious activity type	2019 in (1,000s)	2022 in (1,000s)	Percentage change 2019–2022
Against financial institutions	4	8	100%
Against customers	18	38	111%
Against other parts of financial system	3	8	166%
Total	**25**	**54**	**116%**

Table 4.1 shows three things. First, cyberattacks happen frequently. In 2022 there were over 50,000 cyberattacks that financial institutions reported. That is about 150 attacks per day. Second, the number of attacks is increasing over time. Total attacks more than doubled in just the first four years data were collected. Last, the majority of attacks were focused on the system's weakest link: customers.

The FinCEN data are not perfect. They show attacks seen and recognized, but not all cyberattacks are noticed. They also do not show the number of successful attacks so it is impossible to know the effectiveness of security measures. Additionally, all attacks are given the same weight. An attack infecting one customer's banking app counts the same as a successful attack that shuts down a bank like ICBC for weeks.

FinCEN data, which focus on financial institutions, also do not show other places where electronic payments are vulnerable. Cash registers and more sophisticated point-of-sale systems for major retailers have been hacked, showing payment information used by stores is not secure. Millions of people have had their financial information stolen by cybercriminals after shopping at major retailers like Target, Home Depot, eBay, CVS Health, and Forever 21.[10]

CONCLUSION

Electronic payments depend on three things to operate: steady power, secure communications, and protected computers. Unfortunately, as this chapter has pointed out, power interruptions often happen, communications networks are not available everywhere all the time, and cybercriminals are constantly attacking computers around the world.

In a world where steady power, secure communications, and protected computers do not exist 100% of the time, paper money provides a low-cost, secure, and simple alternative. Paper money ensures transactions continue when the power goes out, communication is lost, or computers are hacked. Plus, after using paper money there is no worry cybercriminals have stolen your financial data.

CHAPTER FIVE

NATURAL DISASTERS PREVENT CASHLESS PAYMENTS FROM HAPPENING

T he weather around the world has become more unstable. Fires, floods, heat waves, and other natural disasters are becoming more common. The increasing numbers of natural disasters make relying on electronic payments risky. Paper money is a key tool for being prepared for any disaster precipitated by Mother Nature.

Let me tell you a short personal story to show why cash is important. A few summers ago the United States was hit by a series of very long heat waves. Large parts of the country baked under extreme temperatures. Foolishly, I planned a solo multiweek bicycle trip up the East Coast in the middle of this blistering heat. My wife worried that my body would shut down with heat stroke while pedaling, so I promised to call her frequently. She was at the beach during one check-in phone call. Partway through the conversation the line went dead. I was fine, but her phone had gotten too hot and shut itself off. No phone meant her ability to make mobile payments, plus all the other things her phone does, like unlock her car, were unavailable. With cash she could have bought a cold drink at a shady stand to cool herself and the phone down. With her phone suffering from heat stroke, instead of her husband, she was unable to make purchases or communicate with me.

Cash doesn't stop working until the temperature reaches over 450°F or 232°C. That is the point at which paper burns. Because humans die at temperatures well below 450°, cash works in all relevant temperatures. Electronic payments work only in a much narrower temperature range. For example, Apple's iPhones automatically shut off when temperatures get too extreme. Apple states their products should only be used "where the ambient temperature is between 0° and 35°C (32°–95°F)" and the devices should not be stored in places where the temperature is below −20° or above 45°C (−4°F and 113°F).[1]

Fire is another natural disaster in which cash is useful and electronic payments are not. During massive fires, government officials often order mandatory evacuations with little notice. People with full gas tanks can drive hundreds of miles fleeing danger. People with partial tanks need to fill up, which costs money. During massive fires the communications network and electrical grids often break down, preventing people from using credit cards, debit cards, or mobile payments. No money means no gas. No gas blocks your ability to outrun large conflagrations!

For example, let's look at a fire that happened in the Northern California counties of Napa, Sonoma, and Lake, areas famous for their wines. A conflagration called the Tubbs Fire killed 44 people and caused over $14 billion in damages. Beyond the damage to lives and property, the fire demonstrated how fragile communication networks are even in one of the wealthiest parts of the world. The fire completely destroyed or knocked out over 340 cell sites. Not only was cell communication disrupted but surveys found about two-thirds of all landlines failed. Plus, the fire sparked widespread power outages. This meant during the fire and evacuation both communications and the ability to make electronic payments stopped working for many residents.[2]

The fire was very fast moving. After the fire was over, officials surveyed those who survived. About 15% of all people stated they had less than ten minutes warning before evacuating. One-third of all people who fled had an hour or less notice. The combined loss of telecommunications and power meant that when people living in these fire-swept counties most needed to pay for food, fuel, and shelter their ability to buy things electronically disappeared.

Another massive wildfire happened on the Hawaiian island of Maui, destroying the town of Lahaina and killing 100 people. The death toll was higher than expected because emergency managers thought they were sending text message evacuation alerts to everyone, but the fast-moving fire destroyed cell communications so few people received the alerts.[3]

The next section starts with an overview of the increasing trend in natural disasters in the United States. But the rising number of major natural disasters is not just affecting the United States. Problems are occurring around the world.

No matter what type of natural disaster happens, the key idea in this chapter is that when Mother Nature releases her fury, power grids, computers, and communication networks experience major problems. Keeping cash around and using it frequently will ensure when the electricity, phone, or internet go down, both your ability to spend and the overall economy will not grind to a halt.

TREND IN NATURAL DISASTERS

The world has been experiencing an increasing number of costly natural disasters. The US government's National Oceanic and Atmospheric Administration (NOAA) tracks the most destructive weather and climate disasters back to 1980. NOAA classifies a major disaster as one that caused over $1 billion of damage, after adjusting for inflation.[4]

Billion-dollar disasters are unfortunately quite common, as Table 5.1 shows. Over the first 44 years of record keeping, the United States experienced over eight major disasters a year on average. That's over 300 different billion-dollar disasters with a total of $2.7 trillion in damages!

The most troubling aspect of the NOAA data is that the number of billion-dollar disasters is increasing over time. Table 5.1 shows decade by

Table 5.1 Count and Cost of Major US Natural Disasters (Inflation-Adjusted)

Decade	Average number per year	Average disaster cost
1980–1989	3	$22 billion
1990–1999	6	$33 billion
2000–2009	7	$62 billion
2010–2019	13	$99 billion
2020–2023	22	$140 billion
Average all years	**8.5**	**$62 billion**

decade the count and cost of major disasters. In a typical year during the 1980s there were about three major disasters in the average year. The 1990s saw the average jump to six disasters a year. The first decade of the 2000s saw the average increase to seven and during the 2010s the typical year experienced over a dozen billion-dollar disasters. Although the 2020s are not done yet, they are shaping up to be record-breaking with an average of 22 huge disasters per year.

Not only has the number of disasters steadily increased but the cost of damage from each major natural disaster has also risen. The right side of Table 5.1 shows the damages done by a typical storm. During the 1980s the average damage per disaster was about $20 billion. By the 2010s, this had risen to almost $100 billion. In just over four decades the cost of a "typical" major disaster had risen more than fourfold, and this is after taking infla-tion into account!

The rising average number of disasters is not due to a few outlier or unique years. Although there are peaks and valleys, the trend is upward over time. Using an analysis technique called *linear regression* shows the United States gets on average an additional major disaster every three years. The upward trend in the cost of US natural disasters is not caused by statistical mistakes such as ignoring inflation, because the government adjusts the data for changes in consumer prices.[5]

Moreover, if anything, these data understate the problem because the official cost of disasters excludes the value of any lives lost. Even if a storm kills hundreds, no adjustment is made for these deaths. Like the number of disasters, deaths have climbed over time. In the 1980s fewer than 300 peo-ple a year were killed by major natural disasters. By the 2010s over 500 people a year were killed in major natural disasters.

Natural disasters are also getting more frequent around the world. The World Meteorological Organization periodically publishes an "Atlas of Mortality and Economic Losses from Weather, Climate and Water Extremes." A recent atlas found the "number of disasters has increased by a factor of five over the 50-year period, driven by climate change, more extreme weather and improved reporting."[6]

The Atlas shows since 1970 the number of droughts, earthquakes, extreme temperatures, floods, storms, volcanic activity, and wildfires is increasing by about seven a year. In the early 1970s the number of reported natural disasters in the world was in the 60s each year. Recently, the data show almost 370 disasters per year. The world, similar to the US, is seeing a steady rise in natural disasters. Not every disaster wipes out the ability to make electronic payments, but many do.

To summarize, what does the rising number of disasters mean? Even if you are not being affected by major disasters now, you are much more likely to be affected in the future! To give you an idea of the impact of natural disasters, the next few sections discuss specific types such as hurricanes, fires, volcanic eruptions, and solar storms. The goal is not to be fearmongering or excessively morbid. Instead, the point is that although most of the time life proceeds normally, natural disasters occur periodically. Different parts of the world experience different forms of natural disasters, but all disasters are made worse when it is impossible to make purchases or while trying to rebuild shattered lives and communities.

FLOODS: AN EXAMPLE FROM CHINA

China is at the forefront of digital payments. Few people carry cash. Instead most make payments using mobile phone apps like WeChat and Alipay. These phone apps depend on the existence of a robust cell phone network. When cell phone service is knocked out for millions of people who only use their phones to pay, there are massive problems.

Newspaper stories describe what happened in summer 2021 when very heavy rains hit the city of Zhengzhou in central China.[7] Zhengzhou is a city of about 12 million people that sits on the southern bank of the Yellow River. A very slow-moving mid-July rainstorm dropped a year's worth of water on the city in just three days. Cars and people were washed away. Homes, subways, and roads were flooded. The official death toll was over 300 people.[8]

The floods knocked offline 62,000 mobile phone base stations. These stations enable cell phones to connect to the telecommunications network. People could not make purchases when the cell network failed. Banks and ATMs, which could have distributed cash, were shut down because most of them lost electricity.

The Chinese tried novel solutions like using drones for cell towers. Although the drones provided some help, they had limited abilities and could only connect about 650 cell phones to the network at each moment. This was not enough capacity to handle the crush of calls. It took four days to restore the cell phone network. For millions of people in this city who didn't have cash on hand that meant four days without the ability to buy food, water, or pay for transportation.

HURRICANES

Extremely high winds moving through populated areas can come in the form of hurricanes, typhoons, northeasters, or tornadoes depending on where you live. Whatever form they take, these exceptionally high winds knock down electrical poles, topple phone lines, and destroy communication towers.

Two important examples of these winds's destructive force are Hurricane Maria and Hurricane Sandy. Hurricane Maria hit Puerto Rico, a Caribbean Island of 3 million people, in September 2017. The hurricane obliterated the island's entire power grid. One week after the storm, no power had been restored to the island. Two weeks after Hurricane Maria hit, the power was restored to just 9% of electricity customers, mostly in the capital San Juan. The rest of the island was left in the dark. Three weeks after the storm, power was restored to only 11% of customers.[9]

After four weeks the figure had climbed to 19%. This means four out of five customers still didn't have power after a month. It took 11 months – almost a full year – before the power was fully restored to all parts of the island. S&P, the large financial rating and news organization, interviewed Puerto Rican bankers and business owners a year after the hurricane:

> Maria left virtually the entire island without power and wiped out communication networks. That left businesses unable to operate point-of-sale systems, which meant no card payments. The island was suddenly dependent on cash. . . . Hurricane Maria laid bare the banking system's dependence on telecommunications systems, and showed how unprepared banks were for the sudden disruption in cell service.[10]

Although reading about natural disasters in the news might make them seem like quick incidents, Hurricane Maria showed the resulting power and communication outages can last a long time. Maria showed switching away from cash because of the belief damage from a major storm will be cleaned up quickly is not a good assumption.

In October 2012, Hurricane Sandy destroyed parts of the US East Coast. Some of the heaviest damage occurred in New York City and along the New Jersey coast. Sandy is important to understand because it struck Wall Street, the heart of the US financial system.

Major banks, stock exchanges, and even the Federal Reserve all have presences on or near Wall Street. These financial institutions are prepared for disasters with backup generators, redundant data centers, extra communication lines, and remotely located staff. Plus, the East Coast was spared major highway damage when Sandy struck. Because most roads were undamaged, emergency utility crews from all over the country were able to drive repair trucks to the greater New York area as soon as the winds stopped. New York had another advantage: during the storm Michael Bloomberg was mayor. Bloomberg was widely credited with being an efficient and effective mayor who got things done quickly. This meant little political paralysis when the storm hit, and in the cleanup afterwards.

Hurricane Sandy hit one of the most important, but also best-prepared parts of the world. So, given all these positive attributes, what was the outcome? Data from the US government's Energy Information Administration showed the resulting typical New York power outage lasted over one week. After the storm, *Consumer Reports* published an article entitled "Hurricane Sandy Proves Cash Is Still King in Emergencies." The article pointed out[11]:

> Many ATMs in Sandy's path were rendered useless by the storm. Those that remained in operation often had long lines, and some reportedly ran out of cash. Credit and debit cards weren't of much use either, dependent as they are on electronic store terminals.[12]

Hurricanes Maria and Sandy were massive storms that show the need for cash during and after extreme winds. However, it is not only winds that cause problems.

FIRE AND DROUGHT

This chapter started off with the story of the Tubbs Fire, which destroyed parts of Napa, Sonoma, and Lake in California and temporarily shut down communications, eliminating the ability to make electronic payments in a major tourist region. Unfortunately, this fire is not unique. As global temperatures rise, droughts become more frequent. Massive wildfires spread more easily when trees and other vegetation dry out and act as kindling.

Droughts resulting in massive blazes are not a recent phenomenon. One of the biggest US fires on record was the Big Burn of 1910, which occurred during an earlier severe drought.[13] The fire destroyed three million acres of virgin timberland in northern Idaho and western Montana. To give some perspective, three million acres is larger than the entire size of Jamaica, a sunny Caribbean nation.

What is changing is that in earlier times wildfires often happened in remote forests. Today, population growth has resulted in more people living near large forests. In the United States, California is particularly hard hit by wildfires. Cal Fire, the government agency charged with fighting forest fires in the state, has separate lists for the biggest California fires based on: acres burned, deaths, and properties destroyed. The Tubbs fire, discussed previously, is not even California's biggest for property damage.[14]

California's Camp Fire was started by sparks from an electric company's powerline. This fire destroyed nearly 19,000 homes, three times more than the Tubbs fire, and wiped out the town of Paradise. The Camp Fire also eclipsed the Tubbs Fire in deaths by killing at least 85 people. More important, because the fire started from a major powerline, electricity was cut off during the disaster, eliminating the ability to make electronic payments. To prevent being blamed for another conflagration, like the Camp Fire, many utilities are proactively shutting off the power in dangerous drought conditions before fires start. This eliminates the ability to do electronic payments when disasters loom.

Wildfires burning areas where people live and work are not just a California problem. Europe recently experienced years of heat waves and droughts. For example, in summer 2017 Portugal had a series of wildfires that burned half a million hectares, which is about 5% of the entire country. In the face of the growth of wildfires the European Environment Agency states "forest fires coinciding with record droughts and heatwaves have affected regions in central and northern Europe not typically prone to fires. An expansion of fire-prone areas and longer fire seasons are projected in most European regions."[15]

The spread of wildfires in more populated areas is a problem on many levels. These fires destroy not only homes but also the infrastructure that enables electronic payments.

VOLCANIC ERUPTION

Most people think of Pacific Island chains like Hawaii, Tahiti, or Bora Bora as tropical paradises. Many of these islands are located along the "Ring of Fire," which is a path through the Pacific Ocean where most of Earth's volcanoes are located, and where most earthquakes take place. In early 2022 a massive volcanic eruption happened about 40 miles away from the island nation of Tonga. The eruption was heard in New Zealand and triggered a tsunami that killed people across the Pacific Ocean in Peru.[16]

Tonga is small country with about 100,000 people. Nevertheless, it serves as an example of how volcanoes can disrupt electronic money. Electronic payments depend on communication and the volcanic eruption cut the internet connection between Tonga and Fiji, which was the only internet connection Tonga had with other countries. Moreover, the eruption caused an earthquake and a tsunami that broke the internet connections among Tonga's many islands, so within-country communications were also lost. It took five weeks to restore communications.[17]

Tonga's economy was set up to handle this problem better than many other countries, because most Tongans use only cash. Tonga's central bank, the National Reserve Bank of Tonga, surveyed the country's population before the eruption and found the following:

> Cash is king in payments. Income and payments revolve around cash. Both in the private sector and in agriculture the majority of Tongan adults receive income in cash. Only in the public sector do we see employees receiving income into a bank account. Nearly all (98%) respondents report paying utility and school payments with cash instead of digital instruments like bank transfers, debit cards or mobile money; only 10% of respondents reported using mobile money services such as Digicel.[18]

Because so many people use cash in Tonga, transactions after the eruption were able to continue. Tongans use cash because one-fifth of the population doesn't have a photo ID or a birth certificate, a prerequisite in all countries for getting a bank account. Nevertheless, many Tongans receive remittances from friends and relatives abroad. The internet disruption prevented anyone from sending new cash into the country, reducing economic activity.

I do not think Tonga's officials learned the correct monetary lessons from the volcanic eruption. Less than six months after the eruption, Tonga's central bank unveiled a new electronic payment system. The bank trumpeted this move as "marking the beginning of the progressive move toward digitalization of the payment system."[19]

Volcanic disruption is not just a Tongan problem. There are many other countries, such as Japan, that lie in volcanic zones and can suffer the same problems Tonga did. Shifting completely to electronic payments can result in economic disaster when volcanic activity causes a natural disaster.

SOLAR STORMS

Solar storms are one of the most important natural disasters that almost no one thinks about. These storms have not struck recently but could inflict far more damage on electronic payment systems than floods, hurricanes, fires, earthquakes, or volcanic eruptions. Solar or geomagnetic storms happen when the sun erupts and sends out huge bursts of energy and radiation. When these bursts of energy are aimed at Earth they disrupt communication networks, satellites, and electrical power grids.

The impact of solar storms is a relatively recent problem for mankind. Although the sun has been giving off huge bursts of energy for billions of years, until electricity became widespread these bursts of energy were relatively benign. Prior to electricity, mankind primarily noticed these bursts by observing changes in the intensity of the Northern Lights, the dancing patterns of light that occasionally appear near the Arctic after dark.

One of the first times solar storms caused major problems was in 1859. For two days "telegraph systems around the world failed catastrophically. Telegraph operators reported receiving electrical shocks, telegraph paper catching fire, and being able to operate equipment with batteries disconnected." This storm is called the *Carrington event* after the English astronomer Richard Carrington, who was studying sunspots and reported the solar explosion that caused worldwide problems. Another major solar storm happened in 1921 and caused major problems in New York City, where the storm knocked out telegraph service.[20]

Solar storms have affected us more recently. In March 1989 a solar storm hit North America. Within 90 seconds this storm caused Canada's Hydro-Québec power grid to collapse, leaving millions of people in the province of Québec without electricity for up to nine hours, while the grid was restored. The same storm also knocked offline a nuclear power plant in New Jersey, cutting off electricity to people near New York City. In February 2022 a relatively mild solar storm hit Earth and 40 of SpaceX's Starlink satellites, which provide high-speed internet from space, plunged out of orbit and fell to Earth.[21]

There are other ways of detecting solar storms besides watching the Northern Lights or seeing when electrical equipment blows up. Tree rings and ice cores provide records of major solar eruptions. Techniques for decoding these records were pioneered by Fusa Miyake, a Japanese physicist who has been looking for evidence inside ancient Japanese trees.

She has uncovered several solar storms that appear much bigger than the one seen by Carrington and the one experienced by residents of New York City. She found a massive storm, now called the *Miyake Event*, which happened about 1,400 years ago. This storm left behind changes that were more than ten times larger than the Carrington storm.[22] Imagine if a storm of this magnitude were to happen today!

Solar storms are relatively rare. However, when a large one does occur, they are a huge problem because large storms destroy electrical and communications equipment. To quote David Wallace, an electrical engineering professor:

> It is only a matter of time before the Earth is hit by another geomagnetic storm. A Carrington Event–size storm would be extremely damaging to the electrical and communication systems worldwide with outages lasting into the weeks. If the storm is the size of the Miyake Event, the results would be catastrophic for the world with potential outages lasting months if not longer.[23]

Solar storms are very rare events, but if they knock out the electrical grid and communications networks, how will society continue to function? Not well is clearly the answer but having paper money still in use would ensure at least some transactions succeed.

CONCLUSION

The world is constantly beset by natural disasters. In those moments of great need, only paper money works.

Imagine for a moment a storm is forecast. Weather forecasters expect this storm to be nothing out of the ordinary, so no one panics or prepares. Unexpectedly, the storm intensifies, smashing power lines leading to a widespread blackout. Everyone is urged to evacuate the area. Without power the stores, gas stations, and other retailers providing necessities to flee the storm's wrath cannot handle electronic transactions. They can only take paper money. If you only have credit cards, debit cards, or cryptocurrency in this circumstance, you are in trouble no matter how rich you are.

It is not just storms. During earthquakes, antennas and communication equipment topple. Massive fires burn cell towers and communication switching centers. Even if the power stays on during a disaster, businesses often cannot accept electronic payments because the ability to communicate with the banking system is lost.

There is little anyone can do to reduce the number of natural disasters. However, there are simple things that increase resilience in the face of disaster. This is the advice I gave to a friend who moved to Los Angeles and now lives near the San Andreas Fault, an earthquake-prone zone. First, always have a go-bag handy. A go-bag is a prepacked survival kit that contains food, medicine, water, and other supplies ready to go when an emergency strikes. Second, put enough cash in the go-bag to get safely out of the disaster zone even after prices soar.

Cash is not only useful during the disaster but also in the aftermath. Many states institute price freezes after a disaster strikes to prevent price gouging. In general these laws stipulate that key items must be sold at either the pre-emergency price or only a small markup above the pre-disaster price. For example in 2023 the Hawaiian Island of Maui had massive wildfires and instituted price freezes on food, water, milk, vehicles, rent, and many other costs during the recovery phase.[24]

Price freezes result in shortages because the cost of doing business soars after a disaster. People able to pay in cash often get preferred treatment over customers paying with electronic methods. This happens because when companies have more business than they can handle, cash payers give the companies both a higher profit and the assurance payments are not disputed. Plus, dealing with cash payers is simpler after a disaster, because there are fewer steps that need to work.

Keeping and continuously using cash during usual times ensures resilience so when Mother Nature unleashes her full fury on the world, society continues functioning.

CHAPTER SIX

PAPER MONEY BOOSTS NATIONAL DEFENSE

Every major country has enemies and wants to protect itself. Although it might not be obvious at first glance, the switch from physical cash to digital and electronic money is a major national defense problem. One way to boost a country's national defense is by keeping paper money around.

Military planners learned long ago there are many ways of weakening or destroying an enemy without bombing it back into the Stone Age. One effective method of hurting an enemy is by shutting down their economy. In general, the more a country uses electronic payments, the easier it is for an enemy to cause widespread disruption.[1]

During past wars, attackers would blockade an enemy to limit its food supply or bomb its supply and storage centers to disrupt the economy. With a cashless society a simpler and more effective method of disruption is to deny people access to their money and deny people the ability to spend their money. Without money, it is difficult to buy food, pay for medical care, or use transportation. Destroying the ability to move money around grinds an economy to a halt. Using paper money makes it harder for an enemy to disrupt the economy because there are fewer central places to attack.

One example of paper money's usefulness in the face of enemy attacks occurred when Russia invaded Ukraine in 2022. Nine months into the war, after suffering numerous battlefield setbacks, Russian forces switched tactics. They began a systematic campaign of using clusters of missile attacks to destroy Ukraine's electrical grid. These attacks resulted in millions of Ukrainians losing power for long periods of time. Without power Ukrainian credit cards, debit cards, and cryptocurrency transactions did not work, but cash did.[2]

Before the war Ukrainians used paper money called the *hryvnia*. The National Bank of Ukraine, the country's central bank, did not appreciate the usefulness of paper currency and before the war was at the forefront of nations trying to introduce a digital currency. Only a few months before the war the central bank started testing an electronic version of money called the *e-hryvnia* for all kinds of retail payments. Luckily for the country the e-hryvnia was not officially rolled out into widespread use at the war's beginning. If the country had switched over to the e-hryvnia, citizens would have found it is impossible to use the digital currency when they were without power for long periods of time.[3]

It is not just physical bombs but also cyberattacks which threaten electronic payments and money. This chapter will go into more details, but all types of financial institutions are under constant cyberattacks. Most are by criminals looking to steal money, but some are by nation states trying to hurt enemies. For example, Ukraine experienced a wave of cyberattacks just before Russian forces invaded.

For officials in charge of national security, cyberattacks by state-sponsored organizations are far more dangerous than threats from criminals. Enemies are trying to disrupt or destroy the entire financial infrastructure; criminals are not. One of the best data sources tracking these more serious threats lists 66 state-sponsored cyberattacks on financial institutions by enemy states from 2007 to 2022, a time of relative peace in the world.[4]

On average, more than four times a year one state has attacked and attempted to disrupt another state's banking and financial systems. Although 66 might not seem like a large number, this list only tracks state-sponsored attacks that were publicly revealed. There are no data on thwarted, covered up, never discovered, or failed state-sponsored attacks.

Keeping paper money in circulation helps national security by ensuring payments can still be made when an enemy denies citizens the ability to use electronic payments. Just as importantly, when an enemy successfully attacks the financial system and people lose confidence, paper money gives the ability for people and businesses to feel they have some control over their economic lives by letting them pull money out of the financial system and hold it as cash.

MODERN EXAMPLES

Beyond Ukraine there are numerous examples of a nation's enemies attempting to economically disrupt a country by physically attacking banks and other financial institutions. One of the most famous happened on September 11, 2001, when two hijacked planes destroyed the World Trade Center in New York City. Destroying the towers was designed to economically cripple the United States because the towers contained the offices of many financial firms and were physically located blocks from Wall Street, the country's financial center.

The 2001 attack was the second time these buildings were targeted. In 1993 a giant truck bomb was parked under the north tower of the World Trade Center. Exploding the bomb was designed to undermine the building's foundation and cause one tower to collapse onto the other. This bombing failed to bring down either of the towers but killed six people.

Another example where an enemy of the state targeted the financial heart of a country happened during 2014 in the Middle East. ISIS, a terrorist group attempting to create an Islamic caliphate, stormed the Iraqi city of Mosul. One of the group's first targets was the Iraqi central bank. The Iraqi central bank's head office is in Baghdad, but it has four branches in Basrah, Mosul, Sulaymaniyah, and Erbil. News reports focused on the amount of money ISIS took: "500 billion Iraqi dinars," worth about US$425 million, as well as a "large quantity of gold bullion." However, the loss to the Iraqi economy far exceeded the money taken. Targeting the central bank made it almost impossible to move money and make payments electronically in the Mosul region, because the bank at the center of economic activity was destroyed.[5]

These examples were physical attacks. Cyberattacks are also growing. One type of attack is denial of service, when rogue actors prevent access by flooding the internet with requests. This overload prevents legitimate users from accessing financial websites, ATMs, and online payments. For example, in 2018 two Dutch banks, ABN Amro and Rabobank, were attacked and their online banking services were shut down for extended periods. A few months later Spain's central bank was hit by a denial-of-service attack.

Although denial-of-service attacks are obvious when they occur, other types of cyberattacks are more difficult to detect. Occasionally large-scale cyberattacks by foreign governments make the news. In 2020 the US government revealed details of how the "BeagleBoyz," a group of North Korean government hackers attached to an intelligence unit, were attacking banks throughout the world. In a period of five years the BeagleBoyz had attempted to steal about $2 billion. More important, the group had put destructive malware on bank computers that made critical computer systems inoperable.[6]

Banks project an image of extreme safety. Many banks are physically imposing structures and have large guards standing at the doors. After all, who would want to deposit money with an organization that appears weak and untrustworthy? Because of this desire to maintain a strong and secure façade, banks are loath to report less obvious attacks when their systems are breached. Concern over this problem has resulted in US banks now being required to report to federal regulators any outages or cyberattacks that "would pose a threat to the financial stability of the United States."[7]

These reports, plus information from other countries, are collected by the Carnegie Endowment for International Peace and organized into a database of cyberattacks on financial institutions called the FinCyber Project. The Carnegie Endowment created this database to help people understand that "state-sponsored cyberattacks targeting financial institutions are becoming more frequent, sophisticated, and destructive." Although regular criminals seek to steal money, state-sponsored attacks are designed to compromise national security. As mentioned, FinCyber data show 66 state-sponsored attacks from 2007 to 2022. More important, over time the average number of attacks each year is growing. Given state-sponsored attacks are a reality, countries around the world should continue to use paper money for the times when, not if, electronic money is disrupted.[8]

COUNTERFEIT MONEY – DESTROYING FAITH IN THE CURRENCY

History is replete with other examples of a nation's enemies attempting to disrupt the economy. One early method was by printing counterfeit money. Modern printing techniques make this difficult to do today, but there are many examples in the past of enemies flooding a country with counterfeits, causing people to lose faith in paper money. Once faith is lost, people refuse to accept money, putting the economy in jeopardy.

My favorite example comes from the US Revolutionary War. During that war the Continental Congress needed revenue. The Congress was a weak confederation of revolutionary leaders who had little gold or other monetary resources. They also had few methods of earning funds by taxation. The standard story is that the Congress turned to the printing press to create money called the *continental*. Supposedly the Congress printed so much money that the resulting inflation led to the expression "not worth a continental." These problems with the almost worthless continental currency were especially pronounced in Philadelphia, the location of the Continental Congress, where shopkeepers didn't trust the money and workers refused to be paid in continentals.[9]

Although the standard story is interesting, there is an extremely high likelihood it is a fable that doesn't reflect what happened. Eric Newman, an expert in the history of early coins and currency, published a fascinating article laying out evidence that Great Britain sent not only troops to fight the Continental Army but also a special printing press that could create counterfeit continental currency.[10]

The British bought supplies from locals with counterfeit continental currency, resulting in massive inflation.[11] By printing and using counterfeit currency the British secured supplies at no cost to the English Crown. They also destroyed faith in their enemy's currency. The problem was especially acute in Philadelphia because British troops spent eight months occupying the city during winter 1777.

The British forces understood that without a trusted currency, colonial era people were forced to use either scarce Spanish coins or barter. Destroying faith and trust in the continental currency weakened the ability of the Continental Congress to supply their troops and continue the war.[12]

Counterfeiting was not limited to the British during one war. During World War II the Nazis hit the English with a dose of their own medicine. The Nazis created an entire unit to forge British currency. The forgery, called *Operation Bernhard*, was originally designed to destabilize the English economy. Hitler believed dropping fake notes that were indistinguishable from real notes via airplanes flying over England would weaken the British economy.

This plan was not carried out because the Germans changed their goals and used counterfeit money to pay their spies and English people who were secretly trying to help the German cause. The money was such a good replica of British currency that after the war the Bank of England replaced all currency above £5 to restore trust.[13]

In the early 1990s the United States led a coalition of forces to overthrow Iraqi president Saddam Hussein. Before the actual fighting began, coalition forces started injecting a flood of fake Iraqi dinars, the local money, into the country. The goal was "aimed at crippling Iraq's economy." Flooding Iraq with fake money resulted in people being unsure if the money they received was real or not, leading to suspicion and a sharp reduction in purchases.[14]

Newer printing and engraving techniques have made counterfeiting currency very difficult. Since 1994 US currency has included sophisticated anti-counterfeiting measures such as color shifting inks, 3D security ribbons, and watermark images. Other countries have switched to plastic or polymer stock instead of using paper made from cloth rags to print bills. Because of these measures, counterfeiting today is relatively rare.

Given countries no longer worry much about counterfeiting, attacks on money should no longer be a national defense problem, right? Wrong. Although the problem of destroying faith in cash transactions has receded, cashless transactions are still at risk.

POWER

Parts of the next war will be fought in cyberspace. For the United States one potential threat comes from Russia. *The New York Times* published an article in 2021 about this threat and the lead sentence was "Russia's premier intelligence agency has launched another campaign to pierce thousands of US government, corporate and think-tank computer networks."[15]

Military planners try to attack key physical infrastructure like power, water, and communications. However, what you destroy in war needs to be rebuilt after you take over territory. Military planners sometimes look for ways to deprive enemies of food, water, and communications without blowing up power stations, warehouses, and dams. One way is to prevent people from buying necessities.

A cashless economy depends on electricity to function. In times of war the electrical grid is subject to both physical and cyberattacks. Going back to the example of Russia invading Ukraine, one of the early key targets of the Russian military was Ukraine's power stations. In the beginning of the war the Russians captured the Zaporizhzhia nuclear power plant, Europe's largest. This plant provided one-fifth of all Ukraine's electricity. Losing the ability to generate power means lights are off, elevators do not run, kitchen appliances shut off, and electronic money is unusable.[16]

The US, like Ukraine, is also susceptible to widespread electrical disruption, except the United States has a different Achilles heel. Ukraine concentrated its generation in a few large plants. This is not a problem for the United States because the largest power plant, the Grand Coulee Dam, produces less than 1% of the country's trillion kilowatts of generating capacity.

The US electrical system, however, has a different vulnerability, as discussed in Chapter 4. Electricity flows over only three power grids, which are massive sets of wires that move power thousands of miles. Knocking out even one of the three US grids would cause disruption to millions of people and shut down a significant portion of the overall economy. Numerous high-level task forces have been convened to discuss how to harden key pieces of infrastructure. Efforts like creating micro-grids, battery backups, and extensive testing for security problems are good methods of hardening. However, these efforts are like a chess game. As one avenue of attack is blocked, another opening or fault line is revealed.

One of the simplest methods to ensure the economy functions even when the power supply is disrupted is one used for decades: paper money. Paper money needs power to be printed. However, once it is created paper money works without any additional energy.

MOVING MONEY

Another national defense problem is preventing a disruption to how the banking system moves money and other financial assets. Banks across the world move huge amounts of money electronically. They expend extraordinary effort to ensure these movements are secure.

A serious vulnerability to moving money is counterfeit messages. Rogue actors can infiltrate the system and disrupt the system by sending extra messages or deleting some messages.

The financial messaging system is like GPS instructions when driving. Most of us always follow the computer-generated directions when driving from place to place. When the voice navigation system states turn left, we turn left; when it says turn right, we turn right.

Vast numbers of financial messages flow around the world every moment telling banks and other financial institutions to move huge amounts of money. Banks follow these instructions, just like drivers follow GPS directions. The financial system is quick and inexpensive to use because all parties trust the messages. However, imagine a world where some of the messages are fake! The ability to seamlessly make financial transactions electronically would end and the world would need a backup. That backup is paper money.

Before talking about the present day, let's go back in time to 1899 because the past and present are never very far apart. In the 1800s financial messages moved around the world over telegraph wires. Although today's messages are encrypted, those in the past were not. This meant that people with technical expertise could tap into the telegraph wires and listen in on the messages being transmitted. This became known as wiretapping.

Although most wiretappers simply listened to glean confidential information, there were also times when people inserted fake messages. In 1899 cotton commodity speculators created the "wildest panic ever witnessed on the floor of the New Orleans Cotton Exchange" by inserting messages saying that cotton was trading at much higher prices in Liverpool than it actually was.[17]

Rogue traders sent five messages down the telegraph wire and caused pandemonium because farmers, traders, and mills all thought the price of cotton was soaring, when it wasn't. Cotton, which in 1899 traded at an average of 7¢ per pound, supposedly had jumped up by 2.5¢, a roughly one-third increase. The spoofed messages caused a temporary closure of the Cotton Exchange and resulted in lawsuits. Although history has quickly forgotten this episode, it shows the impact a small number of fake financial messages can have on the economy.

Today we no longer use unencrypted telegrams to move money; instead, we use more sophisticated message networks. One of the largest networks for transferring money is SWIFT, which stands for the Society for Worldwide Interbank Financial Telecommunications. SWIFT is a global cooperative that has linked almost all countries' financial systems since the 1970s. The SWIFT network does not actually move money. Instead, SWIFT is a messaging system that enables banks and other financial institutions to securely tell other organizations how much and where to move money and other financial assets.

SWIFT maintains the highest standards of security because millions of messages flow through its systems daily. Nevertheless, the system is constantly tested by rogue actors. In February 2016 the central bank of Bangladesh was the victim of a widely reported SWIFT attack. The central bank lost over $100 million due to fake SWIFT messages being inserted into the system. These fraudulent messages directed the New York Federal Reserve to send money to accounts in Indonesia and the Philippines. The attack could have been more costly, because over US$1 billion was asked to be transferred, but after transferring about 10% bank officials held up the remaining transfers to ensure they were legitimate.[18]

The Bangladesh case shows that although breaking into the SWIFT network is difficult, it is not impossible. A larger compromise of the SWIFT network could prevent money and other financial assets from moving between countries because people could no longer trust the messages. This would dramatically reduce the amount of world trade because exporters and importers could no longer depend on fast and cheap international money transfers.

Policymakers concerned about national defense not only have to worry about moving money between countries but also how money is transferred within a country. Inside the US, one important method of moving money is via the Federal Reserve's Fedwire system. Whereas SWIFT simply contains the instructions for how much to move and where, Fedwire messages actually move money from one account to another.

Fedwire is designed to let banks and financial institutions make large-value, time-critical payments. When a payment is initiated in the system it is processed immediately and cannot be revoked. It is impossible to take the money back. This means once someone wires the money, the person or business receiving knows it is theirs without any question.

The Fedwire moves a staggering amount of money each year. In just 2021, a year when the COVID pandemic still slowed economic activity, almost $1 quadrillion in payments were sent through the system. A quadrillion is 1,000 times $1 trillion. To give an idea of the scale, that is more than ten times the entire world's annual GDP. This vast movement depends on all parties believing every message is legitimate.

Can cash even serve as a Fedwire backup? Each day the Fedwire handles about $4 trillion in transfers. Given the United States has only about $2 trillion of paper currency in circulation, cash potentially could handle only half of all transactions, unless special larger denomination bills were created.

Larger notes were printed and occasionally used. In the depths of the Great Depression the US Treasury printed $100,000 notes. These were not legal tender for the public, but were used by the US Treasury to buy all the gold held by the Federal Reserve. To make the transfer of gold from one government branch to another legal, money had to be created and this money was the largest denomination printed to date. Although these very large notes were printed in the 1930s to help rescue the economy, there is nothing preventing large notes from being printed again to be used as a backup for when large electronic money transfers do not work or are not trusted.[19]

The important thing to keep in mind when thinking about these massive numbers is that the Fedwire is only one method of transferring money. Other methods of transferring large sums are via ACH, which is the Automated Clearing House, or CHIPS, the Clearing House Interbank Payments System, which is a private funds transfer system. All these methods have vulnerabilities that can be exploited by nation state hackers.

Can the Fedwire be compromised? The Federal Reserve System takes inordinate care to make sure the Fedwire is safe and secure. However, Mark Bilger examined the cybersecurity risks and the possibility of a successful attack on Fedwire and its potential impact on the US financial system.

Bilger suggests there is a relatively low likelihood the Fedwire will be compromised but cannot rule it out. However, his conclusion is clear, "if you can't trust Fedwire, you can't trust the Fed. The efficiency of American commerce depends on that trust."[20]

DESTROYING FAITH

Another way an enemy can destabilize an economy is by destroying faith in banks, money, and the financial system. People save money in banks because they believe all their money is secure and can be withdrawn on a moment's notice. People work because they are sure their pay will be able to buy goods and services. Businesses sell items because they are confident customers will pay for purchases. Traders buy and sell in financial markets because they believe counterparties will complete their trades. When faith is gone, economies start shutting down.

Let me ask you a question. Do you have a bank account, stocks, or bonds? How much is in these accounts? All these accounts exist only in electronic form. Much of the world's wealth exists only in electronic form in a variety of databases. If these databases are wiped clean, society has little proof of the existence of this wealth or our corresponding debts. We store our wealth in electronic form because we have faith it is secure.

Hackers around the world have been increasingly using ransomware attacks on all types of businesses. These attacks lock computers and their data, preventing access. More recently hackers have installed software on unprotected computers and servers that wipe away all data.

Financial institutions have always been concerned about this, so they run redundant servers and store backups off-site in secure locations. This means our wealth that is stored electronically is safe for the long term. However, what about short term? Imagine all the computers in a large bank or financial institution are compromised and all data wiped clean. It could take the IT department days to reconstruct all the accounts. For days account holders would have no access to their money.

These situations have happened. On September 11, 2001, two hijacked planes destroyed the World Trade Towers in New York City. A side effect was that much of the telecommunication infrastructure of lower Manhattan was also destroyed and unusable for days.[21]

One of the most affected financial institutions was Bank of New York, nicknamed BoNY, whose main operations center was one block from the World Trade Center. Although BoNY moved to its backup sites outside Manhattan immediately, it took the bank one week to restore services to its customers. During that week BoNY reported it was unable to send $100 billion in payments on the Fedwire and customers could not use BoNY's ATMs!

Another example of a physical attack that disrupted electronic payments happened over Christmas in 2020 in Nashville, Tennessee. The perpetrator parked an RV containing a bomb beside one of the main telecommunications buildings and when the bomb went off, AT&T and T-Mobile services were disrupted. This led stores like Walmart in a wide area stretching all the way into northern Alabama to become cash-only businesses until telecommunications were restored about four days later.[22]

ARE TRANSACTIONS TRUE?

Another way an enemy can destabilize the economy is to destroy faith in the truth of transactions. Large numbers of people swipe, tap, and scan without looking at the actual amounts or requesting any proof of what they are expected to pay. I am often glared at by clerks and restaurant staff who are offended when I request a paper receipt after paying electronically.

When people are asked to sign for purchases, many simply swipe a finger or make a small mark. Few people today treat purchases as something to be suspicious of. The attitude is that banks and financial companies don't make math or transcription mistakes. If an item was scanned and the price is in the right range at the register, then the universal assumption is that this amount will show up on the monthly statement.

What if that assumption was wrong? The current focus for many is to defend against hacking, which is where nefarious individuals try to deny service or steal outright. However, to sow confusion and crush an economy, a nefarious enemy state can simply inject randomization into the electronic money process.

Who would use or accept electronic methods of payment if no one was sure what would be charged? If businesses had to double-check every transaction, they would quickly abandon electronic payments, but injecting programs that provide randomness is just as easy or hard as breaking in and stealing information or causing other kinds of problems.

Cash is an important defense against all types of cyberattacks. In general, when financial markets experience unexpected sharp losses, investors quickly shift away from risky assets like stocks, bonds, and cryptocurrencies. They shift their investments into less risky assets like government bonds and paper money. This is called a *flight to quality* or a *flight from risk.*

Another potential way state-sponsored enemies can wreak financial havoc is by cyberattacks on financial institutions that use artificial intelligence (AI) to make trading and lending decisions. As financial markets have grown, humans have become less involved in making routine decisions. In 2018 one financial expert estimated the majority of US stock market trades were done by computer programs executing buy and sell orders without any human interaction.[23]

Many of these trading and lending algorithms use machine learning. This means as more data arrive, the computer updates how it trades and makes decisions. Because machine learning is relatively new, experts are only just beginning to understand these programs' vulnerabilities. For example, one commonly used assumption is that all data being input into financial computers are accurate and truthful. An expert on these programs reported to the *Wall Street Journal* that

"They're very much susceptible to manipulation," said David Van Bruwaene, an AI expert who heads compliance company Fairly AI Inc. "Figuring out a way to trick models at overleveraged banks, then have them take massive losses, that would be a kind of large-scale nuclear bomb on our economy."[24]

Many computer algorithms make trading decisions based on momentum. When a stock or bond is rising or falling it often continues in the same direction. Momentum algorithms tend to exacerbate market movements. For example, the CFA Institute, which trains many investment managers, discusses algorithmic trades and states, "When the market starts to trend, these 'algos' often switch into trading faster than others or more aggressively in the same direction of the trend. Selling more or before others drains liquidity and can create a flash crash."[25]

When algorithms are making trading decisions, it is possible to cause a market crash by hacking into the networks that report financial trades and broadcasting a series of fake trades that appear to show the value of financial assets are steadily falling. Seeing this happen, the algorithms can take over and cause that very result.

Faith in the banking system can be restored, but it is often costly. In 1991 Iraq invaded Kuwait. During the invasion Iraq ransacked banks, businesses, and homes. After Iraq was driven out of Kuwait, the central bank made extraordinary efforts to restore faith in the financial system. "All bank account deposits were restored to their pre-invasion balances. Where forced withdrawals had been made, interest for the period of the occupation was calculated and added to each account."[26]

CONCLUSION

Proponents of cryptocurrency believe that block chain technology can eliminate the problems discussed in this chapter because the data containing the ownership trail of cryptocurrencies is distributed all over the world. Unfortunately, during wars, access to electricity and communications, like the internet on which cryptocurrency rely, does not always work.

Moreover, enemy states as well as hackers and other nefarious organizations might target cryptocurrencies created by governments during a war. This was highlighted in a speech given by Federal Reserve Governor Christopher Waller about creating a central bank digital currency, or CBDC. Governor Waller states, "As cybersecurity concerns mount, a CBDC could become a new target for those threats."[27]

The shift to a cashless economy worries officials in charge of national defense. Sweden is one of the world's cashless societies. Relatively few people in this Scandinavian country use or hold paper money. However, this country is located less than 500 miles from Russia and government officials are concerned about being on the doorstep of a belligerent neighbor.

Sweden has a government organization called the *Civil Contingencies Agency*, whose job is to provide civil defense and emergency management. A few years ago, this agency sent every home in Sweden a booklet entitled "If Crisis or War Comes."[28]

The booklet asks, "What would you do if your everyday life was turned upside down?" and mentions problems like payment cards, cash machines, mobile networks, and the internet not working. Despite being a cashless society, one government recommendation is still that all Swedes should have a reserve of cash. This example shows national defense is not just about planes, tanks, and guns. National defense is also about ensuring the economy continues working during actual and cold wars.

Not all countries worry about attacks from neighbors. However, for those facing these threats, the Swedish idea of ensuring every citizen and business keeps a reserve of cash combined with businesses able to handle paper money makes a country more resilient against enemy attacks.

SECTION III

CASH HELPS PEOPLE

This section of the book shows how using cash helps individuals and covers four main points. First, as discussed in Chapter 7, using cash helps control a person's spending. We all want to be rich. Electronic payment methods like buy now, pay later and credit cards provide the illusion of being rich because people using these methods do not have to deal immediately with the consequences of making a purchase! Swipe, tap, or click and something desired is yours right this instant. What could be better? This frictionless experience turbocharges desires for immediate gratification. Using paper money, however, causes people to experience a moment of regret, called the *pain of paying*. The pain causes people to think about their spending, resulting in more self-control.

Chapter 8 discusses other reasons how cash can help people. Electronic payments cause people to spend more, even without experiencing pain. Using electronic payments ensures you have access to all of the money in your bank accounts, plus any credit you are allowed to borrow. Cash forces people to budget their spending. Electronic payment methods do not.

Chapter 9 discusses how cash provides privacy. Electronic methods of paying result in a permanent record of all purchases. Protecting privacy is important for people's safety, control, and avoiding awkward situations. Chapter 10 describes how using cash reduces business costs compared to many electronic methods. Lower costs means consumers can buy products and services at cheaper prices.

CHAPTER SEVEN

USING CASH HELPS CONTROL SPENDING

W hy use cash instead of electronic means of payment? One of the biggest reasons is that using paper money reduces your spending! Many people have problems with impulse control. Paying for things in cash helps because once you run out of cash you are done shopping. Credit and debit cards loosen these constraints, allowing people to make impulse purchases.

Humans are not perfect calculating machines who make all decisions rationally. Instead, we all suffer from inconsistencies and biases that businesses exploit. There is an entire academic field called *behavioral economics* that investigates the quirks in how people act, and one quirk is that people spend more when paying electronically than when using cash.

One finding from behavioral economics is the idea of present bias: people overvalue instant gratification and undervalue debts or payments they will make in the future. Credit cards and buy now, pay later strategies exploit this present bias: swipe, tap, or click "okay" and you have instant gratification although the bill, whether you've selected to pay in full or are spreading the total out into staggered payments, does not arrive until much later.

A second reason electronic methods increase spending comes from Zellermayer's research, which found many people feel a tiny amount of pain, regret, or guilt when they spend cash, so he coined the phrase "pain of paying." Swiping a credit or debit card or using another form of electronic payments separates you from the physical act of parting with cash and does not cause the same kind or amount of pain. This not only makes humans more receptive to using cashless payments but also makes them willing to spend more. Because spending with a cashless method doesn't cause pain, you are more likely to do it![1]

A third reason why people spend more with cashless payments is because electronic methods enable people to live beyond their means. Many people live paycheck to paycheck, which means spending every bit of disposable income and not saving anything for the future. A recent survey found about 60% of the United States live this way; it is not just the poor. The same survey found many high-income people spend their entire income each month. For poor people, living paycheck to paycheck is often due to not having enough income. For high-income people, however, part of this spend-it-all-now attitude is aided by the rise of electronic payments, which enable people to spend more freely than when using cash.[2]

Spending is boosted by the policies of cashless payment companies. For example, American Express, one of the large credit card companies, has a special program called the "spend-centric" business model. Spend-centric targets card holders with special offers and lower fees. American Express is clear on this program's goal: "This creates incentives for Card Members to spend more on their cards."[3]

Before diving deeper into the details I want to tell you a story that illustrates how much people boost their spending by shifting away from cash. In my mind the cashless economy started in New York City in February 1950 when a mass-market credit card was first used to buy something. This first credit card was Diners Club, which enabled patrons to charge their meals instead of paying with cash.

Diners Club's pitch to individuals was simple; it made life easier. Customers who ate out frequently didn't have to carefully budget their cash during the month. The pitch to restaurants was just as simple. Customers who did not feel financially constrained would eat and drink more. Letting customers charge their meals would boost restaurant revenue.

The first charge happened at Major's Cabin Grill, a fancy restaurant long since closed. The Grill was located a few steps from the Empire State Building in New York City, where the Diners Club offices were located. A postcard from the restaurant trumpets it as known for "Nationally famous charcoal broiled steaks – chops – sea food." The postcard shows large pieces of meat hanging in the front window and rows of tables with white starched napkins, set off with black ashtrays.[4]

At the end of the meal the company's founders pulled out the first credit card and handed it to the waiter, who was confused. The waiter looked at the restaurant's owner and then remembered he had been told this was a valid means of paying for the meal. The rest was history. Diners Club card use and other credit cards exploded in popularity. Diners Club in its first year signed up almost 100,000 members for this new cashless concept. The company was also able to sign up many restaurants even though each got only 93% of the total charge. Diners Club initially kept 7% of all billings by acting as an intermediary.

This number bears repeating. Restaurant owners voluntarily gave up 7¢ from every $1 of income in the 1950s because customers boosted their spending by far more than Diners Club's share!

DO PEOPLE SPEND MORE?

Beyond the Diners Club anecdote it is important to check if using electronic payments, especially credit cards, boosts spending today. One often-quoted statistic showing that electronic payment users spend more is that "McDonald's reports that cash users spent an average of $4.50 per ticket in its restaurants, while debit or credit card users spent an average of $7." This was corroborated by Hirschman, who found holding a credit card boosted spending in department stores, and Feinberg, who found people left bigger tips when using credit cards instead of cash.[5]

The problem with these facts is that richer people have debit and credit cards, and poorer people often do not. Richer people can afford to purchase more than poor. So simply knowing that electronic payment customers spend more than cash buyers doesn't prove that using electronic payments results in increased spending.

Researchers spent time analyzing this problem with relatively sophisticated statistical techniques that held many factors like income, wealth, and education constant. The consensus from this research was clear: cashless payments boosted spending. The problem with considering all these factors is that researchers are never sure they adjusted for every important factor. They might have overlooked an integral factor that no one thought was important.

Lately, researchers have been using imaginative techniques to get around this missing variable problem. Two professors ran some interesting experiments with MBA students. They auctioned off tickets to professional sporting events like professional basketball and baseball games. Half the MBA students were randomly selected and told only cash was accepted if they had a winning bid, and the other half was told only credit cards were accepted for payment. The experiment found students allowed to use credit cards were willing to pay more than double for the tickets than those using cash.[6]

Another group of professors put a small number of adults into a functional magnetic resonance imaging (fMRI) machine to watch what happened when people made purchase decisions using cash or credit cards. fMRI uses magnetic imaging to measure tiny changes in blood flow in the active part of the brain. When subjects used credit cards their striatum, which is the part of the brain that controls rewards, was activated no matter what price was charged. Cash, however, didn't activate reward circuitry for high-priced items but weakly activated it for low-priced items. In simple terms, using credit cards gives people a positive mental jolt especially for expensive items; cash purchases don't stimulate us the same way.[7]

IMPULSE CONTROL

Leaders of protest marches often start chants with "What do we want?" and "When do we want it?" Although the answer to the first question varies, the universal answer to the second question is "Now!" Many people have problems with impulse control. We see something we want, and we do not want to delay. Electronic payments help fuel our desire for instant gratification. Purchasing something with electronic means is as simple as waving your phone or tapping a few buttons. The bill comes much later.

Economists frequently create models in which all humans are rational calculating people. However, humans are not rational and certainly don't calculate all the time. Instead, we often choose immediate rewards, even when they harm us in the future. People don't value things in the future as much as they care about things today. The old expression is apt: a bird in the hand is worth two in the bush. Credit cards and buy now, pay later plans push off the day of reckoning. Paying in the future is no big deal, until the future happens. Giving people the breathing space between buying and paying boosts their spending.

Economists use a tool called the *discount rate* that shows how much people are willing to give up to avoid having to wait. Calculating the discount rate is simple. Which would you rather have: $100 today or $110 tomorrow? People who choose the $100 today are taking a 10% discount to avoid waiting.

I have hypothetically asked many people this question and the results are mixed, with quite a few taking the $100 instantly and others taking the $110 tomorrow. Then I change the question and ask which do you prefer, $100 one year from now or $110 one year and one day from now? The gap in the question is still one day, but all the rewards will occur in a distant future. Almost everyone chooses the $110. There is no real pain in waiting one more day given the reward is far off. However, I am sure that after waiting one year, if I ask the same people the original question, many people will revert to taking the smaller amount. This inconsistency and desire for instant gratification is another reason why merchants love electronic forms of payment, especially those that allow people to defer payment. People are consistently willing to spend more when they can achieve instant gratification.

VISUALIZATION

Visualization is another reason why using cash results in less spending. When paying with cash you count out the bills. This makes it easy to see exactly how much wealth you are giving up. Cashless payments make this wealth loss difficult to visualize because money in a bank account is just digits and not something actually touched or counted. Humans are conditioned to think of paper money as something valuable. In reality it is just pretty pieces of paper, but we treat it as something special. Because our brains view it as valuable, we treat cash differently.[8]

Casinos have understood this for years. Gamblers in casinos play with colored chips, not cash. Before placing a bet, a gambler hands cash over to the dealer or teller for chips. Gamblers who win are handed back chips. Before leaving a casino, gamblers go and "cash out" their chips. This seems totally irrational. Gamblers start and end with cash but must convert everything to chips in the middle. Casinos need a large staff to convert cash to chips and back again. It seems like extra work for nothing. However, this extra work results in gamblers willing to wager very large sums because playing with chips feels as if they are not playing with real money. Losing large numbers of chips on a bad bet results in much less regret than losing the same amount of paper money.

I rarely go to casinos, but one experience stands out clearly. A friend invited me to a casino, so I took cash out of the bank a few days before. Because the cash made my wallet lumpy, I pulled some bills out and put them away. Just before leaving I went looking for the extra money and couldn't find it. I tore my apartment apart looking for the missing bills. It was quite upsetting that I couldn't remember where my cash was stashed. I finally found the money, but it took a while to calm down. Later at the casino I felt "lucky" and put down a bet the same size as the misplaced cash. A few seconds later I lost. I didn't feel very upset, shrugged, and kept on playing. I still think about that day. Losing cash was deeply distressing. Losing the same amount in chips was a minor annoyance.

ENDOWMENT EFFECT

A third reason why paying with cash results in spending less comes from Thaler, who pointed out the endowment effect. Once people are endowed, or given, something valuable, they don't want to give it up. One of Thaler's classic experiments used coffee mugs. Half a group of students were given coffee mugs emblazoned with a university logo. Half were given cash. The group with the mugs was asked at what price they would sell their mugs. The mug-less students were asked how much they would pay to own a mug. The price those endowed with mugs wanted was twice as high as the price the mug-less were willing to pay.[9]

The endowment effect arises because of loss aversion. Giving something up means a person experiences a loss. Most humans experience more pain and regret when faced with a loss than they experience pleasure with an equal size gain. For example, imagine you just won $1,000. How much joy would you feel? How long would you feel happy? Now imagine you just lost $1,000. How much sadness would you feel? How long would you feel upset? I didn't pick these amounts randomly. Five years before writing this book, I had $1,000 stolen from me by a pickpocket on a subway ride. My mind still frequently returns to that moment and the negative emotions, even though I have had many larger financial successes since that day.

Paying with cash triggers the loss-aversion reaction. Paper money is an item of value; holding it in your hands makes it more valuable and less likely to be given up. Although swiping with a credit card might result in the same payment, it doesn't feel the same. For many people, nothing is being given up mentally when electronic payments are used.

An even more interesting research finding is the work of Kamleitner and Erki, who found that people who pay with cash form an immediate stronger attachment to their purchase than those paying by credit card. This means if you want to treasure something now, pay cash.[10]

THE BUDGET CONSTRAINT

Cashless payments boost people's spending power. In economic terms this is called an expansion of a person's *budget* or *liquidity constraint*. This sounds wonderful in the abstract. However, for people who lack self-control it can be devastating. In a cash-only economy people are limited by what they have earned or saved. A cash-only economy keeps people on a relatively tight budget and ensures they live within their means.

Electronic payments, however, enable spending beyond current earnings and savings. Credit cards and other electronic forms that allow borrowing switch the world from "wait until you can afford it" to "enjoy now and pay later." Even electronic methods that don't allow borrowing, like debit cards, boost spending. Spending increases because what you can purchase is not constrained by the amount of cash you are carrying; instead, it is the amount accessible in your accounts.

Let's think first about a store that only accepts paper money. The maximum customers can purchase is the amount of cash they have on hand. It doesn't matter how wealthy a customer is outside this shop. A rich person with little cash cannot purchase much. A poor person with a lot of cash can purchase quite a bit. In this case a poor person with cash is a better customer than a rich person without cash. Given the typical US consumer in 2020 carried just $76 in cash each day, on average the budget constraint is fairly tight.[11]

I used to play in a basketball league with a bar located above the gym. The bar had a strict cash-only policy. To relax the budget constraint and boost patrons' spending the bar installed an ATM near the bathrooms. This machine dispensed cash for people who wanted to spend more but didn't bring enough paper money with them.

This ATM reduced the budget constraint but did not eliminate it because banks and ATM networks have daily withdrawal limits. These limits are designed to ensure large numbers of customers can use the ATM before it is emptied of cash. They are also designed to reduce the impact of theft and fraud. Having a daily maximum limits the amount of financial havoc a thief can cause by stealing an ATM card and its personal identification number, or PIN.

Using electronic payments enables people to spend more by relaxing the budget constraint even more than placing ATMs in stores, restaurants, and bars. Debit cards withdraw money directly from a bank account. These cards expand a customer's budget constraint from the cash on hand to all the money in the bank account linked to that card. Data from the Federal Reserve show the median bank account has about $5,000, which boosts purchases significantly compared to a cash-only restriction.[12]

Although merchants like debit cards, credit cards are even better for boosting spending. Credit cards relax the budget constraint even more than debit cards because they allow customers to spend based on their cash on hand plus whatever free credit balances they have remaining on their cards. In the United States the average general purpose credit card has a $23,000 credit limit, with about a $5,000 balance. This means the typical customer with a credit card has a budget constraint of about $18,000. This dramatically higher spending limit is a key reason why shops, restaurants, and other retailers welcome credit cards.[13]

CONCLUSION

Businesses around the world want customers to spend more money. To boost spending, businesses do many things like advertise and entice customers with new features, colors, and experiences. Another method of boosting customer spending is by allowing customers to use cashless payments. This reduces the "pain of paying" with cash and makes it easier for customers with a credit line to spend money they do not have.

Using cashless methods boosts spending for many reasons. Debt rose dramatically as society made the transition from all cash to also using credit cards. This rise results in problems for many people because a person with a $5,000 credit card balance spends roughly an extra $1,000 a year in interest.

This rise is debt is not benign. Data from the New York Federal Reserve show almost 10% of all credit card balances are delinquent by at least three months. Federal bankruptcy court records show hundreds of thousands of individuals file for personal bankruptcy each year, many because their spending got out of control. If all people managed their finances wisely, electronic means that expand opportunities would be wonderful. Unfortunately, as these figures show, this is not the case.[14]

For readers who want to try weaning off electronic payments, try an old personal finance trick: freeze your credit and debit cards. Literally! Seal the credit cards in a plastic bag of water and place the bag in your freezer. The cards are available for an emergency and for times when cash is not accepted. However, because it takes time to thaw out the card, you experience a tiny bit of the "pain of paying." This gives you time to think about a purchase and often leads to reduced spending.

For decades American Express ran an advertising campaign whose tagline was "Don't leave home without it." The ads convinced people they needed to always have a credit card with them. An academic paper titled "Always Leave Home Without It" spoofs this campaign, but it also provides sound financial advice for those people who want to control their spending.[15]

For those who shop online, many store websites offer to save your credit or debit card information "for a faster checkout next time." Removing your stored payment information from all websites is a less extreme version of putting your card on ice, but it still forces you to physically find your wallet or purse when making an online purchase. Like putting your cards on ice, this gives you extra time to consider if a purchase is necessary.

The personal finance takeaway from this chapter is clear. If you want to reduce spending, use cash instead of electronic payments.

CHAPTER EIGHT

OTHER REASONS WHY USING CASH HELPS PEOPLE

Previous chapters outlined major reasons for using cash instead of electronic means of payment. For example, using paper money reduces your spending. However, there are many smaller reasons why keeping cash around helps individuals. Five issues are important to highlight: saving money, health, cognition, tipping, and being nickeled and dimed.

USING CASH SAVES MONEY

The previous chapters show using cashless payments results in people spending more. Using cash also reduces expenses by helping people avoid fees. Many people charge purchases and then carry a balance. Banks or credit companies charge interest on these balances, which boosts the final purchase cost.

Credit cards have wildly different interest rates. Banks offer high interest rates to people with poor credit scores who don't pay off their balance each month because there is a risk these customers will default on their debts. Individuals who consistently pay off their balances and have excellent scores typically get low interest rates to entice them to borrow money.

The Federal Reserve has tracked the average interest rate on credit cards since the mid-1990s. Their data show that the average annual rate is about 15% for people who pay interest. A 15% interest rate doubles the price paid for something in less than five years if the balance is not paid down. Moreover, the rate tracked by the Fed does not include fees for late payments, exceeding a card's credit limit, or a host of other charges such as annual fees simply to use a credit card.[1]

How much credit card debt is there in the United States? According to the Federal Reserve, revolving credit in the United States is about $1 trillion. Because most people have a hard time grasping figures with large numbers of zeros, spreading credit card debt evenly across every adult in the United States results in about $4,000 per person. At 15% interest this is $600 in extra charges per year, just for interest payments.

The $600 figure, however, is a distortion because the credit card industry deals with three types of customers. The first type is called *convenience users*. These people almost always pay off their entire credit card balance in full by the due date, which means they are not charged interest or late fees.

The second type is called *revolvers*. They are the opposite of convenience users. They typically float a balance from month to month. Many only pay off the minimum amount required to ensure the credit card account stays active and does not incur extra fees. The last type is called *dormant* accounts. These are accounts where the card holder either doesn't use the credit card for long periods of time or stopped using the card and has a balance outstanding.

The Federal Reserve's Survey of Consumer Finances found about 40% of all American families carried credit card debt and 60% either didn't use credit cards or were convenience users. This means the $600 figure is associated just with 40% of US families. The other 60% didn't pay credit card interest. Adjusting the interest rate figure for these different groups means revolvers, who carry a balance each month, are paying about $1,500 a year in interest for the privilege of being cashless.[2]

It is not just interest rates costing credit card holders money. Credit card companies charge annual fees, late payment fees, and a variety of miscellaneous fees. These fees totaled $25 billion in 2023. Although cards with no annual fee exist, many people pay high annual fees to obtain cards with special perks, like the ability to earn frequent flier miles or access airport lounges.[3]

USING CASH KEEPS YOU HEALTHIER

Some of us smoke, drink, gamble, or participate in other unhealthy habits more than we wish because impulse control is tough! Using cash helps cut back on these problems and as a result keeps you healthier. How can this be? Electronic methods of payments are frictionless. They make it easy to overindulge in bad habits because they make it so easy to spend money.

I saw this clearly when a friend invited me to a bar. I had cash in my wallet; they only had a credit card. The bartender asked if we each wanted to open a tab. My friend said sure and flipped their credit card down on the bar. I said no and paid cash for each round. When I ran out of paper money I stopped drinking and went home. My friend stayed until the bar closed and woke up to a very expensive bill and a huge hangover.

When dealing with unhealthy habits, cash limits your spending to the amount of money you are carrying. If you leave to get more money, you have a moment to think, while away from the situation. Cash keeps you healthier by adding friction to the spending process.

Beyond keeping vices in check there is interesting research by Soman and his colleagues showing another way using cash keeps you healthier. Soman asked people immediately after they left a supermarket if he could have a copy of their receipt. The receipts did not contain any personal identifying information but showed how shoppers paid for the items. They then classified all purchased items into two groups: necessities, such as cooking oil, rice, or bread; and discretionary items like chocolate, gum, snacks, and magazines. Credit card customers spent twice the amount of money on discretionary items as cash users. In simple terms using a credit card resulted in customers putting more junk food in their carts.[4]

Soman's research was very interesting, but it potentially had biases. The research was done at a single store and at a single point in time, there was a relatively small sample size, and no information was gathered about the shoppers. Another team of researchers set out to check the robustness of the results. They recruited 1,000 people who all were single-person households and tracked their shopping and payment type over a six-month period. The results were quite clear: "shopping baskets had a larger proportion of impulsive and unhealthy food items when shoppers paid with credit or debit cards than when they paid in cash."[5]

Other researchers wanted to understand why cashless payments cause people to purchase less healthy products. They brought people into a laboratory and simulated a shopping experience while measuring skin conductance on subjects' palms. Skin conductance varies as people's emotions change. For example, when people are nervous, they get sweaty palms.[6]

The researchers measured finer changes using their equipment as people looked at pictures of various healthy and unhealthy food items and decided to put the items in their cart or not. They had half of their participants imagine making a cash payment, and the other half imagine making a cashless payment. They found the mode of payment not only mattered for whether participants said they would buy cookies and candies but they were also able to show that "when such shoppers have to pay by cash, the negative arousal cues their attention to the health risks and makes the risks more salient." This research means if you are thinking about dieting or having healthier eating habits, use cash. This will keep your wallet fat and not your belly.

CASH AND MATH SKILLS

Cognition is another reason why continuing to use cash is useful. Using cash helps create, preserve, and improve math skills. Counting out change and tallying the correct amount of bills are life skills. Overspending is easier to do when individuals have weak or nonexistent numerical or computational abilities. The lack of math skills is easy to see. Hand a cashier paper money and see how many make change without looking at the register's computer screen. The vast majority cannot do the simple subtraction needed in their head.

Beyond cashiers paper money helps math skills for two groups: children and illiterate adults. There is a long-running debate among child psychologists about the pros and cons of using real items, called *manipulatives*, for helping children learn math.[7] It is impossible to say if money manipulatives definitively help all children. However, proponents believe using money helps many children recognize numbers.[8] Also, ideas such as the importance of zeros become real when children learn the difference between being given a $1 bill instead of a $10 bill. Money also helps some children understand fractions because coins are paper money divided into fractional units. Last, using paper money helps some children master addition and subtraction.[9]

Using cash also helps adults. Math skills that are not used atrophy. Using electronic payment methods reduces the need for adults to do math in their heads. Using cash forces people to do mental addition when purchasing multiple items and do subtraction when making change. It is harder to overspend when you are adding up the cost of each item as you put it in your shopping cart.

Some research suggests continuing to exercise the brain by doing simple arithmetic problems during a person's elderly years has many beneficial cognitive effects, such as better attention and less chance of forgetting words. Although the research is not definitive, there is a good chance using paper money helps keep you mentally sharp and helps children become smarter.[10]

TIPPING

Have you ever started to pay for something electronically and been confronted with a tip already preselected? If you wanted to tip, was the tip amount or percentage more than you planned on giving? When the tip is preselected, most people just accept it even when this boosts the amount they meant to pay. Some people are outraged when they are asked to pay a tip at self-checkouts when there has been no employee interaction.[11]

People in some service occupations like waitpersons and bartenders depend on tips to get paid. In Japan and many European countries restaurant staffs are paid a living wage. In the United States servers only need to be paid a small part of the minimum wage as long as the rest is made up in tips. This means the more customers tip, the less restaurant owners need to pay in wages, which is why owners try to get customers to give larger tips.

Tipping was originally designed to incentivize workers into providing great service; the better the service the higher the tip. However, this incentive has disappeared over time because most people now simply tip a standard percentage of the bill, whether the service is good or bad. I have settled on tipping 20% unless the service is exceptionally poor.

Recently I went out to eat with friends. The meal was pretty good, but the experience was marred by terrible service. The waitperson didn't bring all the food, forgot drinks, and made a mistake on the bill. I prefer paying with cash, but I didn't have enough so I used my credit card. The waitperson swiped the card and handed me a tablet to sign. The tip was set on the tablet for an 18% gratuity. I wanted to give less because the service was exceptionally poor. There were options to give a higher percentage but no simple way to specify a lower amount. After pressing several buttons and getting nowhere I was forced to give that amount as a tip. Paying electronically forced me to spend more than I wanted and did not provide any signal to the waitperson that their performance was subpar.

Tipping electronically compared to giving cash is also detrimental to restaurant workers. I have talked to many waitpeople and bartenders and many report they do not instantly get tips given electronically. Instead, they have to wait until the restaurant gets the payment from the bank. Banks do not give restaurants money instantly because they want to make sure chargebacks, refunds, and disputes are all settled first. This means tipped workers often have to wait for electronic tips, but they get cash tips immediately.

I am constantly amazed to hear complaints that "using cash is so slow." Cash is not slow, especially in restaurants. Once I get the bill I typically hand the waitperson the right amount of paper money and start walking out the door. There is no need to wait until the server takes my card away for processing or hunts down the restaurant's charge machine and brings it to the table.

What about paying in other places? Yes, we have all been stuck behind someone slowly counting out bills and coins when we are in a rush. However, haven't you also been stuck waiting when someone ahead of you has their credit card denied or cannot enter their debit card PIN correctly?

NICKEL AND DIMED

Many people live close to the financial edge and constantly worry about being hit with a surcharge, surprise fee, or unexpected extra costs. They worry because although these extra charges are nicknamed *nickel and diming* people, they can add up to significant sums that can wreck a family's budget. Extra fees and surcharges often make electronic payments a more expensive choice than using cash.

The extra expense was made clear when I was driving by the university one day at lunch time and decided to get something out of the office. I was quite happy to find an open parking spot just around the corner from my office. Unfortunately, I didn't have any coins for the meter. Because lunch time is the prime moment for getting a parking ticket, I downloaded the local parking app to my phone and paid electronically to avoid the high chance of a fine.

I needed just 20 minutes to make it upstairs and back to the car. The parking app said 20 minutes cost 80¢ for parking. However, the app added a 40-cent "convenience fee." The price to park increased by 50%, simply by switching from paying with coins to paying with an electronic method.

Now an extra 40¢ will not financially break me today. However, I remember often parking on the same street when I was a poor graduate student, living on a very tight budget. Having to pay this extra fee daily would have resulted in my skipping at least one meal a month.

Credit card companies allow convenience fees to be levied by any merchant, government agency, or organization that accepts multiple methods of payment. As long as the business allows people one way to pay without a convenience fee, then all other methods can have a surcharge.[12]

The method without convenience fees doesn't have to be the most popular way customers want to pay. For example, relatively few tickets to sporting events, concerts, and plays are sold in face-to-face transactions at the event box office. Instead, most people buy their tickets online, yet tickets sold online usually have a convenience fee, but walk-up traffic does not pay extra.

Convenience fees are widespread. My favorite bagel shop in New York City has a sign by the cash register telling customers that using a credit or debit card results in an extra charge of 4%. A gas station near my home offers a reverse convenience fee. People who pay cash get gasoline for 10¢ less per gallon than those paying with credit cards.

Many poor people get into debt and are hounded by debt collectors. To ensure payment, debt collectors provide clients multiple ways to pay off their bills via mail, phone, and online systems. The Consumer Financial Protection Bureau notes that some debt collectors impose additional fees to pay off a debt using debit or credit cards. To stop this practice the Bureau issued an advisory notice that states these types of fees are often illegal. Advisory notices are a lot like warnings when you are pulled over for speeding. They don't actually mean or do anything.[13]

I recently spent a few hours on the outskirts of Montreal, one of Canada's major cities. I left the United States late on Sunday afternoon, spent the night in Canada, and was back in the United States before lunch the next day. I didn't have any Canadian paper money and the neighborhood didn't have any banks or ATMs, so I used my credit card to pay for a hotel room and two meals. Every time I swiped the card my bank added a 3% "foreign transaction fee" to the bill. Using cash would have saved me 3%.

Often the only ways to avoid a convenience fee are to pay with cash, check, or using online bill pay, which is a modern twist on checks. Shifting to a more cashless society where people primarily use credit or debit cards to pay will mean more convenience fees and higher costs for everyone. These fees hit the poor and those living close to the financial edge especially hard.

CONCLUSION

Businesses around the world want customers to spend more money. Financial companies want individuals to forgo cash and use electronic means so they get a cut of every purchase. However, cash has some extra benefits. If you want to eat healthier, stay mentally sharp, tip effectively, and pay less overall, then use cash instead of electronic payments.

CHAPTER NINE

USING CASH KEEPS YOUR LIFE PRIVATE

Privacy is important. Many people do not want their lives to be an open book for all to see. Some of us have minor secrets that we are ashamed to admit like dieting, dyeing our hair, boosting our height, or altering our bodies through plastic surgery. Others have medium-sized secrets about our true age, origin, or education. Some have big secrets such as hiding mental breakdowns, embarrassing illness, gambling issues, drug addiction, or sexual desires. Few people want everything revealed about their lives, even to their most intimate partners. Our purchases, however, reveal many of our deepest secrets to anyone able to see and piece together our transactions.

How can these secrets be protected? Using cash to make a purchase ensures that transaction is private. Using electronic payments instead potentially links that purchase to you forever. Despite widespread belief, even electronic payment methods like cryptocurrency are not actually anonymous.

One of the most colorful examples demonstrating how all electronic purchases are traceable is the case of the Bitcoin Bonnie and Crypto Clyde. In real life the couple's names are Heather Morgan and Ilya Lichtenstein. In 2016, the couple broke into the Bitfinex crypto exchange and stole roughly $72 million, which was about 120,000 Bitcoins. At the time of the theft, people assumed Bitcoin transactions were totally anonymous and it would be impossible to recover the stolen money. The theft happened just before the price of Bitcoins soared, and the value of the pilfered coins grew exponentially as the price of Bitcoin climbed. By 2021 when the price of one Bitcoin hit $65,000, the theft was worth about $8 billion, adding urgency to catching the perpetrators. In February 2022, US agents arrested the couple in New York City. Their mistake was spending some of the stolen Bitcoin to purchase a $500 Walmart gift card that was emailed to their online address. My goal is not to glorify modern-day electronic bank robbery. Instead, the story illustrates a simple idea: electronic purchases are not private.[1]

Proponents of electronic money say if all transactions were traceable, this would reduce illegal acts because many individuals would fear being caught. However, privacy is important even if it increases illegal actions. Without privacy there is a chilling effect on many legal actions people want to take, but not if they are public knowledge.

Here is just one example: Today in wealthy countries, purchasing and listening to popular music like top-40 songs is a legal activity. However, in parts of the world where religious fundamentalism is strong, buying and playing a top-40 song is seen as a mark of deviance. In Afghanistan today, the government frowns not only on top-40 music but even listening to traditional Afghani music. Officials have smashed peoples' traditional instruments. In some places people shut off their radios to avoid being beaten.[2]

For those who think getting in trouble simply by buying or listening to popular music happens only in countries under fundamentalist regimes, let me tell you about examples in more open countries. On June 3, 1956, the city of Santa Cruz, California, enacted a total ban on rock 'n roll at public gatherings. This was followed by bans in Asbury Park, New Jersey, and in San Antonio, Texas. Today these bans seem absurd because places like Asbury Park are very proud they served as the launching pad for world-famous rock 'n roll musicians like Bruce Springsteen and Jon Bon Jovi. You might be thinking that this was years ago; bans could not possibly happen today. Yet while this book is being written, Ukraine, which is fighting Russia, banned any modern Russian music from being played or distributed.[3]

My point is simple. Using cash makes it simple to buy music or any other legal good or service without a trace. Using electronic payments to buy music, or anything else, gives governments and businesses the permanent ability to know who purchases or listens to forbidden tunes.

HOW PRIVATE IS COLLECTING AND DISTRIBUTING DATA?

One of the major problems with electronic payments is that by inserting many intermediaries between the payer and payee, huge amounts of information become available. Professor Josh Lauer points out that in today's economy information becomes quite valuable, especially when linked with other data. Advertisers want this information to provide tailored ads. Marketing specialists want this information to understand who is buying and how to change products or services to boost sales. People in finance want to track purchases to find the optimal price to charge and maximize profits. Politicians want to dig up dirt on opponents. This information is provided by companies called *data brokers*. Data brokers collect information from a large variety of sources and weave it together to create a picture of your life.[4]

When you pay with cash, the ability of data brokers to link purchases to you is lost. Use electronic payments and the purchase is potentially linked to you forever. Cash preserves privacy, and electronic payments destroy privacy.

Many financial firms that facilitate electronic payments make money three ways. First, they make money by charging the merchant for the privilege of letting their customers pay with a credit card, debit card, or participate in a buy now, pay later program. Second, they make money from customers by charging interest and service fees. Third, they make money by selling data to advertisers, marketers, and data brokers. These data are quite valuable. I just typed "buy credit card transaction data" into a search browser and the top entry is an ad from a company offering the "Largest Consumer Spend Panel with 100 million cardholders and billions of transactions." There is a high likelihood you are one of the 100 million credit card holders and your recent credit card transactions are available for purchase.

Before selling this information, companies anonymize the data. This means stripping off your name, address, and any other personally identifiable information. You might think this protects you. However, when real data are sold it is possible to reidentify who made the transactions. In an article in the journal *Science* a group of researchers primarily from MIT took three months' worth of anonymous credit card records for 1.1 million people and were able to reidentify 90% of the individuals. Moreover, they found that women were easier to reidentify using credit card information than men, and that having more income makes reidentification easier.[5]

How can people be identified from "anonymous" transactions? People divulge large amounts of information about themselves on social media. Social media posts are date and time stamped, which reduces the number of electronic transactions needing examination. Merchant codes are quite specific, with almost every airline and hotel chain having a unique code. People tell the world via social media they are staying in a Sheraton hotel on Sunday, which is merchant code 3503; switched on Monday to a Hilton hotel, code 2501; and on Tuesday bought an amazing pair of shoes, code 5661. In the billions of transactions there is likely only one person with that sequence and dates. It is not necessary to know how much was spent to identify the spender. Some payment apps broadcast your spending to social media accounts, making identification even easier and fraught with problems. You might be happy telling friends via social media you just bought an engagement ring, but this is typically not the best way to inform Grandma.[6]

Even without a few specific pieces of data linking datasets, just knowing something about people's habits enables reidentification. My business school has thousands of students and about 500 faculty and staff. It also has a Starbucks coffee shop on the second floor of the building. The shop is very busy at all hours of the day and night. I haven't tried it, but with access to billions of credit or debit card transactions I could probably pick many fellow professors out of the data.

Here's how I could find my colleague's purchases. We don't need to look at billions of transactions. First, we zero in on the transactions from this particular Starbucks location. Even if this Starbucks is not named or identified in the data, it is straightforward to pick out this shop from others in Boston that have the same merchant code 5814. This shop's sales follow a unique pattern, with sales rising dramatically during final exam week and then plummeting the next seven days during graduation.

Once we identify the store, how do we identify people? Most professors use a credit or debit card to purchase their drinks, unlike students who use their meal plan cards. This means credit and debit transactions are primarily from faculty, staff, and visitors. Professors, unlike staff and visitors, often pick up coffee just before they teach. The teaching schedule, with each professor's name, is publicly available so students can choose classes. Linking repeated purchases by a customer to the teaching schedule narrows down the repeat buyers to a small list. Knowing the type of drink my colleagues prefer tells me the price, which can identify the specific professor when multiple people follow the same teaching schedule. I wouldn't do it, but once someone is identified it's possible to return to the billions of transactions and see what else they bought.

Even if very specific pieces of data do not exist, it is possible to use a few rough pieces of information to reidentify people through the process of elimination. Let's assume we have the names and some demographic information about everyone in the world. There are about eight billion people in the world. If I know someone is male, then half the list is eliminated, and the number of possibilities is cut to about four billion. If I know that man lives in North America, I have cut the possibilities down to 250 million. Just two coarse pieces of information have reduced the number of people considered by a factor of 32. If I know a rough age, like child, teenager, young adult, middle-aged, or elderly, I can reduce the list by a factor of five from 250 million to 50 million. With three pieces of vague information, we have gone from considering eight billion people to only considering 50 million. Throw in a few more pieces of information like education, marital status, and the number of people in their household, and the list of likely suspects gets small enough that it becomes easier to identify someone.

Reidentification is even easier if you don't have to consider the whole world but instead start with a smaller group. Knowing that I am a professor somewhere in the greater Boston area means the list doesn't start with eight billion people. Instead, the list starts with only 20,000. Adding a few more pieces of information like my gender and rough age shrinks the pool of candidates further. The key idea is that knowing anything from one very specific detail to a moderate amount of imprecise information can identify someone with a high degree of certainty in a sea of electronic payment information.

WHO NEEDS DATA PRIVACY?

Economists typically divide society into three groups; households, businesses, and governments. The need and desire for privacy within and among these three groups show why continuing to use cash is important. The next sections look at three of many reasons. First, privacy is important in households. Not all families are happy and well-functioning. Some couples are in abusive relationships, and hiding cash from a spouse or partner enables people to leave or escape. Second, people don't want businesses to know everything about their lives. Do we really want major retailers identifying and targeting pregnant women before these women have had a chance to tell friends and family? Third, do we trust our government to not prosecute us for actions that might be legal one day and illegal the next? I will go into more details on all three of these cases.

Privacy Within Households

Financial privacy is important within households because not all individuals want to be completely financially open with their family or roommates. Let's start off with some relatively innocent reasons for needing privacy before getting to the more important cases. I use cash when purchasing gifts for my wife so she doesn't know where I shopped and how much I spent. Hiding purchases even has its own name: *stealth shopping.*[7]

Beyond gifts, my wife and I are often at loggerheads about food. My wife tried for years to get me to lose weight by eating healthier, so I promised to give up eating donuts. Donuts are a legal product to purchase anywhere in the world by people of all ages. I used to swipe my credit card to pay for the donuts, forgetting that each month my wife dutifully checks our statements. The statements provided irrefutable evidence that I was still eating these forbidden items. No one in the world besides my wife cares that I enjoy eating chocolate covered, cream filled donuts. However, there was a matter of trust. By using electronic payments, I left a trail of evidence that I was breaking my promises. Using cash would have hidden my indiscretions. Data show I am not the only one in this situation; many people are "cheating" on their partners with food.[8]

More important reasons are easy to find. The National Endowment for Financial Education[9] (NEFE) has been running, with the Harris Poll, a series of surveys about US financial infidelity. The five surveys NEFE has fielded since 2010 ask random samples of thousands of US adults if they have ever combined their finances with another person. About two-thirds of all respondents stated they had comingled their finances.

All people who combined their finances were asked about two types of financial infidelity. The first was hiding finances such as purchases, bank accounts, statements, bills, or cash from their spouse or partner. The second was lying to a partner or spouse about debts that are owed, how much money was earned, or other financial topics that would give the other party a truer understanding of the respondent's financial situation.

The NEFE surveys show widespread financial infidelity. In the typical survey, well over one-third (38%) of all people who combined their finances admitted to some type of financial deception. Moreover, the trend has shown increasing deception, not less, over time. In the 2010 survey 31% stated they either lied or hid finances, but by 2021 the figure had risen to 43%.

These financial infidelity surveys ask about eight specific actions. The most cited indiscretion was hiding cash. One in five adults who had combined their finances at some time stated they had hidden paper money from their spouse or partner. Why did they do this? Some people reported being embarrassed or fearful. Others knew or guessed their spouse or partner would not approve of something they did.[10] However, the most common reason stated by 35% of the people who committed financial infidelity was that they believed "some aspects of my finances should remain private, even from my partner." Some back of the envelope calculations using these surveys suggest almost 12 million US adults are hiding cash from their spouse.[11]

The data show there is a desire for cash to maintain privacy within the family. This is not illegal or necessarily immoral. My own actions when eating donuts showed I wanted privacy. The fact that millions of people in the United States use cash to provide financial privacy within the family is another reason to keep cash around.

It is not just in the high-income world that privacy is prized. An experiment in India found "25% of spouses choose to keep (some) money private when given the opportunity." In Senegal when people got extra cash no one else knew about they hid a quarter of it from their kin. Philippine experiments found giving men money resulted in them putting it into a private account if their wife controlled the family's savings.[12]

Privacy is important also with your extended family. I like to buy and drink wine. Since I am well over 21 years old, purchasing and consuming wine is quite legal. However, I often pay cash for wine. Some people in my family are aghast at how much I have spent for various bottles, and others are insulted when I didn't spend enough on the wine they were served. Paying cash and throwing away the receipts has eliminated both problems.

Spousal and Partner Abuse and Infidelity

Another important reason for privacy within the family is the need to escape from spousal or partner abuse. This is a serious problem in many countries. Data from the CDC's National Intimate Partner and Sexual Violence Survey show about two in five women and one in four men in the

United States have experienced physical violence sometime in their life at the hands of an intimate partner. Moreover, about one in five homicide victims are people killed by an intimate partner.[13]

Imagine being in a long-term relationship with a partner who is physically or mentally abusive. Leaving is not easy. Many times it is important to get advice or counseling before leaving to ensure children are protected or ensure the victim does not become destitute. What happens if the abuser sees a charge from a divorce lawyer or a prepaid hotel room set up as an escape? It is legal to see a divorce lawyer and legal to stay in a hotel. However, either of these activities can lead to further abuse. Paying cash ensures these activities stay discreet and there is a chance of escaping.

Not all relationships end because of abuse. Sometimes relationships end because of sexual infidelity. *New York Magazine* ran an interesting article about the billionaire investor and dealmaker Ron Perelman, who owned Revlon Cosmetics, among other companies.[14] In the 1980s Mr. Perelman was married to Faith Golding. Ms. Golding suspected Mr. Perelman of sexual infidelity and "claimed that her husband had charged at least $100,000 on gifts and lavish trysts." Worse, he had charged them "to the company she had loaned him the money to buy." Ms. Golding was tipped off to the infidelity by seeing charges for jewelry that she did not receive. These credit card charges helped prove Mr. Perelman was having an affair with a local florist and secured Ms. Golding her divorce.

I am not encouraging sexual infidelity. However, if you are going to cheat on a spouse, do not charge expensive gifts that they will not receive. These suspicious purchases leave an electronic trail and are a simple way of being caught.

It is not just abusive relationships and infidelity. Many couples just feel differently about money. I know a husband who is relatively frugal. His wife likes expensive items, especially shoes. The wife works and earns her own money. Nevertheless, she feels it is important to pay cash for her designer shoes so that the high purchase amounts do not upset her spouse.

Privacy Between Households and Businesses

In many households it is important to keep our purchases private from businesses. Businesses want to know what you are buying. Rossi and his coauthors says it quite clearly: "there exists a tremendous potential for improving the profitability of direct marketing efforts by more fully utilizing household purchase histories."[15]

Privacy extends to many types of purchases. Do you really want businesses to know when you are dieting? Many people find it hard to diet simply by reducing calories, so they purchase diet meals and plans. Trying to reduce your weight is a legal activity but many of us don't want to proclaim loudly that we are doing it. Being able to track purchases provides businesses with the ability to know when a customer is dieting and then flood them with ads, sample products, and advice whether they want it or not.

Do people want others to know when they or their partner are pregnant? There are many reasons to keep pregnancy a secret. Some expectant mothers are concerned they might not have a successful pregnancy. Announcing to the world that you are pregnant and then having a miscarriage is hard on many levels, from the emotional pain of losing a child to the social pain of first announcing a happy event and then bearing bad news. Announcing your pregnancy can stall your career. Some managers are not interested in promoting a person if they think that person will take time off to care for a newborn or will be distracted at work after caring all night for a newborn.

Businesses that sell to consumers have a strong desire to know when people are pregnant. There are a small number of times in people's lives when their routines change, and their shopping habits are malleable; when children are born and when someone moves are two big ones. Think about the last time you moved. Moving, even only a few miles, likely means you switched which stores and restaurants you frequent and the type of things you buy. Having a new child means people start using new products and often switch preferences. Pinpointing this moment is key for marketers.

One of the largest retailers in the United States is Target. Target is a Minnesota-based company that has very large department stores spread across suburban America. These stores sell everything from perishable food to long-lasting furniture and clothing. Target also does direct marketing by sending fliers and emails to customers.

Target, like many other retailers, has an extensive customer purchase history, which it uses to deliver targeted ads. It builds up this purchase history by giving "each shopper a unique code – known internally as the Guest ID number – that keeps tabs on everything they buy." One way it identifies shoppers is via their credit card. Each purchase made via a credit card can then be linked to a customer's Guest ID.[16]

Charles Duhigg shows how Target is able to identify with a high degree of precision which of Target's customers are pregnant and when they are due to give birth. Target gives customers the ability to create a baby registry. Using this registry, the company was able to see the purchase history of expectant mothers and more important the timing of purchases. For example, expectant mothers start purchasing newborn disposable diapers just before or just after the baby's birth, but few purchases of newborn diapers happen much after the birth.[17]

Once Target knew this purchase history pattern, it was a straightforward data analysis exercise to compare expectant mothers on the registry with other similar but likely not pregnant Target customers to see what items are specially bought when pregnant. Not surprisingly, Target found that pregnant mothers bought extra-large sizes of unscented lotion and supplements like calcium, magnesium, and zinc, particularly around their 20th week of being pregnant.

With this information Target can identify which customers are pregnant. It then begins sending targeted ads to expectant mothers to get them into Target stores. Although Target's motives are relatively benign – simply to shift consumers to make more purchases – the information that they wield on when a person is about to give birth is not benign. Target realizes this and tries not to upset pregnant customers. By mingling advertisements for baby products with other items, they ensure fewer potential customers understand that Target is spying on them by using their own purchase history.

The reason for doing all this is profits – big profits. Duhigg suggests that a major reason why Target was able to boost sales by $2 to $3 billion a year was use of targeted information. If a Target customer doesn't want their data linked to a Guest ID number, there is a very simple method of ensuring privacy. Pay cash when shopping in person. Using paper money breaks the ability to connect purchases to a particular individual.

Households and Businesses versus the Government

Many people want privacy from the government. Societies create rules. Some of these rules are very serious, like not committing murder. Other rules are designed to protect individuals and enforce societal norms, such as forcing people to cross streets only at marked places. Breaking rules means a person is committing an illegal activity. To reduce illegal activities, writers like Ken Rogoff advocate banning cash.

The problem with blanket proposals to reduce illegal activities by banning cash is that these proposals make no distinction between serious and minor illegal activities. Later in this book there is an entire chapter devoted to understanding the relationship between serious illegal activities and cash. That chapter finds little relationship between cash and illegal activities because it is clear gangs, mafias, and drug cartels all can flourish with or without cash.

This section focuses on using cash in minor rule breaking. Every day large numbers of people buy illegal products and services. People don't want to be associated with making these purchases; no one wants evidence linking them to a crime. Banning cash makes it harder and riskier for people to engage in illegal activities because it removes the veil of privacy. However, I doubt increasing the risk and difficulty results in less criminal activity.

The desire for privacy is understandable for individuals engaging in illegal activities. For example, there are penalties for purchasing and using illegal drugs. Buying sex is not allowed in most countries. Even gambling is proscribed in many parts of the world. Using electronic payments is dangerous and makes little sense when paying for illegal activities because it leaves a trail that links an individual directly to a crime.

The problem is that what is legal or illegal is constantly changing. It is hard for individuals to support governmental bans when the government is constantly changing the definition of what is illegal. This lack of support means people need cash.

The United Nations Office on Drugs and Crime publishes the "World Drug Report." This report shows what is legal or illegal changes depending on time and location. For example, the "World Drug Report" estimates that there are 200 million people in the world who use cannabis, some illegally and some in parts of the world where cannabis is being deregulated and becoming legal to use. Canada, Uruguay, and some US states have decriminalized possession and use.[18]

When I grew up in Boston cannabis was illegal and those who used it could be arrested. Today, I live within a short walk of two cannabis shops that allow any adult to purchase their products. Moreover, both shops regularly hire the local police to control crowds when there are long lines. The police in my neighborhood have gone from arresting marijuana users to bantering with people waiting to buy marijuana.

There are many other activities that have become legal recently. When I was young most forms of gambling were prohibited in Boston. There were just two places that could legally take bets: the horse and dog racing tracks. Both were only open part of the year and even then, only for a limited number of hours. Betting in any other place or betting on anything other than horses or dogs was illegal.

Today, legalized gambling is available 24 hours a day in a massive casino located on the edge of Boston. Plus, the state government runs many different lotteries and even has thousands of locations offering Keno, a type of bingo game. The state Keno games run every four minutes from early morning until late at night. Additionally, my state allows online betting on almost every type of team sports.

Only a short time ago gambling was illegal. A desire by the government for more revenue and a shift in societal attitudes has made betting legal today. For people who don't have a gambling addiction, there is no longer the need to hide their betting by using cash.

Many items that were previously legal are now illegal. In 1898 the German company Bayer Pharmaceutical introduced two new legal over-the-counter products: aspirin and heroin. Both of these new drugs could be sold to any person without a doctor's prescription. One of Bayer's early ads lists heroin as a "sedative for coughs" and many early users lauded its effects. Today Bayer aspirin is still a legal drug everywhere in the world and can be bought without a prescription. Heroin, however, which started off legal, first became a controlled and then an illegal substance. For two decades, when heroin was a legal drug, all heroin sales were officially sanctioned. Imagine if you had bought heroin with a credit card; that record would be easily traceable.

Last, some payments are legal and encouraged in some places, but illegal and discouraged in others. In my neighborhood teenage girls are encouraged to sign up and pay for driving lessons. By learning how to drive they reduce the burden on parents of chauffeuring them to school, activities, and friends. For many years in Saudi Arabia, women were banned from driving. Paying for driving lessons was an illegal activity and frowned on by both the government and many families.

In the United States abortion is legal is some states and not legal in others. It is unsettled legally if a person who lives in a state where abortion is outlawed can travel to another state to end their pregnancy. Some people are very concerned that by using electronic payments to pay to end pregnancy, they can be charged with a crime when they go back home.[19]

PROBLEMS OF BEING INCORRECTLY IDENTIFIED

Using cash prevents goods and services from being linked to an individual. But there is another benefit beyond privacy. Businesses do targeted advertising. What if the data compiled from your purchase history misidentify you? I first shopped online with a giant retailer when it was still a young company, not the behemoth it is today. At the winter holidays I needed a gift for a relative who loved Japanese warriors. Online I found some beautiful Samurai swords at a reasonable price. Because I wanted to present the gift in person, I had the sword shipped to my home as a regular, unwrapped purchase. For decades this giant Internet retailer consistently misidentified my interests by constantly showing me guns, knives, and swords, things I don't have any interest in purchasing.

This misidentification was benign until my children started watching me use the computer and then began using it themselves. My wife and I had agreed that our children would not have toy weapons. Having their father repeatedly receive suggestions to buy the real items led to problems, because the children didn't understand why they were forbidden to play with these items when pictures of them were always on Dad's computer.

There are ways to correct errors in a credit report or your insurance claims history. However, once a computer model puts you into a particular category, there is little you can do to avoid being flooded with ads and suggestions that don't match your interests. The only way is to wait years or even decades for the algorithms to forget the original purchase.

POTENTIAL SOLUTIONS

One privacy solution touted by companies in the digital financial world is a service that generates a unique virtual credit or debit card number for every transaction. This makes it difficult for a merchant to link purchases from the same customer. This might sound good. However, although the merchant can no longer link purchases, the bank and the credit card company still have a complete record. If they didn't have a record, you couldn't be charged for the purchase!

Virtual credit cards provide some, but not complete anonymity. Using a virtual card means the specific items cannot be tracked to you. However, the merchant is still identified. For some purchases simply knowing the merchant code and the dollar amount is enough to identify the items bought. My wife knows that donuts cost slightly more than $1; seeing that charge enabled her to determine I was still buying this forbidden food simply by looking at where and how much I spent.

Another technique for hiding purchases is the use of multiple accounts. The average US adult has two credit cards.[20] This average masks a wide divergence, with some people having no credit cards and others having large numbers. Some people with many credit and debit cards rotate through them when making purchases so it is more difficult to tie purchases together. The problem is that not all people can get multiple cards. Moreover, once you get multiple cards there is an enticement to use all of them up to the credit limit, giving you privacy, but ruining your finances.

CONCLUSION

In 1948 the United Nations released the "Universal Declaration of Human Rights," which states everyone in the world has a right to privacy. Continuing to ensure paper money is available does not guarantee privacy because paper money cannot conceal everything. However, using cash ensures people still have some ability to keep their purchases private from the prying eyes of other people, businesses, and governments. Electronic money, however, doesn't conceal anything.

CHAPTER TEN

USING ELECTRONIC PAYMENTS BOOSTS PRICES

U sing electronic payments pushes up the prices paid for goods and services. I see this every time I drive by a gas station that advertises one price for credit card payments and a lower price for cash. Businesses end up paying about 2% of their sales to handle electronic payments like credit cards. To cover this 2% surcharge, many merchants simply raise the price of what they are selling by 2%.

Now 2% might not seem like much when talking about buying one apple or a cup of coffee. However, the average US family spends about $75,000 a year. A 2% reduction in the prices families pay means a savings of over $1,500 a year! If all 130 million families in the United States used credit cards to pay for all purchases, this would increase their costs by almost $200 billion.[1]

Most people cannot grasp very large numbers. It is hard for me to comprehend $200 billion. A stack of dollar bills in that amount is over 10,000 miles high. With $200 billion every single person in the world could get a gift of $25. With $200 billion a year it is possible to fund the annual budget of the US Department of State, as well as the Departments of Commerce, Interior, Energy, Housing and Urban Development, and all the space exploration done by NASA.[2]

Cash is not costless for businesses to handle. However, before cash went out of fashion several central banks did studies and most found cash was less expensive for businesses to handle than accepting electronic payments. This means bringing back cash will make things cheaper for businesses, reducing their need to boost prices to cover electronic payment charges.

This chapter goes deep into the weeds and examines in detail the fees merchants pay to accept credit and debit cards. Not everyone cares about the details, so feel free to skip this chapter if numbers are not your cup of tea. The big picture of this chapter is that it shows store managers often find electronic money makes their jobs easier, but store owners find electronic payments cost them money versus cash payments. You don't think it makes any difference which credit card you use, but different credit cards have widely different fees. Cards that offer rewards charge merchants much higher fees, reducing their profits.

The bottom line? Cash saves stores money, which could be passed on to the consumer. Although consumers like the convenience of using electronic payments, a simple way of encouraging consumers to use paper money is to offer cash discounts.

MERCHANT FEES

All kinds of merchants, from the biggest to the smallest, pay fees when they accept electronic payments. The fees vary dramatically depending on which kind of credit card, debit card, or buy now, pay later method you use.

The most important fee paid to process electronic payments is called the *merchant discount rate*. This name is a misnomer because it implies that the merchant gets a discount for using electronic payments. Unfortunately for merchants and their customers the name is the exact opposite of what it implies. Merchants don't get a discount. Instead, they only get paid a percentage of their actual sales. How much is taken off is the merchant discount. Calculating the exact merchant discount is very difficult for two reasons. First, electronic payment companies have very complex fee schedules. Second, as Chapter 4 on electronic payments showed, there are many different steps in the electronic payment process. Fees are added at multiple points.

Let's look at the merchant discount charged by PayPal because PayPal has one of the simpler fee schedules to understand. PayPal charges sellers anywhere from 1.9% to 3.5% of each transaction's value as part of their discount rate. PayPal also charges a fixed fee on each transaction that ranges from 5 to 49¢. The simplest method to determine PayPal's typical charge is to look at the company's financial reports. In 2023 PayPal reported $1.5 trillion of payments flowed through their system. PayPal made about $30 billion by moving all that money around, which is 2%.[3]

Figure 10.1 shows a simplified version of how fees affect merchants. Let's say someone uses their credit card to buy an item that costs $100. The credit card issuer takes $100 from the individual and then sends $98 on to the merchant's bank or credit card processor. That organization then takes a fee, in this case 50¢, to cover its costs of handling the transaction and deposits $97.50 into the merchant's bank account.

The fee from card issuers is not always 2%. Mastercard publishes a book of fees that is 12 dense pages. Visa's US book is 26 pages long, and American Express's fee structure is also complex. Part of the reason for the additional complexity is that all these companies issue a variety of cards with different levels of benefits. Some cards come with relatively few benefits, and others provide a range of benefits like "free" insurance when you

Figure 10.1   How fees affect merchants.

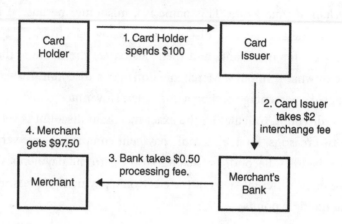

rent a car. Travel is one of the high merchant discount fee categories. Mastercard charges airlines 2.55% of the ticket price plus 10 cents for its top cards with the most benefits.[4]

To give an idea of the range of discounts, Table 10.1 shows the cut, or discount, rate Mastercard takes from supermarkets, Visa and American Express's fees are roughly similar. Supermarkets are a low margin, high-volume businesses. The Food Industry Association has tracked profitability of supermarkets for years and their data show supermarkets' profit on each dollar of sales is about 2% before taxes. That means if a customer spends $50 then after all expenses, the grocery store earns about $1 in profit.[5]

The top row of Table 10.1 shows the rates the largest supermarket chains pay, and the bottom row shows the rates the smallest are charged. Cards with the least benefits are on the left, and those with the most are on the right. Because most banks rebrand credit cards with their own program name, it often takes a minute of looking at your physical card to find the hidden words identifying which type of card you have.

The lowest discount rates are found in the top left corner. These are when low-benefit cards are used in giant supermarket chains. Mastercard takes 1.15% of the transaction's value, plus a fixed charge of 5¢. The highest

Table 10.1 Amount Mastercard Charges Supermarkets for Credit Card Purchases

Supermarket annual Mastercard charges	Least to Most benefits			
	Core card	Enhanced value card	World card	World high-value card
Over $2 billion	1.15%+5¢	1.15%+5¢	1.25%+5¢	1.25%+5¢
$750 million to $2 billion	1.22%+5¢	1.22%+5¢	1.32%+5¢	1.32%+5¢
Under $750 million	1.45%+10¢	1.60%+10¢	1.70%+10¢	2.10%+10¢

rates are found in the bottom right corner. These are when high-benefit cards are used in smaller supermarkets. The maximum rate for Mastercard is a 2.1% fee plus a 10¢ fixed charge.

To put these percentages into context, on a $50 supermarket purchase the store earns about $1 profit after Mastercard takes anywhere from 63¢ to a $1.15. This means the merchant discount rate is roughly the same as the supermarket's profit.

Not everyone uses a credit card to buy their groceries; some use a debit card instead. The discount rate is simpler when a debit card is used. Debit cards with a Mastercard logo cost supermarkets a maximum of 35¢. Supermarkets would prefer you use a debit card, not a credit card when buying groceries, but they have no method of incentivizing you to do so.

Not all debit card transactions are fixed at such a low amount. Supermarkets and a few other essential categories in the United States, like gas stations, are capped by government rules. Many other categories are not capped. The Federal Reserve tracks debit card discount rates each year. The data show the typical debit card fee in an uncapped category is about 1.4% of the transaction's value, and the typical capped category fee is 0.5%. The average debit card transaction costs a business about 0.8%.[6]

Cryptocurrency payments do not have fixed fees like credit or debit cards. Instead, their fees fluctuate based on market conditions. This means the discount fee a business pays today is not necessarily the same tomorrow. The *Wall Street Journal* tracked cryptocurrency discount fees during 2021 and found a very wide range. A quote from the article shows how dramatic the range of fees was: "On the Bitcoin network, the average daily transaction fee this year has been as low as $1.78 and as high as $62, according to bitinfocharts…. If you are buying a cup of coffee at Starbucks, paying $1.80 in fees for a $3 coffee is excessive. Paying $60 is insane."[7]

Discount fees, however, are not the only cost merchants need to think about when accepting electronic payments. Merchants must buy or rent point-of-sale systems that can accept electronic payments, plus they pay annual or monthly fees to connect these systems to the electronic networks as well as processing fees to send in batches of transactions.

HOW COMPANIES PRICE

The previous section showed credit, debit, and crypto discount fees plus point-of-sale processing fees are a significant cost to companies. These costs affect the price consumers pay, because when companies price products, "The most common strategy used involves adding a markup on the product costs. Many companies compute the cost of producing a product and add a specific margin."[8]

For example, Mark Cuban, a serial entrepreneur, has created a cost-plus pharmacy. The pharmacy buys drugs directly from manufacturers. To the cost of the medicine it adds a 15% markup, plus an $8 shipping and handling fee. Another example is Costco; the large chain of warehouse stores adds a markup of about 12% to most products.[9]

Most businesses are not charities. Instead, they exist to make money, which is why they pass on these processing and interchange fees. These fees are another cost of doing business. The higher the cost of doing business, the higher the price the customer pays.

But wait, doesn't handling cash also cost merchants money? Yes! However, the cost structure is different. In business terms cash is primarily a fixed cost for merchants, whereas electronic payments are a variable cost. A fixed cost does not vary based on the amount spent, but a variable cost does.

Let's take a small store as an example. If the store accepts cash, the manager has to go to the bank periodically to get cash or deposit cash. There are costs associated with counting the cash at the beginning and end of each shift. There is the cost of theft or robbery. Most of these costs are in the form of a fixed amount of time taken out of the manager's day.

These costs are one reason why many business managers don't like cash. However, these costs for the store do not change very much. If the store does lots of business or does relatively little, the costs are similar because it takes the manager about the same amount of time to handle $1,000 of cash or $10,000.

Because most of cash's handling costs are fixed, the more business the merchant does, the lower the average cost of handling paper money for each transaction. Table 10.2 has a simple example that shows this point. The top part of the table is when the store is cash only; the bottom part assumes the store is credit card only. Let's assume the store owner and manager are different people, with the manager being an hourly employee who doesn't share in the profits.

Table 10.2 Merchant Cost to Accept Cash and Credit Cards When Customers Make Purchases About $100

	Number transactions	Value of all transactions	Total payment cost	Cost per transaction
Cash only	100	$10,000	$50	$0.50
Credit card only	100	$10,000	$210	$2.10

In the top part of Table 10.2, which is cash only, let's assume the manager is paid $50 per hour and it takes one hour per day to handle all the aspects of cash like getting it from the bank, counting it, and redepositing it at the end of the day. During each day the store typically does 100 different transactions about $100.

The top line of Table 10.2 shows being cash only means the business pays $0.50 to handle each customer payment. Now let's switch the example and assume the store only accepts credit cards. Let's assume the store needs to pay a $0.10 fee for each electronic transaction plus pay 2% of the transaction's value.

The store manager is overjoyed to accept credit cards. By not having to handle cash they gain an extra hour each day to do other tasks. This extra hour might mean more sleep for the manager, because they can come into the store just when it needs to open, instead of going to the bank first. It might mean more time at night with the manager's family or friends, because they don't have to count cash at the end of the day or deposit money in the bank.

For the manager, using credit cards is superior to using cash because the manager has fewer overhead tasks to run the store. However, the store owners do not see it the same way. The store owner gives up 10¢ times 100 transactions, which is $10. They also give up 2% of their sales, which is $200. Accepting credit cards costs the owner $2.10 per customer purchase in transaction costs, which is a $1.60 more than the cost of using cash. For most store owners this higher cost needs to be recouped, and they typically do this by raising prices.

MERCHANT VIEWS

The previous example was illustrative but did not use real world data. Is paying with cash really cheaper? About the time when societies started making the transition from cash to electronic payments several central banks and other groups did studies to determine the cost of the various payment methods. The result, especially for smaller value transactions, matched the previous example. Cash was found to be either the cheapest or one of the cheapest forms of payment.

One of the best and longest running studies is done by the British Retail Consortium. The Consortium is the trade group that represents retail shops from the smallest to the largest stores. They ask retailers to tally up all the costs of each form of payment. For cash, that includes getting it delivered to the stores and getting extra money back into the business's bank account. The data show cash costs stores one-half of what debit cards cost and one-fifth what credit cards cost. They found that "the average cost to a retailer of processing a cash transaction remains well below the costs associated with handling card payments."[10]

Other surveys have the same findings. The Bank of Canada ran a survey of retailers and asked merchants how much it cost them to handle each type of payment. "A key finding of the survey is that most merchants perceive cash as the least costly form of payment and, in comparison, find debit cards only moderately costly and credit cards the most costly."[11]

Data from Belgium showed, "Costs are lowest for cash, at about 53 euro cents, but this instrument is closely followed by Proton (54 euro cents) and debit cards (55 euro cents). For credit cards, the costs are noticeably higher (2.62 euros)." Proton was one of the early electronic wallets. It was created in the mid-1990s as a low-cost electronic replacement for cash, but met with limited success and was shut down two decades later.[12]

The Federal Reserve Bank of Kansas published a study that compared the costs of various forms of paying in four countries: Australia, Belgium, the Netherlands, and Norway. Cash was the lowest cost method of payment in three of the four countries. Only in Norway were debit cards cheaper than cash for businesses to use. One reason for this result is that cash was used relatively infrequently in Norway when the survey was done.[13]

SURCHARGING AND STEERING

The strongest evidence for businesses wanting cheaper payment methods comes from the payment industry. Merchants want to steer or incentivize customers to use the cheapest payment methods, like cash. However, for decades credit card companies had strict rules preventing steering.

The simplest way to steer customers is showing a higher price or surcharge for particular payment methods. I recently went by a skate rental shop with a sign that captured steering. The shop accepted cash and Venmo mobile payments. Customers using mobile payments were charged 50¢ or 6.25% extra to cover the additional cost of handling mobile payments.

The legality of steering and anti-steering rules is so contentious the legal disputes went all the way to the US Supreme Court. In 2018 several states, led by Ohio, sued American Express, which typically charges merchants some of the highest discount fees. In 2018 the Supreme Court ruled that American Express's merchant agreements, which prevent steering, were legal.[14]

This means businesses that accept American Express cards must sign an agreement stating they cannot "try to persuade or prompt Cardmembers to use any Other Payment Products or any other method of payment." Merchants must also agree not to impose "fees when the Card is accepted that are not imposed equally on all Other Payment Products, except for electronic funds transfer, or cash and check." This means most merchants cannot recoup American Express', higher fees, except by raising prices for all customers.[15]

Visa and Mastercard do not have anti-steering language in their US merchant agreements. They struck the language in 2010 to avoid being sued by the Department of Justice. However, these credit card companies' merchant agreements are so complex many businesses are reluctant to surcharge. For example, Visa and Mastercard both demand 30 days' notice before surcharging begins. They also require clear notices about surcharging at the store entrance and at checkout. Additionally, the surcharge amount must be shown on the receipt as a separate line item.

Behavioral economics provides a solution to recouping electronic payment fees. Give customers a discount for using cash instead of adding a surcharge for electronic payments like credit cards. Charging customers an extra fee to use electronic payments makes many angry because they feel penalized. However, businesses can reframe this by raising all prices slightly to cover the cost of electronic payment fees and then giving cash paying customers the fees back. Providing a discount makes paper money customers feel like they won. This discount would encourage people to use cash, resulting in more profit for the merchant.

CUSTOM PRICING

The computer revolution has created the ability to create custom products cheaply. It is easy to have customized clothes made. Three-dimensional printing enables customized parts. The cashless society is setting us up for customized prices. Customized pricing, where each customer receives a different price, is a holy grail for businesses because it results in maximum profits. With customized pricing, individuals who are not price sensitive receive a high price and those who are price sensitive get a lower price.

The ability to create a vast number of customized prices only happens if merchants have data on what and where people make purchases. Pay for something electronically and you are providing businesses with the data to create customized prices. Pay for something with cash and that ability is severed.

Knowing just a few facts like where you shop and how much you spend is enough to be able to calculate a rough customized price. Let me give you an example. In my neighborhood I can shop in three different types of grocery stores. One is a very high-end chain, owned by a major technology company. It has fancy fresh produce, expensive imported cheeses, and lots of eager help who know copious amounts of information about even the most obscure product. The prices in that store make me wince.

The second place is a big box store that is owned by one of the world's largest brick-and-mortar retailers. The stores are huge, and one side is devoted just to groceries. It isn't easy to find staff who can answer questions, but that is part of the appeal. The place is clean but relatively bare-bones and the prices are low.

The third place is a mid-market chain. It is a cross between the high- and low-end stores. The prices are not cheap, but they also don't make me blanch. The selection is good, but not amazing. The produce has some life but wasn't handpicked that morning.

Let's imagine for a moment you run a business that has nothing to do with grocery stores and need to calculate a customized price. The customer will be quoted $50, $75, or $100. Your cost doesn't change no matter what price you ask; however, your profits change by a lot. If the customer is not price sensitive, they will pay $100. If they are very price sensitive, they will only pay $50.

Now imagine for a small fee, say $1, a financial-tech company can tell you how much the customer has spent over the past year in each of the three grocery stores. Would you buy this information? Most merchants would jump at the chance. Although knowing where and how much people spend doesn't guarantee which of the three is the optimal price to charge, knowing someone doesn't mind paying top dollar for groceries makes them more likely to accept the $100 price. Conversely, knowing a person primarily shops at the bare-bones big box store doesn't mean they wouldn't pay more than $50 but most people who look to buy groceries cheaply look for bargains in other aspects of their life.

Does customized pricing happen in real life? Yes, it happens all the time. Rafi Mohammed in a *Harvard Business Review* article discusses looking at a vacation package of flights and hotel on a popular travel website. He was quoted $117 or over 6% more on the travel company's website versus using an app on his phone for the identical package. Then he asked a friend who he felt consistently overpaid for everything to try a test. Together they both used the same app at the same time to book the same vacation. The friend received a price that was $50 or almost 3% higher.[16]

It is not just travel companies and it is not just recently. One of the first articles that I remember reading about custom pricing came from the *Wall Street Journal*. The story starts off with a great line; "It was the same Swingline stapler, on the same Staples.com website. But for Kim Wamble, the price was $15.79, while the price on Trude Frizzell's screen, just a few miles away, was $14.29." Customized pricing is slowly taking over. Knowing where, when, and how you spend enables businesses to optimize prices. Using cash reduces the amount of information businesses have. Although customized pricing can still use other data like your location, reducing what businesses know about your purchase history helps defeat it or, as the end of this chapter shows, enables you to confuse the algorithms so they think you should get an even lower price.[17]

For those still not convinced, in July 2024 the Federal Trade Commission issued civil subpoenas to Mastercard, JP Morgan Chase, and other financial companies demanding to know "how artificial intelligence and other technological tools might allow companies to vary prices using data they collect about individual consumers' finances and shopping habits." The Commission is worried that the hypothetical example outlined in this section is not hypothetical.[18]

EXAMPLES OF CUSTOM PRICING

Car dealers have been doing custom pricing for years. The dealers negotiate a different price for every car and truck they sell, even though many vehicles sold are the same except for minor differences, like the paint color. The price paid for a vehicle depends on both the amount of desperation and the bargaining skills of the buyer and the dealer. Economists call what car dealers do "first-degree or perfect price discrimination." *Perfect price discrimination* results in the seller charging each customer the maximum price they are willing to pay. This is a dream scenario for business because it results in a company earning the most money.

It is not just car dealers who do custom pricing. In many developing countries posted prices are the exception, not the rule. People bargain in the market for most purchases. Locals who know the best price or who have a connection with the vendor get good deals. Outsiders and tourists get the worst deals. When I was in China a man outside a large park was selling kites. He shouted out prices in both English and Mandarin. The English price was double the Mandarin price, in a clear example of custom pricing.

In wealthy countries prior to computers and the data collected as part of the cashless society, custom pricing was only possible for items or services people purchased infrequently and at a high price. In addition to cars, homes are bought by negotiating to arrive at a custom price. Because homes cost so much, many people use real estate brokers to help negotiate the purchase.

The data collected via electronic transactions enable businesses whose products or services cost much less than homes or cars to start using custom prices. Let's talk about grocery stores. These places have large numbers of relatively inexpensive items. Moreover, many states have laws that require retailers to display an item's price on the product or shelf.[19] How can a grocery store do custom pricing?

Let me give you a quick example. I shop at one grocery store near my home quite a lot. Don't tell the manager of the store, but if I come in on a weekday, I never look at the prices. I am typically late, out of food, and out of time. Within reason, I just don't care what things cost. On weekends when I visit this store, I look at prices. If the store did custom pricing, they should charge me a lot for items on weekdays and much less if I show up on weekends. Doing this would boost their profits.

How could the grocery store know what to charge me? It is simple if they have my purchase history over the past few years. They, or more specifically their computer's artificial intelligence programs, will notice whether the price goes up or down I purchase roughly the same amount during weekdays. On weekdays I lack any meaningful response to price changes, but on weekends prices do affect my decisions.

With the widespread adoption of cell phones and computers, custom pricing is starting to show up everywhere. Grocery stores in my neighborhood are doing this by sending custom coupons, which reduce the price of a product. Stores that understand I am not price sensitive on weekdays should never send me a coupon that works during a weekday. Giving me items on sale then only lowers their profits. However, although I should never be sent a weekday coupon, they can boost their sales and profits by sending me coupons that trumpet, "Sale This Weekend Only."

Sending coupons with custom prices gets around item pricing laws because thrifty customers have used coupons for years to get deals. The only difference between people clipping coupons out of newspapers and magazines in the 1950s versus today is that people in marketing can send coupons to specific groups or individuals and can vary the amount of the discount. Today coupons are being distributed digitally, which lowers the cost to marketers. Data also allow coupons to be targeted in a much finer granularity today.

CONCLUSION

Using cash instead of electronic payments saves merchants money by avoiding the fees charged by credit card companies and clearinghouses. To make the same profits, stores charge higher prices. Offering discounts for cash purchases, when legally allowed, encourages customers to use cash and can increase profits.

Prices are one of the most important signals in market economies. We often judge the quality of similar items by looking just at their price. Expensive items are viewed as high quality, and lower priced items are viewed as inferior. This signal is distorted when businesses mark up their prices to cover the higher costs of handling electronic payments.

The signal is also distorted when businesses use custom pricing. In a custom pricing situation seeing a high price doesn't mean something is higher quality. Instead, a high price simply means a business views the customer as not price sensitive. The easiest way to defeat custom pricing and remove the distortions when businesses mark up prices to cover the costs of electronic payments is simply to use cash. Using paper money eliminates issues of steering, surcharging, and surveillance all in one simple act. What can be better than that?

SECTION IV

CASH HELPS THE VULNERABLE

A ll societies have vulnerable populations like the poor, immigrants, refugees, and the elderly. Paper money is a powerful method of helping these vulnerable groups. The next three chapters go into more detail about how the vulnerable primarily face two problems.

Chapter 11 points out that many vulnerable people are not able to access electronic payments. Governments around the world require financial institutions to collect identification documents and addresses from customers. These know-your-customer rules make it difficult or even impossible for many vulnerable people to get accounts.

Chapter 12 shows that electronic payments are expensive, especially for the vulnerable. Numerous people have scoffed when I make this statement by pointing out they send money electronically for free or have a free bank account. Unfortunately, there is no free lunch in modern society; everything has some cost.

Electronic money is created, moved, and tracked using an incredibly large and complex system of computers and communication networks managed by highly talented and highly compensated people. What appears "free" to a user costs huge amounts of money to build and maintain and that money has to come from somewhere. If the government is providing the network for "free" the money typically comes from taxes. If private businesses are providing the network, the "free" services are paid for by charging someone else.

For example, my bank provides me with a "free" checking account. However, this free account comes with a catch. I must leave a relatively large amount of money in the account, on which the bank gives almost no interest. I pay for this "free" account by giving the bank a large interest-free loan.

Chapter 13 looks at the elderly, another vulnerable population. Many seniors have saved money for their retirement. Central banks around the world in recent years have pushed interest rates below zero. This takes money away from savers and punishes those who prepared for their golden years. The chapter explains how cash protects the elderly from central bankers' actions.

Before jumping into all the details of how cash benefits society's vulnerable, let me share a message I received highlighting how hard the cashless society is for one vulnerable part of the population, the mentally ill.

I am an inpatient psychiatric nurse at a state adult mental health hospital and part of the discharge plan is how they [the patient] are going to manage financially. A portion of them are on disability and their checks go into an account they have, but accessing the account is hard if you no longer have transportation, valid identification, a cell phone, a permanent address, an email, or the knowledge of how to use technology. I have been told by numerous clients that they can survive better on the streets with cash than they can with a government card. . . . To remember a "pin," to have ID which usually gets stolen, coupled with a chronic mental challenge is too much.

CHAPTER ELEVEN

ELIMINATING CASH HURTS THE POOR

W ould you patronize a store that has a large sign out front saying "Blacks, Jews and Irish Not Allowed"? Most people would walk away in disgust on seeing a sign preventing people from entering based on their race, religion, or ethnicity. Although segregation and exclusions were prevalent in the past, they clearly do not exist today … right? Wrong.

Today, there are new signs popping up in windows saying, "No Cash Accepted." These signs effectively say, "Poor People Are Not Allowed!" Millions of people don't have bank accounts and most of these people are poor. Without access to a credit card, debit card, or mobile payment, poor people are unable to make a purchase when merchants refuse cash. Can we solve this problem by giving or forcing everyone to have a bank account?

As pointed out in this chapter, this will not work because surveys show millions do not want a bank account.

Eliminating cash does more than deny the poor the right to shop; it creates a reverse Robin Hood world. Robin Hood was a legendary heroic outlaw who lived in England's Sherwood Forest. Robin Hood took money from the rich and gave it to the poor.

Today many rich people use rewards cards and programs that accumulate miles, points, and cash back. These rewards promise to provide holders with free travel, vacations, and meals, but they cost someone money. Where does the money come from? As I will explain, rewards programs are funded by taking money from the poor and financially unsophisticated. The poor are charged higher prices, high interest rates, and high fees. This means the modern credit card system is a reverse Robin Hood society, taking from the poor and giving to the rich every time a purchase is made.

Let's jump into the details and see why keeping cash around empowers poor people.

EXCLUSION FROM STORES

I often visit Seattle, which many people think of as a wealthy city, because it is a thriving center of high-technology and progressive business where companies like Microsoft, Amazon, and Starbucks have their headquarters. Although the Seattle area has some very rich people, it also has a large poor population. The poorest of the poor are quite visible in Seattle because there are many homeless people living in its parks and alongside its highways.

The neighborhood where I stay is very trendy and rapidly gentrifying. Many stores proudly display signs in their windows declaring that all racial groups and sexual orientations matter. Right beside these proclamations of tolerance are signs saying, "No Cash Accepted."

Not accepting cash prevents homeless people and many other poor people from buying anything at the neighborhood's restaurants, stores, and shops. The coffee shop where I get my morning bagel doesn't accept cash. The Asian restaurant where I often buy lunch doesn't either. The store where I pick up beer or wine for dinner doesn't accept cash. None of these places are high-end or expensive shops. All serve common needs. However, their prominent signs saying "No Cash Accepted" exclude anyone who does not have a credit card, debit card, or mobile payment plan. The people who don't have electronic payment methods are primarily poor. The signs and policies of refusing cash are a simple way of saying, "Poor people aren't welcome here."

The reasons local business owners give me for not accepting cash range from "it is more convenient for customers" to "it reduces the chance of us being robbed." Not a single owner has ever said or even implied that they want to keep out the poor, but that is the impact of their policies.

The stores' refusal to accept cash has other impacts. Economists worry a lot about monopolies, which is when one store or organization has exclusive control. Monopolies use their power to boost prices because the lack of competition removes constraints on what they can charge. When most stores in a neighborhood shift to a "no cash accepted" policy there will be a large incentive for one to continue accepting cash. That remaining store will have a monopoly serving customers who use paper money. The lack of competition will result in higher prices paid by poor people who have only one place to shop even when surrounded by a sea of stores.

REDUCTION IN CHARITY

Eliminating cash also reduces spontaneous charity. While I was writing this chapter my doorbell rang. It was a group of athletes from the nearby high school asking for donations. I pulled some cash from my pocket, handed it to them, and went back to work. The athletes were happy, and I was proud to support the local kids. Because I used cash the entire episode took about one minute, which let the athletes canvas more homes and let me go back to work.

Cash enables spontaneous charity without concerns about any follow-on contact or issues. I recently pulled into a highway rest area and stopped next to a man with his car hood open. I said hello. He started showing me his car's problem and asked if I had the tool to fix his engine. It was clear he did not have the money to fix the problem.

I wondered if this was a scam. However, having once been poor and knowing the frustration of keeping a dying car alive for as long as possible, I decided to help. I pulled some cash out of my wallet and wished him luck fixing the car. If it was a scam, I didn't have to worry about him having my cell phone number, credit card, or debit card number. I also didn't have to worry about ending up paying some local repair shop an inflated bill. Instead, I helped the best I could and did not worry about any follow-on financial entanglement.

Let's go back to the neighborhood I often visit in Seattle where many businesses refuse cash. The local supermarket is one of the few neighborhood places still accepting cash. There is usually at least one person asking for spare change standing outside the supermarket's entrance. Because so few neighborhood businesses accept paper money many locals do not carry any cash or coins, resulting in few people giving spare change when asked, reducing spontaneous charity.

Bringing back paper money will not solve the long-term problems of poverty or the root causes of homelessness like mental illness or drug addiction. However, giving cash to people panhandling outside a supermarket eases some of poverty's immediate problems, like a homeless person going hungry that day.

How important is cash for helping the homeless and doing charitable work? The Federal Reserve's Survey of Consumer Payments asks a random group of respondents to keep a diary of all their spending during a short period of time each October. Using some advanced statistical techniques on the diary data can indicate national averages.

The most recent data show not a lot of US citizens make cash donations. Slightly less than 2% of all adults gave cash and among those who did give paper money the average amount was $25. These figures don't seem like much. However, there are over 250 million US adults. When slightly less than 2% of that many people gave $25 cash in just October it adds up to over $1 billion annually given to charities, the homeless, and religious organizations using paper money.[1]

Sometimes people want to help the poor by making a large donation but doing it electronically means less money actually gets to the poor. GoFundMe, a favorite method of raising money online, currently charges 2.9% plus a 30¢ fee for each credit or debit card donation.[2]

These charges add up. While writing this book I made a pledge to a charity to donate $3,000 within two months. I procrastinated on paying right up until the moment the money was due. This gave me no time to drive over with a check, hand them a bundle of cash, or even send money using my bank's online bill pay. Because I procrastinated the only choice left was using the charity's website to make a credit card donation. The delay was costly because the charity lost 3% covering their credit card fees, resulting in my donation being cut by $90.

LEGAL AND OTHER SOLUTIONS

People in high-tech are trying to solve the problems of charity and access. One group has created a phone app that sends money to either a poor person's phone or a small beacon they are holding. The concept is novel and means well. However, given we already have a low-tech and low-cost solution, paper money, do we really need to replace it with a high-tech and high-cost solution?[3]

Many others places besides Seattle have storefront signs saying cash is not accepted. This has angered advocates for the poor and homeless. A few cities and states, like Massachusetts, have pushed back and passed laws requiring stores to accept cash to ensure the poor are not shut out of society. These rules, covered later in Chapter 18, on legal tender, sound wonderful but as will be pointed out, have problems limiting their usefulness.

Cash acceptance laws usually cover only retail establishments, which are typically brick-and-mortar stores. This means the regulations don't cover restaurants, medical providers, or transportation. If Seattle passed the identical law that Massachusetts enforces, the bagel store where I get my breakfast and the Asian restaurant where I often eat lunch would still not have to accept cash. Only the liquor store where I get drinks for dinner would have to change its policy. Ensuring the homeless can drink alcohol, but not eat, doesn't seem like a true improvement.

Additionally, although laws can ensure cash is accepted, the rules say nothing about making cash payments convenient or easy. Waiting for a store manager, who might be the only person authorized to take cash, discourages paper money use because it takes time and draws extra attention to the payer. As a professor who advocates for cash, I don't mind extra attention and use these moments to educate people about the power of cash. However, many homeless and poor people don't want extra attention when inside a business. They simply want to get in and get out as fast as possible.

HOW THE POOR SUBSIDIZE THE RICH

Everyone loves something for nothing. As pointed out in this chapter's Introduction many credit cards offer points, miles, and other rewards. Extensive advertisements for these cards imply things like free travel are available for doing nothing more than switching from cash to paying with a rewards-based card. For those people not enticed by "free vacations," other credit cards offer the ability to help a favorite cause or charity, promising a percentage of every charge to the affiliated organization by swiping a card.

Unfortunately, in modern society there is no such thing as a free lunch. Someone pays for the billions of dollars' worth of points, miles, rewards, and donations being given away. Unsurprisingly, the payments are not coming from generous banks and kind financial institutions. Instead, these rewards are paid for by the poor and the financially unsophisticated.

In simple terms when people brag about how many frequent flier miles they earned or how much money they got back from using their credit cards, they are unknowingly bragging about taking advantage of the poor or financially unsophisticated.

Several different groups of economists have investigated this problem.[4] A research group at the Boston Federal Reserve stated, "What most consumers do not know is that their decision to pay by credit card involves merchant fees, retail price increases, a nontrivial transfer of income from cash to card payers, and consequently a transfer from low-income to high-income consumers." They found the amount of these rewards earned by the wealthy are large; the "highest-income household ($150,000 or more annually) receives $750 every year." The money received by the rich comes from low-income credit card users and cash payers.

Researchers at the Bank of Canada found "credit card transactions are cross-subsidized by cheaper debit and cash payments.... We find that consumers in the lowest-income cohort pay the highest net pecuniary cost as a percentage of transaction value, while consumers in the highest-income cohort pay the lowest."

A group of researchers at the US Federal Reserve analyzed millions of credit card accounts and concluded that "credit card rewards transfer income from less to more educated, from poorer to richer, and from high- to low-minority areas, thereby widening existing spatial disparities."

The total amounts transferred are staggering. The researchers from the US Federal Reserve calculated the average card got about $10 worth of rewards during the single month they analyzed. They calculated the average reward card was charged about $22 in fees and interest in the same month. These researchers were only able to get data from 19 banks, which issued about 120 million rewards cards. In annual terms just these 19 banks gave customers over $14 billion in yearly rewards but charged them about $32 billion a year for the privilege of using reward cards.

What is especially notable from these figures is that most people receiving "rewards" are paying more in fees than they are receiving in benefits.

There are several different ways reward cards and programs take money from the poor or financially unsophisticated and move it to the rich or more sophisticated. The first method is through higher prices. Electronic payments are expensive for businesses. As pointed out earlier in Chapter 10, merchants recoup these extra payments by boosting prices. People who earn frequent flier miles or who get cash back from their credit card company are not affected because they get back some or all the extra amount they pay. However, poor people who pay with cash, use debit cards, or prepaid cards end up paying more and don't get any benefit back.

Additionally, high-value rewards cards cost merchants more than plain credit cards with no extra features. As Chapter 10 points out, paying with a high-value rewards card costs the typical merchant about 1% more than if a customer pays with a basic no-frills credit card.

This means as more people switch from plain vanilla credit cards to fancy reward cards, merchants need to boost prices even more to cover the extra costs. One percent more for rewards cards doesn't seem like much. However, US consumers spend trillions of dollars yearly using rewards credit cards, boosting the cost of living for everyone by billions.

Another way the poor and financially unsophisticated transfer money to the rich and sophisticated is through interest and fees. As pointed out in Chapter 8 there are different types of credit card users. Convenience users typically pay off their balances every month, pay no interest, but receive rewards. Revolvers only pay off part of their balance each month. They incur fees and pay interest, which pay for the credit card network, and subsidize the convenience users. Not surprisingly research shows convenience users have higher income and higher financial sophistication than revolvers. The revolvers, by paying for the credit card system, give convenience users a free ride.

Rewards credit cards take from the poor and give to the rich. Switching back to a more cash-based society reduces one method of forcing poor people to subsidize the rich.

UNBANKED AND UNDERBANKED

Eliminating cash is a major problem for the unbanked and underbanked because these people primarily use cash. Unbanked people do not have accounts at banks or other institutions. Underbanked people are individuals who simultaneously have a bank account but also use alternative financial services, like check-cashing outlets. The unbanked and underbanked are primarily poor people. In the United States about one-quarter of those earning less than $15,000 per year are unbanked. The richer a person is, the more likely they are to have a bank account. Among those earning more than $75,000 per year, almost every person had some type of bank account.

Why would people not have a bank account? The Federal Deposit Insurance Corporation (FDIC) asks unbanked people all their reasons for not having bank accounts. People can respond with service issues like the bank has the wrong hours, which affects people working night shifts, or the bank's location is inconvenient, which affects people living in remote areas. Other responses are financial, such as being too poor, or the fees banks charge are too high.[5]

Many people who don't have bank accounts say they are too expensive or banks are too far away to be convenient. Numerous financial technology, or fintech, companies are trying to solve these problems by providing access to bank-like products for people without bank accounts. They trumpet that using their technology will result in financial inclusion for all.

However, the FDIC surveys also track four other reasons people do not use banks. Each reason is why fintech solutions will be not moving everyone into the cashless financial system:

- Avoiding a bank gives more privacy
- Don't trust banks
- Don't have the personal identification required to open an account
- Cannot open an account due to problems with past banking or credit history

Among people providing a reason why they don't have a bank account about 40% avoided banks to get more privacy and 40% just did not trust banks. About 15% did not have enough identification to open an account, and about 15% said they had past banking problems.

These figures add up to more than 100% because people could state multiple answers. There were about eight million people stating at least one of these four reasons and these people lived in over three million households. This means that even with the best cashless solutions there are millions of people and families who still need or want to rely on paper money.

Beyond fintech some advocates for the poor believe a better solution for the millions who are unbanked is to give everyone a free bank account. In my city the government gives poor children free lunches and gives poor adults free housing and free transportation. Why not simply give the poor no-cost bank accounts? This solves the problem of paying for fees, but doesn't address the issues of people who lack trust in banks or who lack identification or addresses.

THE UNBANKED PAY EXTRA FEES

People lacking a bank account are forced to use cash. They have little or no access to credit cards, debit cards, or other bank-related products. There are several ways to get around being unbanked or underbanked and needing to use electronic payments. Unfortunately, workarounds are expensive. One simple method is buying a prepaid card. Prepaid cards act just like a credit card or debit card. Many are sold by major electronic payment companies like Visa, Mastercard, or American Express.

If someone purchases a prepaid Visa, Mastercard, or American Express card they can use the prepaid card anywhere regular credit or debit cards are used. This enables an unbanked person to make purchases in places where cash is not accepted like on internet websites or while flying in an airplane.

The problem with prepaid cards is that there are up-front costs. Target is a large retailer that sells many types of prepaid cards. Anyone can walk into Target with paper money and purchase a prepaid Visa card.[6]

Currently, Target sells a $25 prepaid Visa card; to purchase it the buyer pays an extra $4 activation fee, which is a 16% surcharge. Target also sells $50, $100, and $200 prepaid Visa cards. The $50 card has a $5 fee, and the $100 and $200 cards have a $6 fee. This translates into an up-front 10%, 6%, and 3% surcharge simply to use electronic money.

To prevent money laundering Target's prepaid Visa cards cannot be reloaded and cannot be used to get cash back from ATM's or merchants. This means people who rely on prepaid cards need to pay up-front fees each time they purchase a card, because once a card is emptied of money, it cannot be reloaded.

For another example, Walmart, one of the largest US retailers, offers a reloadable basic debit card. The card costs $1 to buy, $6 per month in fees, and $3 to load with cash at Walmart's registers and a higher fee to reload elsewhere.

Another way to get around being unbanked is using electronic bill payment services. I live a few blocks away from a drug store. The drug store is part of giant chain that has a partnership with a payments company. The store advertises that I can come in with cash and electronically pay any bill at thousands of companies for fees "starting at $3.49." Once again, not being able to use cash means the unbanked are forced to pay more.[7]

It is becoming increasingly difficult to be unbanked. In the past it was relatively easy to avoid being part of the formal banking system. Employers used to pay workers in cash. In the past workers could use their cash to pay bills in person and to shop in brick-and-mortar stores. Today it is much harder to avoid interacting with the banking system because places to pay bills in cash are bygone relics and online shopping takes only electronic means of payment.

HOW MANY UNBANKED ARE IN THE WORLD?

What is it like in other parts of the world? Are the millions of unbanked in the United States who still need to use cash an outlier? Data from the World Bank show over a billion people are unbanked and rely on paper money.

The World Bank tracks the percentage of people in each country with access to financial services. The World Bank's definition of having a bank account is broader than what is used in the United States because it also includes anyone using a cell phone to send and receive money as being banked.[8]

Table 11.1 shows the World Bank's estimates. Overall, about one-quarter of the world's adults do not have access to a bank or mobile phone account, with dramatic geographic differences. If you are reading this book in Europe or the United States the number of unbanked people is relatively small, with the Euro zone having an unbanked rate of just 1%. However, in the Middle East and North Africa, only about half the population has an

Table 11.1   Percent Adults Unbanked in the World

Area	Percentage unbanked
Euro area	1
North America	5
Europe and Central Asia	10
East Asia and Pacific	17
Latin America and Caribbean	26
Sub-Saharan Africa	45
Middle East and North Africa	47
World	24

account, with an unbanked rate of 47%. In general, the higher a country's average income, the more likely the populace has a bank account.

UNABLE TO PAY FOR A PHONE

Many financial technology companies believe mobile payments are the solution for the poor and unbanked. Before ending I want to point out problems with this belief. For mobile payments to work, people need a working phone. As discussed later in Chapter 17, in less stable parts of the world people cannot count on the communications network being available, because sometimes for security reasons governments shut down phones and the internet.

In more stable countries the preconditions for making mobile payments are purchasing a cell phone and paying for cell service. Unfortunately, phones are often shut off because the phone owner cannot pay for their service. This means when a person has financial difficulties, they are likely unable to make or receive mobile payments.

How big is this problem? In the United States two of the biggest cell phone companies are Verizon and T-Mobile. In 2021, an economically good year, Verizon expected 2.6% and T-Mobile expected about 3.5% of all cell phone plan revenue to be uncollectable. In simple terms about 3% of cell phone customers were going to have their cell phones shut off because of inability to pay their bills.

The US government is aware of this problem, and the FCC, the agency in charge of telephones, has a special program called Lifeline. Lifeline provides over $9 per month to people with low income to pay for their cell phones. However, to get this support, poor individuals must provide three months of documentation proving they have little or no money. This means people who suddenly become poor aren't covered until months after their income or wealth disappears.[9]

In a society where almost all payments are electronic and many people use mobile payments, losing the ability to use your phone not only eliminates your ability to communicate with friends and family but also prevents making purchases. In a society that still uses cash, people can still make purchases even if they lose the ability to use their phone.

CONCLUSION

Modern society is becoming increasingly unequal economically. The elimination of cash is not one of the primary drivers of economic inequality. However, as this chapter has shown, eliminating cash makes the problem of economic inequality worse. Eliminating cash hurts the homeless and poor by reducing the number of stores, doctors, and restaurants they can do business with. Eliminating cash reduces spontaneous charity. The elimination of cash forces the poor to subsidize the spending of the rich. Last, it causes people who don't trust or like banks to become part of the financial system and pay high fees. Keeping cash around empowers the poor.

Proponents of a cashless society claim being cashless will promote lofty goals like financial inclusion and equity. However, cash already provides a simple, low-cost, and equitable method of ensuring people can buy and sell goods and services easily and cheaply.

CHAPTER TWELVE

CASH HELPS IMMIGRANTS, REFUGEES, AND TOURISTS

The world is on the move. The United Nations estimates over a quarter of a billion people migrated to a different country in the latest report (2019). Some of these immigrants and refugees come legally. Many come illegally. However, all face similar problems with a cashless society.[1]

First, these immigrants often face language barriers. Many do not speak or read the local language or have less proficiency than native speakers. Electronic transactions come with a host of things that must be read, understood, and signed, from phone screens to long legal agreements.

For example, the consumer agreement for American Express's "EveryDay® Credit Card" is ten pages of densely packed text. Using cash is much simpler and almost no language skills are needed. Instead, all an immigrant needs to recognize are a few commonly used digits.[2]

Second, immigrants often lack experience dealing with banks or other financial institutions. Although many readers have used banks and other financial intuitions for most of their lives, a large proportion of the world's population rarely interacts with banks because they live in rural areas far from any bank or live in a poor country where only a few rich people use banks. This lack of familiarity means many immigrants are more comfortable using cash.

Third, some migrants come from countries where the financial sector is not trusted. While writing this book I talked with a banker from Bangladesh. He mentioned many people in his country did not have faith in banks. A few months after our chat, the reason for the distrust became clear. Bangladesh's central bank "ordered the merger of 10 of the country's 61 private and state-owned lenders in a bid to fix their battered balance sheets and keep them afloat, leading to a crisis of confidence among savers." If you were a brand-new immigrant coming from a country where the banking system collapsed, would you suddenly trust banks in the new country? Obviously the answer is no. This lack of trust leads many migrants to prefer cash.[3]

The last reason, which affects both immigrants and many other vulnerable groups, is that financial institutions all over the world are required by governments to follow "know-your-customer" requirements. These laws are designed to reduce crime, terrorism, and money laundering. However, one unintended consequence is they make it harder for legal and illegal immigrants as well as people on the margins of society to get a bank or financial account.

Although the rules are complex, financial companies typically need three things to satisfy know-your-customer rules. First is a verified identity, which is typically a passport, driver's license, or other type of government-issued identification with the person's photograph. This is often the easiest hurdle to overcome.[4]

Second is a verified address where the person lives. Verification is often done with an electricity, gas, or water bill. Because utilities like water service do not move, but are fixed in place, a bill proves a person's ties to a location. This is often harder for an immigrant to obtain because many migrants don't know where they will live when they enter a new country. For immigrants living with many others in the same apartment or home, there is also the issue of deciding whose name goes on utility bills.[5]

Know-your-customer rules are also a problem for transients and homeless people. Having a stable address is easy for the middle class and rich but there are quite a few people who don't have a permanent mailing address. Homeless people lack a verifiable address. Know-your-customer rules mean many of the half million homeless in the United States cannot open an account and will be unable to function if society makes a complete transition to electronic money. Transients are not homeless but are people who constantly move. These people live in marinas, RV parks, campgrounds, motels, carnivals, and racetracks. The United States has over 100,000 transients; without a permanent address many are not eligible for accounts.[6]

The third and often the hardest know-your-customer requirement for migrants is a tax identification number (ID). There are millions of people entering countries illegally. Entering illegally means not having the paperwork to work and get a tax ID. It is possible to buy stolen or fake tax ID numbers. People who buy stolen and fake numbers provide government programs like Social Security and Medicare with billions in extra revenue. However, the key point is without a tax ID number it is difficult for the over 11 million illegal immigrants residing in the United States to open a financial account, resulting in many operating in a cash-only economy.[7]

VULNERABLE TOURISTS

Immigrants are people making a long-term move to another country. A related group of vulnerable people are foreign tourists. Tourism is a major source of revenue in many parts of the world and some businesses see these visitors as a group from which it is easy to make extra money. Tourists, ranging from broke backpackers to rich retirees, are vulnerable because they need to get and use money in unfamiliar locations and, like many migrants, in a different language. Electronic payments make tourists vulnerable. It is easy to rack up large unauthorized charges as indicated by newspaper headlines like "Help! A Gas Station Charged Me $1,500 and My Bank Won't Believe It's Fraud."[8]

Even if fraud is not occurring, using electronic payments in a foreign country is often more expensive. For example, swipe, tap, or insert a credit or debit card in a local store and the amount charged shows up on the monthly bill. Make the same transaction in a different country and you run the chance of incurring an international transaction fee. American Express charges 2.7% of the transaction amount as an extra fee for using their cards in a different country. Major banks like Bank of America, Chase, and Wells Fargo charge a 3% fee when using some of their credit cards abroad.[9]

The United Nations estimates tourists will spend $3.3 trillion in 2024. Let's say one-quarter of that money is charged an international transaction fee of 3%. That is about $25 billion in transaction fees, which is roughly the size of NASA's annual budget. What the United States spends on sending people and machines into outer space is roughly the same as the extra charge faced by people on earth just to use electronic money outside their own country.[10]

Some travelers prefer using cash and get paper money while in a foreign country. I have used local ATMs when abroad to get paper money to avoid using a credit or debit card. Unfortunately, ATM machines in other countries typically charge out-of-network fees. As an example, Bank of America charges a 3% conversion fee, plus a $5 use fee, while the local bank often charges an additional fee. Pull out $100 from an ATM in a foreign country in the local currency and you might end up paying roughly an extra 10% for the privilege.[11]

This section's point is simple – if a country wants tourists, make it simple for them to spend money. Countries making it hard to pay discourage visitors, depriving the country of a major economic boost.

China is an example of a country where tourists have difficulty paying. Cash is rarely used in China and ATMs are disappearing, making obtaining cash hard.

Foreigners are now allowed to make purchases with their mobile phones using WeChat Pay and Alipay. However, to use either of these services a foreign visitor first needs a mobile phone that works in China. Second, foreigners need a credit or debit card. Then to create an account a person needs to upload their passport, credit card, and other personal information.[12]

After an account is created, a foreigner needs to watch their spending because any purchase is limited to a maximum of 6,000 yuan, a bit over US$800. Plus a visitor's total monthly spending is limited to 50,000 yuan, a bit under US$7,000.

Last, visitors must prepare for sticker shock since the Chinese companies add a 3% service fee for all transactions over 200 yuan, a bit under US$30. This service charge is above and beyond the tourist bank's fees for foreign transactions, making paying for a vacation an ordeal.

The cashless society is touted as more convenient, but for the causal tourist paper money is often simpler and faster to use. Recently, I needed to travel from one Dutch city to another. The online directions offered two options. One was a scenic countryside route. However, the mapping program preferred another, urban route that was 20 minutes longer. Investigation showed why the longer route was preferred. The scenic way included a brief ferry ride where no cash was accepted. Taking the shorter route meant finding the ferry's app in an online store, downloading it, creating a user account, and inputting financial information with all instructions in Dutch. The extra 20 minutes of travel was faster and less of a hassle than setting up to do this one-time cashless transaction.[13]

DYNAMIC CURRENCY CONVERSION

Although I like bringing and using cash abroad, many people do not feel safe doing this so they prefer using electronic methods. Savvy travelers who don't carry cash try to avoid extra charges by using cards that promise no international fees. However, even these people are vulnerable to paying more by falling prey to "dynamic currency conversion."

In the past when traveling abroad, transactions were always done in the local currency. Today, an increasingly common practice is for shops, restaurants, and ATMs to offer travelers the option of immediately converting a payment or withdrawal into their home currency. This service is called *dynamic currency conversion*. For example, an American tourist visiting London is able to use their credit card to pay for a beer at an English pub in US dollars instead of British pounds. This might seem both convenient and harmless, but agreeing to use your home currency in a foreign land can significantly inflate the cost of every purchase.

Dynamic conversion is happening because banks are now offering more credit cards with no foreign transaction fees. Plus "free ATMs" are popping up around the world, which do not charge local transaction fees. To cover the costs of these "free" transactions businesses are offering the travelers the option of paying in a tourist's home currency.

If you elect to pay with the local currency your bank or financial institution typically converts the transaction into foreign currency at the day's wholesale market rate midpoint. If you elect to convert to your home currency you pay an extra fee for the privilege, which might be as much as 10%.

I first discovered the dramatic difference when I was in London's Heathrow Airport and needed some British pounds. There were numerous ATMs with signs proclaiming they were free. As someone who is always suspicious of "free" offers I tried different machines, each of which asked me if I wanted to lock in the exchange rate and each let me know exactly how many dollars would be debited from my bank account.

Checking the foreign exchange market before inserting my card told me the current market rate was US$1.29 for each British pound. I wanted £100. The first ATM offered to convert my dollars into British pounds at 1.34, which was almost a 4% markup over the market rate. The second ATM offered a rate of 1.42, which was a 10% markup. I rejected both offers, did the transaction using the local currency, and ended up with a total charge of just $129 from my bank. While I was taking money out, an Italian family was standing at the next ATM arguing over what to do. After a very loud debate they picked the dynamic conversion button and paid an extra 10% more for their trouble.

Why do travelers pay more by accepting a worse exchange rate when they could simply say no? When people travel to a country with a different currency they often mentally keep track of their total spending using their home currency. Many travelers also mentally convert all prices from the local currency into their home currency. This is what economists call using a *mental unit of account.*

When an ATM or credit card terminal asks if you want to pay for something in your mental unit of account currency, your brain says yes. It is natural to want to keep track in a familiar currency. Resisting your natural inclination to say yes to dynamic currency conversion saves money and makes trips abroad less costly.

It is not only immigrants and travelers who are vulnerable to extremely poor exchange rates. The next section talks about how countries with exchange rate controls often take advantage of their own citizens.

FOREIGN EXCHANGE RATES AND BLACK MARKETS

The previous two sections discussed the problems faced when people move from one country to another. Sometimes it is not people moving, but instead money that is moving from one country to another. When money moves across international borders, there are places and times when paper money is more powerful than using electronic methods.

Money moves across borders to facilitate international trade. People around the world want French wine, Chinese tea, South African diamonds, Argentinian beef, Japanese cars, as well as natural resources. To get these products plus services like foreign travel, education, and health care people and businesses need to convert money from their local to a foreign currency.

The conversion happens using the "foreign exchange rate." In an open and free system without any controls the process of swapping from one currency to another is not something most people think about. Rates vary constantly. However, many countries have fixed foreign exchange rates. If these countries' central banks are unwilling or unable to meet all the demand for foreign exchange at the official rate then black markets arise.[14]

In a black market the price to swap currency is often much better than the official government price. Using paper money, it is possible to evade government foreign exchange controls by trading currencies on the black market. These controls cannot be avoided using electronic payments because foreign exchange transactions either go through the government's central bank or through banks the government monitors and controls.

Using cash provides a simple measure to evade foreign exchange, or FX, controls. But wait, isn't evasion of these controls illegal? In some countries trading in the black or unofficial market is legal. In other places, where it is illegal, the International Monetary Fund points out black markets or "the 'parallel' market might be the only reliable source of FX for the majority of participants in the economy." In simple terms when a government does not have enough foreign exchange at the official rate, private parties using paper money can still conduct foreign exchange transactions using the more favorable, unofficial rate.[15]

An example of many participants being shut out of the foreign exchange market happened in Egypt. The government banned anyone with an Egyptian-issued credit or debit card from using it to make purchases outside the country, unless they were physically traveling abroad. This meant buying items from foreign merchants or websites located outside the country using a credit card suddenly became impossible for most Egyptians. For this and other reasons a thriving black market for currency popped up. The International Monetary Fund showed the unofficial rate was almost double the official rate in early 2024. The gap existed because each year the Egyptian government imports tons of wheat to feed its large population. Buying this wheat takes lots of hard currency, like dollars or euros. To hoard the available hard currency for purchasing wheat, the Egyptian central bank began enforcing the debit or credit cards prohibition. To get around these government controls many people gave friends or family traveling abroad black market cash to make prohibited purchases.[16]

Cash is also useful for being able to transfer money from one currency to another in countries with high or hyperinflation, like Zimbabwe, Venezuela, Cambodia, or Argentina. By keeping cash around people are protected from their government's mismanagement of their local currency, because citizens are able to switch their money into another more stable currency like the US dollar or the euro.

Although black markets sound very sketchy, in some countries they are not. Argentina has a thriving foreign currency black market to avoid government currency controls. Interestingly, using the black market is not illegal in Argentina under current laws. In Buenos Aires and other large cities there are many "Cueva," or caves. These are businesses that swap hard currencies like dollars and euros for Argentinian pesos. Although the word *cave* suggests a dark and seedy place, I used one that was on a main street in a fashionable part of town, whose location was pointed out by a policeman. It had marble floors, wood paneled walls, plus a more private back room for larger scale transactions. It was nothing like a dark and damp cave and was the antithesis of a sketchy business.

Black markets flourish when governments have a system of tiered exchange rates. Tiered rates mean there are different foreign exchange rates depending on the circumstances. Tiered rates enable governments to subsidize favored industries or ensure favored people get a good deal when purchasing foreign products. However, if some industries and people are favored, this means nonfavored groups are penalized by getting a worse foreign exchange rate.

One example of subsidizing favored industries happened in Argentina, a country that is one of the world's major suppliers of soybeans. When farmers export their soybeans, buyers wire the payments through the Argentinian central bank and then into the farmers' bank accounts. Many farmers, however, did not like the price they were getting for soybeans. Instead of exporting the beans, they harvested and put the beans into storage.

To boost exports and earn more hard foreign currency the government declared that instead of getting the official rate, soybean exporters would get a rate boost that earned exporters one-third more. If a farmer was going to get 100 million pesos by selling soybeans to a foreign buyer before the announcement, afterward they would get 133 million pesos. This special program only lasted five weeks. Soybeans exported after the five-week period expired got just the regular official rate.[17]

This sounds like a wonderful deal, but soybean farmers were outraged. The government offered a boost of one-third. However, if farmers exported soybeans to a buyer willing to pay in paper money like US dollars, the "Cueva" would provide pesos using the black market rate, which was 90% higher. It was hard to find cash buyers so farmers were forced to take the special government boost that was almost 60% less than the black market rate.

Another reason for black markets is that some countries tax foreign trade and tourism by using the foreign exchange rate. When I visited Argentina, foreigners were required to pay a 21% lodging tax. However, the government offered an inducement. If I paid for my room with a credit card the tax was waived, which could save me some money. However, by taking my cash to the "Cueva" and getting the black market rate I received a 90% discount, which was even greater than using electronic payments. By controlling the foreign exchange rate the government is able to extract a large tax from every foreign transaction, above and beyond all the other taxes, like a value-added tax. Special rates and promotions reduce the tax but don't eliminate it. Cash often provides a way to get much better prices than electronic payments.

Some countries have been able to maintain a fixed exchange rate for very long periods of time, without a black market arising. For example, since the early 1980s the Hong Kong monetary authority has been willing to trade 7.80 Hong Kong dollars for each US dollar. Other countries have not been as successful as Hong Kong and have seen black markets arise. While I wrote this book, black markets for foreign exchanges also appeared in Russia, Nigeria, the Maldives, Iran, Uzbekistan, Lebanon, Syria, and Venezuela to name some of the countries beyond Egypt and Argentina. The existence of cash ensures when a country's official foreign exchange market is broken there are still ways international trade can happen.[18]

CONCLUSION

Every society has vulnerable people. Immigrants are a vulnerable group that is hurt by the shift from a cash economy to a cashless. It does not matter where you stand on the issues of immigration. Whether you are for a wide opening of your country's doors or a complete shutdown, it is impossible to ignore the fact that millions of people are on the move across the world. These people need to buy food, medicine, and pay for transport. Unfamiliarity, fear, confusion, and know-your-customer rules prevent many migrants from making cashless transactions. Keeping cash around helps these vulnerable individuals and families.

Although tourists are less vulnerable than immigrants, many businesses still view them as fair game to exploit. Vacations are expensive. Paying international transaction fees, foreign exchange fees, out-of-network fees, and dynamic currency conversion fees make every trip abroad even more expensive. Cash does not solve every problem when traveling abroad, but in many countries it can reduce the visit's cost and keep the tourism industry vibrant.

Last, numerous countries in the world have tried to manage their exchange rates or even prevent people from using foreign currency. When a country mismanages the foreign exchange rate, an "official" government rate and an "unofficial" black market rate often arise. Only people with paper money can obtain the black market rate because the "official" rate is only available to select groups who the government deems worthy. Keeping paper money around ensures everyone has a chance at the better market rate. Eliminating paper money helps only the politically favored do well when making foreign exchange transactions.

Paper money is not a panacea for solving the world's immigration problem. Paper money does not suddenly make vacations cheap for all, nor does it solve every problem in a country with a broken foreign exchange system. Nevertheless, keeping cash around helps improve the lives of all three groups by giving them choices in how they can act.

CHAPTER THIRTEEN

CASH PUTS LIMITS ON CENTRAL BANKS HURTING THE ELDERLY

Elderly people are another vulnerable population that is helped by the existence of cash. Many elderly people have spent most of their working lives saving up money for their retirement. They expect to earn something on these savings. However, central banks around the world have pushed interest rates below zero in recent years. Negative interest rates were common in Europe from 2014 to 2022 and also in Japan for many years. As explained in this chapter, negative interest rates take money away from savers, punishing the elderly and others who have stored money. Cash can act as a brake on these policies, and when used, it prevents government officials from taking money away from the elderly.

To make the problem concrete, imagine saving a large amount of money for a big event, like an upcoming wedding. As this chapter shows, negative interest rates mean some of your savings are arbitrarily confiscated while waiting for the big day. There is a simple way to avoid having some of your savings taken by negative interest rates: keep the savings in paper money. Paper money pays no interest. This is a problem when interest rates are positive, but a blessing when rates are negative.

Paper money not only puts limits on central banks' attempts to push interest rates into negative territory but also protects savers when a nation's financial institutions face a "bank run." Bank runs are rare but catastrophic events when large numbers of depositors suddenly remove all their money. In 2023 the United States saw three banks collapse simultaneously: Silicon Valley Bank, First Republic, and Signature Bank. Keeping savings as paper money protects depositors who suspect a large-scale bank run is imminent.[1]

Banks are important to modern economies. Banks can dramatically boost economic growth by channeling money from savers, those with excess funds, to borrowers, those who need funds. Central banks are important for ensuring the stability of the financial sector. Nevertheless, although banks provide some of the modern economy's most important plumbing, banks and central banks periodically make massive mistakes that not only hurt economic growth but also threaten the world's economic conditions.

THE POWER OF INTEREST RATES

Central banks oversee the world's financial system. Central banks, like the Federal Reserve, the European Central Bank (ECB), and the Bank of Japan, are some of the most powerful institutions in the world. They are powerful because a small group of politically protected people are given the power to raise and lower interest rates.

Interest rates might seem a dry technical subject that few care about, but they have a huge influence over our lives. Interest rates determine if and when companies can expand their business. Interest rates determine whether individuals can make major purchases, like buying a home or car, or when people can afford to retire. Interest rates even determine if it is feasible for governments to borrow money to fund large public projects.

For thousands of years the world's economies rested on some simple concepts. One idea is that there is a reward for saving money and showing restraint in spending. Another idea is that there is a penalty for borrowing, which is spending money you do not currently have. As this chapter will show, eliminating cash enables overturning these two fundamental ideas. By eliminating the use of cash, central banks can push interest rates below zero. Negative interest rates punish thrifty people for saving money and reward borrowers for taking out loans.

NEGATIVE INTEREST RATES

For most of human history when people saved money, they were paid interest to induce them to give up their money. For example, if interest rates were 5% and someone saved $10,000 for one year, at the end of the year they were given their original $10,000 plus an extra 5% or $500 to compensate them for letting others use their funds.

Interest rates were rarely constant. They rose and fell depending on macroeconomic conditions. However, even if they were low, savers were given at least a small amount of extra money as an inducement to save.

One of the best sources of the history of interest rates is by Homer and Sylla. In this tome they track interest rates from ancient to modern times around the world. The numerous tables in the book show positive interest rates from ancient Rome to modern Argentina.[2]

Even the suggestion of negative interest rates was considered newsworthy. One of the first attempts at setting negative interest rates happened in Hong Kong in December 1987. In 1983 Hong Kong officials tied their currency to the US dollar (USD) at a fixed rate of 7.75 Hong Kong dollars to every 1 USD. By November 1987 many investors were convinced this fixed exchange rate was going to be broken. Foreigners started buying Hong Kong dollars and depositing the money in local banks, making the revaluation more likely. To stop the inflow of money, officials stated they were planning on putting negative interest rates on all large deposits in local banks. Planned rates ranged from −5.5% for deposits of US$1.3 million up to −88% for deposits of US$25 million or more.

Simply announcing plans for negative interest rates caused foreigners to reverse their currency trades and take their money out of Hong Kong banks. The need to revalue the Hong Kong dollar disappeared and negative interest rates were not implemented. Nevertheless, even the consideration of negative rates was considered shocking at the time.

In 2008 a deep global recession slowed businesses. To combat this recession central bankers in many countries pushed interest rates down. Before 2008, many people assumed, except for unusual experiences, like the currency attack on the Hong Kong dollar, zero was the lowest possible interest rate. This was formally called a *zero lower bound*. However, as the recession dragged on, central bankers broke this bound and pushed rates below zero.

One key interest rate is how much the ECB paid on money that member banks left with the ECB overnight. In October 2008, at the beginning of the recession, the interest rate was over 3%. The ECB slashed rates to zero during 2012 and 2013. Then from 2014 until 2022 rates were negative!

Negative interest rates mean savers are punished for saving. If interest rates are −0.5%, like the rate the ECB set from October 2019 until June 2022, then someone who saved $10,000 for one year is charged $50 for the privilege of letting others use their money.

Negative rates also happened in other parts of the world. The Bank of Japan kept rates in negative territory for eight years until winter 2024 by periodically issuing statements like, "The Bank will apply a negative interest rate of −0.1% to the Policy-Rate Balances in current accounts held by financial institutions at the Bank."[3]

Negative interest rates discourage savings. They act as a tax on thrift. This tax encourages people to immediately spend any extra money because the longer money is held, the less valuable it is. Central bankers used negative interest rates in a recession because these rates encourage people to consume, boosting economic activity.

The concept of kick-starting an economy with rising consumer spending and investment makes sense as a temporary or short-term solution. The concept is similar to starting a balking gasoline-powered car. Sometimes a car that won't start can be coaxed into roaring back to life by injecting a little extra fuel into the engine. The problem with cars is that adding too much fuel chokes the engine, causing other problems.

The analogy with a car is apt because central bankers kept interest rates depressed at either close to zero or in negative territory for a long period of time. The ECB ran a policy of zero or negative rates for a decade, until raising them above zero at the end of 2022. When interest rates are depressed for a long period of time, it changes people's habits, discouraging saving and encouraging spending.

PAPER MONEY IS A BRAKE

Bankers, especially central bankers, dislike paper money because cash acts as a brake on their ability to create negative interest rates. Let's assume central banks are allowed to push interest rates down to −5%, which means saving $10,000 for one year results in a $500 charge. At the end of one year the person saving has just $9,500 to show for their efforts. However, if the saver takes their money out of the bank as cash, and stores it somewhere safe for one year, at the end of the year they still have their original $10,000. While the money has not grown, it also has not shrunk.

While some individuals and businesses can convert their savings into cash in a negative interest environment, many don't. People don't take their money out because converting small bank accounts into cash and then redepositing the money into the banking system when it is needed is time-consuming. Storing small to medium amounts of cash is also relatively expensive. People need to buy safes or rent deposit boxes. If they simply stuff money into a mattress to save on storage costs, they might lose the cash through theft or if the mattress is accidently thrown away.

Storing very large sums of cash is even more expensive. Investors with millions or billions cannot stuff that amount of money under a mattress or bury the cash in the backyard while waiting for positive interest rates. Buying or building vaults to hold large amounts of cash is expensive as is hiring security services to patrol and protect the cash after the vault is built.

These problems mean that individuals and businesses are willing to bear some negative interest rates. However, the lower rates go, the more likely people are to abandon the banking system and switch to cash. Thus, paper money serves as a brake or check on every central banker's ability to drive interest rates as low as they desire. The easier cash is to use and move in and out of the banking system, the more likely the zero lower bound on interest rates will hold. If cash is eliminated, there is no check on the ability of central bankers to push interest rates into negative territory.[4]

How much power should central banks have? Negative interest rates provide central bankers with more control over the economy. Ensuring that paper money continues to exist gives central bankers less control but gives individuals and businesses more power. There is no easy answer to this trade-off. Negative interest rates are not a magic bullet for solving economic downturns because they remove the incentive to save. Negative rates are an attempt to solve one problem, a recession, but result in another, a lack of saving.

SAVINGS PROBLEMS

How many people in the United States don't save money? The Survey of Consumer Finances is a nationwide random sample of families run by the Federal Reserve every three years. The survey asks people to describe their savings habits and intentions. Respondents are given three choices: not saving, saving if there is money left over at the end of the month, and having a regular savings plan. Since the new millennium less than half of all families reported the third choice, saving regularly.

Intentions don't always match reality, so this survey asks a follow-up question to respondents. Over the past year was the family's spending greater than, less than, or the same as their income? Similar to the intentions data, less than half of all families reported they saved in the past year.

Savings are not needed if someone is already wealthy. If you are rich and content, there is little need to save more. Unfortunately, many people in the United States have very little wealth, which is why it is a problem that under 50% of the population saves.

In addition to asking about savings attitudes the survey asks every respondent about their wealth. The questions are designed to uncover even small amounts, like half-forgotten bank accounts. The survey then determines each person's wealth by subtracting their debts from their assets.

Averaging all the surveys from the 1980s to the present shows about 10% of families in the United States didn't have more than $1 in wealth. One out of every ten families had either a negative or zero net worth! The most recent survey data show half of all families have saved less than two years of income.

Low or zero net worth, combined with relatively low savings rates, is a national problem. It indicates many people in society are wholly dependent on government retirement programs for support in their old age. Small financial shocks like unexpected bills can result in financial disaster. The less people have in savings, the more dependent they are on the government's social safety net for support during times of trouble.

The widespread existence of low, zero, or negative wealth means governments need to incentivize people to save. Politicians and government policymakers have clearly seen this need. They have created many programs that encourage workers to put aside money tax-free for their retirement into private savings plans. For example, in the United States there are a raft of specialized programs with names like IRA, SEP, and 401K, designed for this very purpose. There are also special savings plans for education in the US, like 529 plans and special savings plans for health care expenses.

However, the simplest and clearest incentive to save is providing savers with a positive rate of return on their investments. Putting money in the bank is traditionally one of the simplest, safest, and easiest ways of savings. Put money into a bank account, and the money grows until you take it out. It is simple enough even for children to understand, as long as interest rates stay above zero.

CASH LIMITS THE DAMAGE OF BANK RUNS

Banks runs also show the power of cash. Holding cash is the ultimate insurance policy when the entire banking sector faces a financial meltdown.

Banks project an image of strength. In past decades banks projected strength by creating imposing buildings that looked like Greek temples. In modern times banks tout strength by bragging how much excess capital they hold and how long they have been in business. Banks project strength because periodically the entire sector's viability is questioned, and large numbers of banks face a simultaneous financial meltdown. For example, Lehman Brothers, a large Wall Street investment bank, collapsed in fall 2008. Three hundred US banks collapsed in the ensuing financial turmoil over the following two years.[5]

When a bank's viability becomes suspect, a bank run happens. Years ago, people physically ran to the bank to pull out their money. Today, many bank runs occur virtually, with large amounts of money being moved electronically. A virtual bank run happened during spring 2023, when rising interest rates squeezed three US mid-sized banks, Silicon Valley Bank, First Republic, and Signature Bank. All lost large amounts of their deposits overnight and collapsed. The collapse of these banks and rising interest also toppled Credit Suisse, one of Switzerland's biggest banks, and regulators forced Credit Suisse to merge with its long-time rival UBS.

Bank runs were a frequent occurrence a century ago. In recent times they have become rarer for two reasons. First, the creation of central banks provides a source of credit for troubled banks. Central banks loan money when private businesses and individuals don't or can't provide loans. Second, many governments have created deposit insurance programs. Deposit insurance simply means that if a bank collapses, depositors get back some or all of their money. The largest US program protecting depositors is the Federal Deposit Insurance Corporation, or FDIC.

The FDIC insures depositors' accounts up to $250,000 per person, per bank. This means if someone has $100,000 in a bank account and their bank collapses the government will return all their money.

Personal experience showed me the system works for people with small accounts. In the late 1980s I had money in a Boston bank located a few blocks from where I teach. One Saturday morning I opened the mailbox and found an envelope with a check from the FDIC. There was no note, letter, or other explanation, just a check from this government agency. When I looked at the news the top story was about how my bank had collapsed the previous afternoon and was immediately taken over by the FDIC. I got my money the next morning, plus interest.

Although small depositors are quickly protected, larger depositors must wait. My favorite example of waiting is the First Bank of Beverly Hills. Beverly Hills is one of the wealthiest places in the world. Many of show business's most important and richest actors and entertainers live there. This bank, which failed on a Friday in April 2009, had about $1.5 billion in assets. The FDIC mailed checks the next Monday up to the deposit insurance limit. But what about people with bigger accounts, plus people and businesses owed money by the bank?[6]

The FDIC paid out 99% of all claims against the bank! This is an amazing figure. People who had large deposits or other claims against this bank lost almost nothing. However, there is a big caveat to this 99% figure. The first payment beyond the deposit insurance limit was made by the FDIC in March 2011, two years after the bank collapsed. The last payment occurred in September 2022, 13 years after the collapse. The FDIC is clear on their website that some people have to wait:

> While fully insured deposits are paid promptly after the failure of the bank, the disbursements of uninsured funds may take place over several years based on the timing in the liquidation of the failed bank assets.[7]

Getting all your money back is great. Waiting years to get all the money back is a problem.

When just one bank is experiencing stress and potentially could fail, the prudent measure for individuals or businesses with money over the deposit limit is to move the funds to a stronger bank.

When all banks are experiencing stress and many might fail, moving money from one bank to another does not guarantee the funds are protected because the money might accidently end up in a collapsing bank.

For those who believe mobile payments are a way to safeguard money during a bank run, it is not. The Consumer Financial Protection Bureau (CFPB) points out that people have stored billions of dollars on their phones using nonbank payment apps like PayPal, Venmo, and Cash App. During a bank run many people might be tempted to pull money out of banks and store it on their phone. The problem is not all the payment apps automatically sweep funds into accounts protected by deposit insurance. This means during times when the financial system is stressed, mobile payments increase the risks consumers face because billions of dollars are in jeopardy if a company behind a major payment app collapses.[8]

There is a simple way to ensure the money is protected. Move the funds into paper money and redeposit the money when the banking crisis is over. By doing this, funds are not tied up in bankruptcy court and are not subject to capital gains or losses associated with owning government bonds while interest rates fluctuate.

Cash provides society with an additional layer of low-cost protection during a banking crisis beyond deposit insurance and crisis lending by the central bank.

REAL INTEREST RATES

This next section is for those readers who want a more nuanced understanding of the problem. Feel free to skip this part if all you want is a high-level view.

The previous discussion is simplified because it doesn't consider inflation or deflation. A positive 5% interest rate might seem great compared to a 0% interest rate, but even 5% might not cover the increase in prices happening in an economy.

Adding inflation or deflation shows the existence of paper money does not prevent a zero lower bound from happening. Instead, paper money acts as a partial, but not complete, brake on a central bank.

The posted or nominal interest rate used by banks is not actually the most important rate for savers. Instead, what savers really care about is the real interest rate, which is the posted rate adjusted for inflation. The real interest rate shows how much a saver receives in extra purchasing power for giving up the use of their money.

If the real rate is 5%, then the saver can buy 5% more goods and services after accounting for inflation or deflation in exchange for not using their money. If there is no risk of a loan defaulting then the nominal rate is computed by the following formula, formally called the Fisher equation[9]:

$$\text{Nominal Rate} = \text{Real Rate} + \text{Expected Inflation Rate}$$
$$+ \left(\text{Real Rate} \times \text{Expected Inflation Rate} \right). \quad (13.1)$$

For example, if the real rate is 3% and the inflation rate is 5% then the nominal rate is equal to $3\% + 5\% + 0.15\% = 8.15\%$. Because the (Real Rate × Expected Inflation Rate) term and the risk of default are usually small it is possible to rewrite the formula. The simplified formula is that the real interest rate is approximately the nominal interest rate minus the expected inflation rate.

$$\text{Real Interest Rate} \approx \text{Nominal Interest Rate} - \text{Expected Inflation Rate}.$$
$$(13.2)$$

For example, if a borrower is quoted a 6% rate on a loan, then 6% is the nominal rate. If the expected inflation rate over the next year is 4%, then the real interest rate is about 2%.

$$\text{Real Interest Rate} \approx 6\% - 4\% - 2\% \quad (13.3)$$

The difference between the posted or nominal rate and the real interest rate is seen by comparing the two lines in Figure 13.1. The solid line in Figure 13.1 shows the posted or nominal rate on five-year US Treasury notes. Purchasers of these notes are loaning money to the US government for five years. Because the US government can print its own money, the risk of default on these notes is zero. The solid line shows the interest rate paid is consistently above zero. At the end of 2018 the 3% rate is relatively far from zero. In mid-2020 the 0.27% rate is close to zero. However, no matter what year is looked at, investors earned a positive nominal return.[10]

The problem with Figure 13.1 is that consumer prices during this time were constantly changing. Because inflation was not constant, the figure gives a false representation of a saver's true return.

The dotted line in the figure graphs the real or inflation-adjusted interest rate. The real rate comes from the US Government's 5-Year Treasury

Figure 13.1   US Treasury five-year posted and inflation-adjusted interest rates.

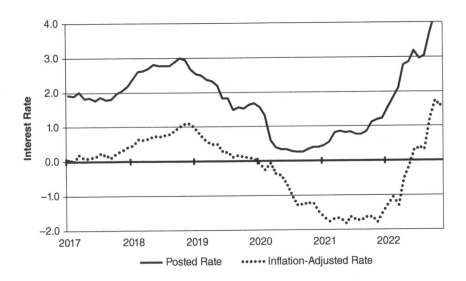

Inflation-Indexed Securities, or TIPS. TIPS are special bonds that automatically adjust the principal for inflation. For example, if someone buys $10,000 of TIPS today and inflation rises by 10% over the next year, the government calculates interest on the inflation-adjusted $11,000, instead of on the original $10,000 amount.

The dotted line shows that during some years, savers experienced negative *real* interest rates. These negative rates started in 2020 and reached almost negative 2% in 2021.

Understanding real rates is important because even if nominal rates are positive, it is still possible for the real rate to be negative. This means central bankers who are prevented from breaking the nominal zero lower bound by the existence of paper money can still punish savers and encourage consumption by boosting inflation.

The situation gets stranger when a country experiences deflation. During deflation prices are falling. This means the expected inflation rate is negative. Looking at Eq. (13.2) shows the real interest rate is calculated by subtracting the expected inflation rate. When subtracting a negative number, the mathematical operation becomes an addition.

This means converting a bank account into paper money during a deflation earns savers at least the rate of deflation. Let's assume a country is experiencing a 2% deflation each year. Savers able to turn their money into cash do not experience any deflation because their cash at the end of the year buys 2% more goods and services.

Paper money prevents central bankers from creating large disincentives to save. Cash keeps central bankers at bay by enabling them to force interest rates into negative territory only with inflation, instead of both inflation and negative nominal interest rates. Because having relatively high inflation rates is not politically popular, paper currency combined with a robust political process constrains central bankers and ensures negative interest rates do not get out of control.

CONCLUSION

Central bankers are an extremely powerful group of people who set short-term interest rates and wield other tools that control the monetary systems of the world. Although these bankers have attempted to do the right thing, they are not infallible. For example, in the middle of the 1930s during the Great Depression, the US Federal Reserve, in a well-meaning but mistaken move, raised interest rates because it was worried about inflation. This mistake doubled the length of time the world endured the Great Depression. In the modern world there have been numerous hyperinflations. It is impossible to have a hyperinflation unless the central bank dramatically increases the money supply.

By design the public have few controls over central bankers' decisions. The political process is long and slow. Central bankers can change interest rates and other monetary policy levels instantly. By the time the political process catches up, long-lasting damage can be done. However, paper money provides one brake on the actions of central bankers.

Central bankers' primary focus is on controlling inflation. Personal savings are neither their focus nor part of their stated mandates. However, when actions by central bankers destroy saving incentives, the economy is hurt. Savings are needed to fund companies, build factories, construct homes, improve lands, and pay for a host of other expensive projects. Savings ensure people are not entirely dependent on government handouts by providing insurance against unexpected financial expenses. Savings also reduce people's stress and anxiety by providing a financial buffer.

When central banks set negative interest rates, they discourage saving. Keeping a robust paper money system intact provides a partial brake on central banks' ability to force negative interest rates on society. By holding cash people earn 0%. There is an old saying "something is better than nothing." This saying gets turned on its head in a negative interest rate environment, because getting nothing with your cash is much better than losing money.

CASH IS NOT CAUSING CRIME, TERRORISM, OR TAX EVASION

Many opponents of cash point out that criminals, terrorists, and corrupt politicians all use cash to fund their activities. The news is full of stories about corrupt politicians with hidden bundles of cash and vast amounts of cash seized when drug lords are taken down. There is no dispute – crime and cash go hand-in-hand. The important question, however, is does cash cause crime? If cash is eliminated, will crime go down?

This section of the book investigates what happens to crime, terrorism, corruption, and tax avoidance as society shifts from a cash to a cashless economy. The answer is clear. The amount of crime doesn't fall by eliminating cash; instead, it changes form.

For example, Chapter 14 points out, in the United States there is a dramatic fall in the number of bank robberies. Bank managers today face far fewer weapon-toting thieves walking in the front door and demanding cash than a few decades ago. This is a positive sign. Thieves are asking why stick up a bank if the bank has less cash to steal? However, although banks are not seeing thieves walking in, criminals are robbing banks via the internet. Thieves are breaking in electronically, stealing credit card numbers and ATM pins, and redirecting deposits. Banks are not facing less crime as cash disappears, but more crime, in different types.

The second important point in Chapter 14 is that most people assume there is no risk using cashless payments. If something goes wrong, a quick phone call reverses the charges or restores the money and any problem disappears. Unfortunately, this perception no longer matches reality. The risk versus reward trade-off has changed and customers are increasingly left holding the bag when criminals use their accounts.

Chapter 15 checks if using cash facilitates corruption, terrorism, or organized crime. Chapter 16 checks if eliminating cash use reduces cheating on paying taxes. Both chapters show the extent a country uses paper money has little relationship to these major problems. Even without cash government officials can be corrupted with expensive gifts, sexual favors, or promises of lucrative future work. Terrorists do not need very much cash to create havoc. Organized crime will not stop preying on society simply because cash disappears. Last, there are many ways to cheat the government's tax collector; using cash to hide transactions turns out to be a relatively small method.

CHAPTER FOURTEEN

DOES CASH MAKE MORE PEOPLE AND BUSINESSES VICTIMS OF CRIME?

Many people tell me they do not want to use cash because they feel it makes them susceptible to being robbed, and no one wants to be a victim of crime. It is true that some people and businesses are robbed of cash each year. Being robbed is an upsetting and frightening experience that makes victims feel scared and vulnerable.

However, cash by itself does not make a society vulnerable to crime. One of the most cash-centric countries in the world is Japan. Cash in large and small amounts is used everywhere there. Even though Japan uses large amounts of cash, it is extremely safe. For example, the United Nations reports Japan had one-tenth the burglaries and one-fifth the thefts per 100,000 people as the United States, which is a much less cash-centered society.[1] If cash caused crime, Japan would not be one of the safest countries in the world!

This chapter's key point is that abandoning cash and shifting to electronic payments doesn't reduce crime. Instead, it makes it worse! Using electronic payments makes thefts easier to carry out, instead of harder. To rob someone or a business of cash, the criminal must be physically present. With electronic money, distance is no longer a factor. Criminals can act from anywhere in the world and target anyone. The results of shifting to electronic payments are startling. This chapter shows the amount of money stolen electronically is much greater than what is stolen in cash form. Moreover, when a criminal is caught, the punishment they receive in the United States for stealing electronically is far less than if they had stolen cash.

I often show my students how eliminating cash does not get rid of crime by asking them two questions. How many times has someone ever stolen cash from you or your immediate family? Plus, how many times have you or someone in your family had their credit card, debit card, or bank account information used fraudulently? A small number of my students raise their hand saying they had cash stolen, but almost everyone raises their hand when asked about credit card, debit card, or bank account theft.

The next sections explain in detail how much and how often money is stolen in both paper and electronic forms. Before jumping into these detailed sections let's look at where electronic methods have resulted in a burst of criminal activity: identity theft, fraud, and scams. This analysis shows, if a key societal goal is to keep people safer from crime, then using electronic payments is making matters worse, not better than using cash.

FRAUD, SCAMS, AND IDENTITY THEFT

The US government tracks frauds, scams, and identity theft via the Consumer Sentinel Network. The Network is a large law enforcement database aimed at combating these types of crimes. The Network has recorded a massive explosion in problems. In 2,000 a bit less than a quarter of a million frauds, scams, and identity thefts were recorded. In 2023 over five million problems were entered into the database, a 20-fold increase.[2]

There are a couple of reasons for this dramatic increase. First, to steal cash a criminal or their accomplice has to come face-to-face with a victim or the victim's belongings. Electronic means of payment break this geographic relationship, enabling thieves and crooks to target individuals and businesses anywhere in the world, not just those physically close. Second, the information revolution enables criminals to reach out to massive numbers of people using phone calls, emails, text messages, and fake websites very cheaply and quickly.

About half of each year's Sentinel reports are for fraud. Fraud is when a criminal deceives a victim by pretending to be something they are not. Examples are when a criminal pretends to be a government official, offers a fake job, acts like someone looking for love, asks for help moving imaginary piles of money, or doing something else like providing fake technical support. The amounts lost to fraud are staggering. Recently people in the United States lost over $10 billion a year, with just 5% of it lost using cash.

Even when a fraud is well known, new victims are continually found. When email first came out in the 1990s many people received messages purporting to be from a "Nigerian prince" who needed financial help. This scam has existed in various guises for over a century.[3]

The "prince" is entitled to a large sum of money, but the money is locked up. If the victim sends the "prince" a small sum, supposedly this will enable access to the money and in gratitude a share of the windfall will be split with the victim. Unfortunately, no matter how many people send the "prince" money, the windfall stays in limbo. After three decades in circulation, the prince's email messages are still bringing in about three-quarters of a million dollars a year from unsuspecting victims. Technological advances that lowered the cost to contact people and simplify getting payments means this and other scams now affect millions of victims instead of hundreds.[4]

Identity theft is another large Sentinel Network category. The number one purpose in stealing someone's identity is opening or taking over a method of electronic payments. The Network reports half a million cases a year in which an identity thief hijacked a credit card, debit card, or online payment account.

Sentinel Network data show as cash use in the United States has declined, the number of people affected by frauds, identity theft, and scams has skyrocketed. The network shows very little is lost using cash, yet billions of dollars are stolen, and millions of people are affected using electronic methods of payments. However, correlation does not mean causation. The Sentinel Network is opt-in, which means only people who decide to report a problem are found in the database. The next sections use less biased reporting methods to look in more depth at how much cash is stolen and how much is lost with electronic methods. Because not a lot of cash is used today, the next sections compare how much cash was lost in the early 1990s, when cash was king, with the amount of money lost today using electronic payments.

THE AMOUNT OF STOLEN CASH

How much cash is stolen each year? Sentinel Network and police reports provide biased numbers because sometimes the amount stolen is too small to bother reporting to authorities. Sometimes it is too painful to report that cash was stolen because the thief was a close relative. Sometimes people know cash was stolen but do not know the amount. Because of these reasons the US government runs a survey each year to track better information on victimization and the different types of crimes people experience, and this is called the National Crime Victimization Survey.

Although much of the survey covers physical assaults and sex crimes, one section asks respondents if they experienced a theft. These questions provide the ability to see exactly how much money was stolen and recovered.

Figure 14.1 shows results from the Victimization Survey. In general, individuals are reporting losing less paper money as time goes on. This matches the idea that fewer people are using and carrying cash. In 1992, when the data began, slightly more than $1.5 billion was stolen, after adjusting for inflation. By 2022, the figure had fallen to about $360 million.

The dramatic reduction in cash stolen is primarily due to fewer people being robbed, not because the average amount taken fell. In 1992 almost five million people reported having cash stolen. This number plunged to 1.4 million victims by 2022. Because of population growth a better way of looking at these figures is in percentage terms. In 1992, when cash was king, about 3% of adults reported being robbed of paper money; by 2022 the figure plunged to 0.5%.[5]

The typical victim lost about $320 in 1992 after adjusting for inflation, which is close in value to the 2022 figure of about $260. Sadly, the crime

Figure 14.1 **Amount of cash stolen each year in the United States (inflation adjusted).**

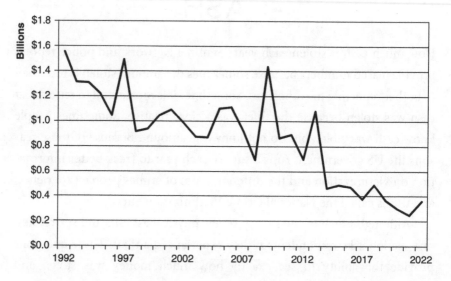

victimization data over the whole time show only about $7 of the money stolen is recovered by victims, which is a dismal 3% recovery rate.[6]

Since 1992 individuals lost about $870 million of cash in a typical year. That sounds like a lot of money but as the next sections show it pales in comparison to the amount stolen each year from credit cards, debit cards, and bank accounts.

CASHLESS WAYS TO COMMIT CRIMES

There are many different ways to commit cashless crimes. Let's start off with some ways crooks steal debit and credit cards. One of the most common methods is to steal a currently active card's number and identifying information like the CVV (card verification value) code. The news is filled with examples of data breaches where detailed customer information was stolen. With this information, thieves can pay remotely for items or services, like buying things on the internet, until either the customer or card issuer notices a problem.

Another way is physically stealing cards. Criminals sometimes intercept newly issued cards that are sent through the mail and start using them before the cardholder ever has a chance. Criminals also submit fraudulent applications for new cards. These applications are based on someone else's identity, but criminals send the new card to a different address. Criminals even make counterfeit cards by altering or cloning an existing card.

Although criminals have a variety of methods, most individuals in the United States don't worry when their credit card is lost or stolen because of a federal law called the Fair Credit Billing Act.[7] This act limits a person's liability for unauthorized use of their credit card to a maximum of $50, but in practice some credit card issuers wave all liability to retain customers.[8] Credit card companies can afford to be generous because they make large profits on most credit cards. Banks are not as generous when theft occurs with debit and ATM cards because the profits on these payment methods are much lower than with credit cards.

However, the Fair Credit Billing Act does not ensure all fraudulent charges will be removed. Any charge that is more than 60 days old is yours to pay, whether you or a thief made it. The 60-day provision means people who only periodically check their statements are on the hook for any false charges.

Moreover, if the credit card issuer does not believe the charge is fraudulent, the credit cardholder must pay no matter how much they complain. The *New York Times* Travel section wrote a story about a tourist in Mexico. After returning home the tourist found an unexpected $1,500 credit card charge on their statement for a restaurant in Mexico City, which was over a 1,000 miles from where they were vacationing. The tourist's bank did not believe this was a fraudulent transaction and refused to cancel the charge until pressured by a major newspaper's reporter.[9]

Some people pay known fraudulent charges because of embarrassment. A few years ago Hollywood released a movie called *Hustlers*, starring Jennifer Lopez, Lizzo, and Cardi B. The movie is based on a true story from New York City about a small group of women who stole money. The women met Wall Street traders and CEOs at bars and restaurants, added drugs to the men's drinks, took them to strip clubs, and maxed out the men's credit cards. The strip club gave a percentage of sales back to the women. The group photographed the men "having a good time." Most victims were too embarrassed to dispute the charges and ended up paying for a night they could not remember.[10]

I hate being the bearer of bad news, but when a thief uses your credit card illegally it really does cost you something. Even if there are no personal consequences, someone must bear the theft's cost. When a theft happens and the amount is wiped off your bill, the bank typically charges the merchant for the illegal purchase. Merchants are not charities. In response to these charge-backs, they raise the prices on all goods and services to make up for these illegal transactions, making living more expensive for all of us.

CREDIT CARD CRIME

How much crime happens with credit cards? One set of estimates comes from the Nilson Report, a bimonthly newsletter tracking payment industry trends. Nilson estimates that in just 2021 US credit card crimes amounted to almost $12 billion ($11.91 billion). This cost is almost 50 times larger than the amount of cash lost shown in Figure 14.1 for that year.[11]

The 50 times figure is skewed because fewer people today carry cash; instead, many carry credit cards. A fairer comparison uses cash stolen decades ago, after adjusting for inflation, versus recent credit card crime. Even this comparison shows credit card crime dwarfs stolen cash, with the amount stolen using credit cards in 2021 being eight times the cash stolen in 1992.

Nilson also calculates that the amount of credit card fraud outside the United States was over $20 billion in 2021. Combining the inside and outside the US numbers means credit card fraud cost the world over $32 billion in 2021. Beyond the high amounts, the Nilson data show credit card fraud is growing fast, doubling roughly every decade in the United States and roughly every eight years worldwide.

Another way to compare cash theft with credit card crime is to look at the number of people affected. Using this different measure also shows electronic payments are more dangerous than cash.

The Federal Reserve asked all respondents to the "Diary of Consumer Payment Choice" who had at least one credit card if they had experienced any fraudulent activity or use of their credit card in the last year. It also asked a similar question if the person held a debit card. Over 10% of credit cardholders and almost 8% of debit cardholders said they experienced fraudulent or unauthorized use of at least one card. This means the typical person has a credit card stolen roughly once a decade and a debit card stolen roughly every 13 years.

The Victimization Survey data analyzed previously show that when cash was king back in 1992 about 3% of adults had cash stolen each year. This is a vastly lower percentage than the 10% of credit cardholders and almost 8% of debt cardholders experiencing a theft each year today.

Overall, if society is worried about crime, these figures show shifting to cashless payments is making matters worse, not better. However, electronic payment crime is even bigger than the Nilson figures show because credit cards are only one type of electronic payment. The next section investigates debit card crime in more detail.

DEBIT CARD CRIME

It is important to track how much is stolen with debit cards because customers bear more of the costs when these cards are stolen or used fraudulently. The Federal Reserve tracks debit card use as part of its Payment Card Network and Debit Card Issuer Surveys.[12]

The surveys show the amounts spent using debit cards tripled in a short period of time. In 2009, when the surveys start, debit cards paid for $1.5 trillion worth of purchases, but by 2021 this figure jumped to over $4.2 trillion.

With this increase in use came a dramatic surge in fraud and theft. In 2009 about a half-billion dollars of fraud and theft was committed using debit cards, but a dozen years later fraud had risen to $4.6 billion, nine times more.

This dramatic increase is not just due to more people using debit cards. Instead, a significant portion is due to rising fraud rates. In 2009 the typical loss by fraud or theft on a debit card was 4¢ for every $100. A dozen years later, theft rates were 11¢ per $100.

Customers are not held blameless when a debit card theft occurs! These cards and ATM cards are covered by a different set of consumer protection rules. Depending on how fast theft is noticed, a debit or ATM cardholder could lose no money or everything in their bank account.[13]

When a debit or ATM card is stolen there are two possible outcomes: customers who report a card missing before a thief uses it lose nothing, except being unable to access their account until a new card arrives. Any spending using the card after the customer immediately reports it gone must be reimbursed by the card issuer.

However, the rules are not as generous if you wait. Customers reporting a card lost or stolen within two business days of the theft face a maximum loss of $50. Reporting a card lost or stolen after 2 business days but within 60 calendar days pushes the maximum loss to $500. Wait more than 60 days to report the theft and the maximum loss is all the money in the bank account tied to the debit or ATM card, plus any linked accounts![14]

These rules have resulted in consumers absorbing an increasing amount of damages from fraudulent use of their cards. In 2011 debit cardholders absorbed just 2% of debit card losses. By 2021 the figure had jumped to 19%, which means about one-fifth of all fraudulent activity, or almost $1 billion, was charged to debit cardholders.

It is not just debit cards where consumers are at risk. Many people use apps like PayPal, Venmo, Cash App, and Zelle to make person-to-person payments. These payments often happen instantly and once done are very difficult to reverse. Over time, criminals are increasingly targeting people using these programs because once a payment is authorized, the money is gone. The title of a US Senate report summarizes the problems with these instant payment apps: "Facilitation Fraud: How Consumers Defrauded on Zelle are Left High and Dry by the Banks That Created It." The report shows just 10% of requests for refunds were honored.[15]

DOES THE CASHLESS SOCIETY REDUCE BANK LOSSES?

Banks, the primary guardians of society's cash, are a key target for thieves. One of the most famous US bank robbers was a man named Willie Sutton. When asked why he robbed banks, he supposedly replied, "Because that's where the money is."[16]

Shifting to a cashless society has not resulted in less bank crime. Although this section shows that losses from bank robbery, when thieves enter via the front door, have declined dramatically, thieves entering through the back cyber door are making off with a far greater share of money.

One the best sources of data on bank crime is the US Sentencing Commission. The Commission was created in the 1980s to reduce federal judges' discretion by ensuring all people charged with breaking a particular federal law received roughly the same sentence. Table 14.1 uses the Commission's data to show the number of people caught, the amount they stole, and how long they were jailed in the 2010s.[17]

The table's far left-hand group are bank robbers. These are often masked individuals who walk into a bank and pass a note to a teller demanding cash.[18] In the past, bank robbery made people like Bonnie and Clyde famous and Willie Sutton temporarily rich. Today, bank robbery is neither lucrative nor a path to fame. Bank robbers steal less than $50,000 (mean $49,000; median $5,500). When caught, the typical bank robber goes to prison for eight years (96 months).

Table 14.1 Summary of People Sentenced for US Federal Bank Crimes in 2010s

	Bank robbery	Credit card theft	Financial institution crime
Mean stolen in thousands $	$49	$462	$1,268
Median stolen in thousands $	$5.5	37.6	$53.9
Total stolen in millions $	$38	$262	$898
Avg. number of people sentenced per year	787	565	712
Prison sentence average months	96	30	24
Effective hourly pay rate using mean $	$3	$89	$305

To give an idea of bank robbery's futility, the table's last row shows the pay rate needed to earn the amount stolen if the criminal worked a legal 40-hour-a-week job. If a bank robber earned $3 per hour, much less than minimum wage, they could net $49,000 working over the 96 months of their sentence.

Compared to walking into a bank with a gun and a mask, stealing money from a bank's credit card customers, shown in the middle column, is vastly more rewarding. The typical thief absconds with almost a half-million dollars (mean $462,000; median $37,600). Moreover, if a credit card thief is caught, they serve on average only 2.5 years behind bars, which is dramatically less than a bank robber's 8 years. Together, this means a credit card thief needs to find an honest job paying at least $89 an hour to top their cost of serving prison time.

The table's far right hand column shows financial institution crime, which includes other bank fraud schemes like putting a skimmer in an ATM, stealing debit cards, fraudulently obtaining non-mortgage loans, and check fraud. This column shows taking money from a bank in these ways is the most lucrative (mean $1.3 million; median $53,900) and least penalized (24 months' time). Criminals stealing from financial institutions "earn" the most at over $300 an hour. The dramatically different amounts of time for bank robbery, card theft, and financial crimes suggest the penalties associated with stealing money need to be rethought.

Is society better off by switching from cash to electronic methods? Commission data show each year society lost only $38 million to bank robbers caught demanding paper money. This is a tiny fraction of the $262 million stolen by credit card thieves who were caught or the $900 million stolen in other financial institution crimes. Commission data indicate paper money is not cursing society with high rates of crimes.

At the risk of oversimplification, Commission data show stealing paper money from a bank is less profitable and potentially faces a harsher punishment than stealing electronically. Is it any wonder that thieves love the switch from cash to electronic methods of payment?

THE CASE OF SWEDEN

The previous sections looked only at US data. Before ending this chapter let us look at Sweden, a country at the forefront of the cashless society. The impacts on crime of removing paper money from society are unambiguous. Crimes that involve cash have plummeted. In 2012 the Swedish police recorded over 50,000 cases of pickpocketing. Ten years later there were just 17,000 cases, a drop of more than a factor of three. In 2012 Sweden had over 20 bank robberies; a decade later it had just 4.

Although crime directly involving cash has fallen, Sweden has become neither safer nor more dangerous. Instead, total crime recorded by the police has been roughly constant. However, the specific categories of criminal activity have shifted. Fraud increased by 50% since 2012 in Sweden. The biggest part of fraud in Sweden today is payment card fraud, which is when criminals steal credit or debit card numbers.

The data from Sweden show removing cash from society switches the type of crimes people and businesses face. Removing cash does not eliminate crime.

CONCLUSION: HOW TO AVOID THESE TYPES OF CRIME?

For those worried by the vast increase in fraud and identity theft, there is a simple way to avoid having your credit card, debit card, or mobile payment information stolen. Use cash to make purchases. Using cash reduces exposure of financial account information. Cash does not have to be used all the time. Using cash half of the time means exposing your financial and personal information to thieves half as often.

Many places tout the convenience of creating an account and leaving your payment information online. Near my office is a Mexican restaurant that is part of a large national chain. If I want to order in advance, I need to pay up-front. Both the app and the online ordering system used to have an option to pay in the store, but the company removed that feature to make things more streamlined. From the business's view, requiring people to pay up-front makes a lot of sense. Prepaying ensures the restaurant is paid whether or not a customer ordering food picks it up. However, this company had a massive data breach a few years ago in which customers' financial information was stolen from every location. Paying in cash means I cannot preorder, which takes more time, but it ensures my financial information is protected.[19]

I protect my financial information because dealing with fraud has taken me a long time to clean up. A few years ago, I was cleaning out my desk and uncovered a credit card that I had not used in a long while. I wondered if it still worked. Calling the bank and waiting on hold seemed a waste of time. Because I had lunch plans at a fancy restaurant, I took the card along and simply handed the card to the waiter to pay for the meal. The waiter disappeared with the card for a long time, but eventually came back. A few days later that dormant card suddenly started racking up expensive charges in places I have never been. It took a lot of time and effort to clear up the fraudulent charges. Paying cash would have kept my account information from that crook and my meal would not have come with a side order of credit card fraud. Using cash can protect you from similar swindles, fraud, and identity theft.

CHAPTER FIFTEEN

DOES CASH FACILITATE CORRUPTION, TERRORISM, OR ORGANIZED CRIME?

C ash is linked in the public mind with crime. The public's general perception is that getting rid of cash will reduce or eliminate crime. It will not. Although crime takes many forms, this chapter deals with organized crime, corruption, and terrorism. The link among these three is simple. People believe cash is the fuel driving all three and that cutting off the fuel will cause these crimes to wither away.

Before diving into data and anecdotes let me ask a hypothetical question. Pretend we could wave a wand and make all cash instantly disappear. Would the disappearance of cash cause groups like South American drug lords, Central American gangs, Eastern European sex traffickers, Mediterranean mafias, African scam artists, and Middle Eastern terrorists to disband and no longer prey on society?

The answer is obviously no. Eliminating cash would have little or no effect because cash does not cause organized crime, corruption, and terrorism. Criminals use cash because it is easy. Eliminating paper money will simply result in these same groups switching to other means of payment such as cryptocurrency, gold, jewelry, fancy wines, or something else.

Using stories and data, this chapter shows there is little or no relationship between being cashless and having less corruption, terrorism, and organized crime. Although cash is linked in the public's mind to these problems, paper money doesn't cause these three types of crime.

CORRUPTION

Corruption of public officials is associated with cash. Stories abound in the media of politicians being paid off with bags stuffed with cash. One of my favorite stories comes from Chicago, where a city employee received over a half-million US dollars of paper money in plain manila envelopes, periodically handed to them while eating lunch at a local deli.[1]

The city employee was paid the cash to ensure only one company was given the right to install red light cameras, which capture drivers who don't stop at intersections. The company paying the bribes promised their equipment would capture on film anyone who broke a traffic law. Apparently, company management thought preventing people from breaking traffic laws was a more serious problem than corrupting public officials.

Another interesting story involving cash and corruption happened outside the United States. Cyril Ramaphosa, the president of South Africa, was involved in a bizarre scandal. President Ramaphosa is very proud of his game ranch, where he breeds rare wildlife. A Sudanese businessperson visited the president's ranch carrying almost US$600,000. On a whim he decided to purchase 20 rare buffalo, which were never delivered because of the COVID pandemic. People at the ranch were supposedly worried about the security of the ranch's safe, so they hid the money inside a sofa. Local people heard about the cash in the sofa, broke in, and stole the money. Whatever the true story, this large amount of cash appearing and disappearing in mysterious circumstances strongly suggests corruption.[2]

However, if this was an attempt to bribe South Africa's president, the Sudanese businessperson didn't need cash. Rare and exotic animals have very high prices. The president could have simply doubled or tripled the price he charged the Sudanese businessperson, compared to what he would have charged anyone else. Overpaying is just as effective, and a far less newsworthy method of giving the president money.

Another of my favorite bribery stories is about Glencore, one of the world's major mining companies. Glencore has admitted in court to paying millions in cash bribes to several African leaders. Glencore used private jets to ferry the cash from Switzerland to various African countries. One Glencore trader stated in court that they paid bribes 25 different times. Each bribe was authorized by senior-level managers. What is shocking is that one of the people who signed off on the cash bribes "was a Glencore 'business ethics officer' and the other was a member of the company's 'business ethics committee.'" Even the people charged with ensuring a corporation acts ethically cannot be trusted.[3]

Although these kinds of stories are scandalous, there is also much bribery and corruption for smaller amounts of money. Following are some examples clarifying why eliminating cash likely will not clean up government at the lowest or highest levels.

Low-level government officials often seek bribes to look the other way for minor infractions. I once spent time traveling in an East African country. I was amazed at how many police checkpoints there were on the roads for a country with relatively few traffic accidents, few cars, little crime, and no discernible terrorism. I discussed it with an astute local businessman who explained the police were underpaid and the checkpoints were a simple method of extracting cash bribes from any driver whose vehicle did not pass inspection.[4] The cash bribes ensured the police earned a livable wage.

Although my experience in East Africa clearly showed officials seeking paper money, there is no need for cash to ensure a bribe is paid to a low-level official. I have a friend who lives in South America. The friend was stopped at a police checkpoint on the way to the beach. The police were willing to overlook the fact my friend was speeding, but in exchange wanted lunch delivered to their checkpoint. A local restaurant already knew the police's order. Because the restaurant accepted all types of payments, no cash was needed to bribe the officers. Instead, my friend paid the restaurant electronically. Hot food was quickly delivered to the checkpoint, which the police even offered to share with my "generous" friend before letting them go.

Mid-level government officials can be bribed without using cash. Starting in 2013, China embarked on a widespread anti-corruption campaign after the press showed many mid-level government officials wearing expensive imported luxury brands of watches, jewelry, handbags, and clothing that were impossible to afford on their salaries.

Researchers looking at this Chinese anti-corruption campaign found in the first six months luxury jewelry imports fell by more than half, yet overall imports to China did not change.[5] The anti-corruption campaign also reduced imported cognac sales in China, because giving gifts of expensive bottles of alcohol is another way of providing noncash bribes.[6]

Bribes don't need to be paid in cash or with physical items; they can also be paid in services. Another way of bribing low- and mid-level Chinese officials was to invite them to lavish banquets that often ended with prostitutes entertaining the honored guests. To combat excessive banquets, all government officials were told to limit themselves to a maximum of four dishes and a soup when entertaining.[7]

Did all this effort prevent Chinese corruption? Transparency International surveys people in many countries about the level of corruption. Seven years after China embarked on their anti-corruption campaign this organization still found 62% of people in China "think government corruption is a big problem" and 28% "paid a bribe for public services in the previous 12 months." Because banning banquets and expensive gifts did not stamp out corruption, why will banning cash?[8]

Cash is not needed to bribe officials at even the highest level of government. Vladimir Putin, the head of Russia's government, likely controls a $700 million super-yacht called the *Scheherazade*, which is 459 ft long, though the actual owner is shrouded in mystery.[9]

High-level politicians don't need to give expensive items as bribes. Instead, supplicants purchase yachts, mansions, planes, and cars and then allow a politician to use them any time they wish in exchange for political favors.

CORRUPTION DATA

Anecdotal stories like these are interesting because they suggest cash is not needed for corruption, but data are needed to back up these anecdotes. To see the relationship between corruption and cash two data sources are used: one from Transparency International and the other from the Bank for International Settlements.

Transparency International has created a corruption index that ranks every country on a scale from 0 (highly corrupt) to 100 (very clean). The index is based on 13 sources of data that track things like bribery and the diversion of public funds and is based on the opinions of experts and business people within a country. The left side of Table 15.1 shows the average corruption score for two dozen countries since 2012. At the top of the list are the least corrupt countries like Sweden and Switzerland, with scores in the mid-80s. At the bottom are countries perceived as extremely corrupt, like Russia.[10]

The right side of Table 15.1 has Bank for International Settlement data on both the number[11] and volume[12] of cashless payments. Small numbers in the cashless payments columns mean relatively few cashless transactions, and large numbers mean many. For example, the top row of Table 15.1 shows the typical Swede makes over 400 cashless payments a year and cashless payments comprise over one-fifth of gross domestic product (GDP).

If corruption is caused by access to cash, then places with high numbers of electronic payments should be associated with less corruption. Instead, these data show no simple relationship. At the top of the table is Sweden with very little corruption and large numbers of cashless payments. South Korea, in the table's middle, has more corruption than Sweden, even though it has more cashless payments per person and cashless payments comprise a bigger percentage of GDP. If eliminating cash reduced crime then South Korea should have less corruption, not more than Sweden.

Another example that shows cash and corruption are not linked is comparing Japan and the United States. Both countries have a similar score of about 73. This puts both in the table's middle, suggesting moderate amounts of corruption. However, Japan is a cash-heavy society but the United States uses far more cashless payments. If cash use drove corruption, the two countries' corruption scores should be very different.

Table 15.1   Average Corruption Score and Cashless Payments

Country	Corruption index	Cashless payments number per person	Cashless payments % GDP
Sweden	86.7	426	22%
Switzerland	85.4	227	12%
Singapore	85.0	740	20%
Netherlands	82.8	440	17%
Canada	80.9	332	30%
Germany	79.9	253	9%
Australia	79.1	457	32%
United Kingdom	78.4	402	35%
Belgium	75.7	320	21%
Japan	73.8	62	12%
United States	72.4	468	30%
France	70.0	328	22%
Spain	59.9	216	14%
South Korea	56.0	462	43%
Saudi Arabia	49.0	37	7%
Italy	47.4	98	12%
South Africa	43.6	75	20%
Turkey	43.0	120	22%
China	39.4	98	81%
Brazil	39.0	152	19%
India	38.9	12	5%
Argentina	37.4	44	11%
Indonesia	35.9	29	4%
Mexico	31.2	36	8%
Russia	28.4	168	34%

Russia is ranked the most corrupt society among the roughly two dozen shown. However, cashless transactions make up a much bigger percentage of Russia's GDP than in Switzerland, which is one of the least corrupt countries in the list. Overall, the data in the table do not show a strong link between being cashless and experiencing less corruption.[13]

THE CASE OF SWEDEN

Before ending the section on corruption, it is important to look at Sweden, a country that is often a financial innovator, and today is at the forefront of the cashless society. The Swedish central bank proudly points out that it was the first European country to issue banknotes, which gave people a more convenient option than carrying around coins made of copper.[14]

Does the current push to make Sweden more convenient by eliminating cash have an impact on corruption? In 2008, when cash was still prevalent, Sweden was tied for the least corrupt country in the world, along with Denmark and New Zealand. If cash is associated with crime, then Sweden's shift to a cashless society should be accompanied by a continued position at the top of the anti-corruption charts.

Table 15.1 shows a single composite average corruption figure. Looking at individual yearly figures shows corruption growing over time in Sweden. In 2013 Sweden had a score of 89 out of 100. However, by 2022 Sweden's score had fallen to 83, a statistically significant drop. Going cashless did not reduce corruption.

TERRORISM

Terrorism involves violent acts designed to topple governments and upset the social order by intimidating large numbers of people. The most recent numbers show over 8,000 terrorist attacks worldwide, with about 25,000 people killed, in just one year. Will shifting to a cashless society reduce terrorism?[15]

The European Union believes it will. The Union declared it would slowly remove the €500 paper note from circulation.[16] The media claimed this was the end of the "Bin Laden" note. The €500 note is called that because Osama Bin Laden, the mastermind behind using airplanes to take down New York's World Trade Towers and part of the Pentagon, allegedly passed out €500 notes to his suicide bombers.

This section argues becoming a cashless society will not affect terrorism for two reasons. First, there is no relationship between how little or much a country uses cash and the number of terrorist attacks. Second, terrorism is not expensive. Many major attacks have not cost much money.

The University of Maryland maintains a detailed database of terrorist incidents happening around the globe since 1970.[17] On the left side of Table 15.2 is the average yearly number of terrorist attacks over the past decade in about two dozen countries.[18] At the top of the list are countries like India, with roughly two attacks a day, and Turkey, with roughly one attack every two days. The list's middle has countries experiencing roughly one attack a month, like China, Sweden, and Italy. At the bottom are countries that rarely experience terrorism, like South Korea and Singapore.

The right side of Table 15.2 has the same Bank for International Settlement data on both the number and volume of cashless payments used in the previous corruption section. Small numbers in the cashless payments columns mean relatively few cashless transactions per person, and large numbers mean many. For example, the top row of Table 15.2 shows India has almost 800 terror attacks per year, but the typical Indian makes a cashless payment just a dozen times a year and cashless payments comprise only 5% of GDP.

Again, Table 15.2 shows no simple positive relationship between terrorism and cashless payments. At the top of the list are two cash economies

Table 15.2 Average Annual Terrorist Attacks and
Cashless Payments

Country	Terrorist attacks	Cashless payments number per person	Cashless payments % GDP
India	779	12	5%
Turkey	185	120	22%
United Kingdom	101	402	35%
Saudi Arabia	58	37	7%
Russia	56	168	34%
United States	55	468	30%
Indonesia	30	29	4%
Germany	29	253	9%
France	29	328	22%
South Africa	20	75	20%
Mexico	17	36	8%
China	13	98	81%
Sweden	11	426	22%
Italy	10	98	12%
Netherlands	8	440	17%
Canada	7	332	30%
Australia	6	457	32%
Brazil	4	152	19%
Japan	3	62	12%
Spain	3	216	14%
Belgium	3	320	21%
Argentina	2	44	11%
Switzerland	2	227	12%
Korea	1	462	43%
Singapore	0	740	20%

(India and Turkey) but also one relatively cashless (the United Kingdom). In the top third of Table 15.2 Germany and France have the same number of terror attacks, but are quite different in cash use. At the bottom of the list Japan, Spain, and Belgium are all relatively safe countries, but there are dramatic differences in cash use. If being cashless prevents terrorism, then neither China nor Sweden should be in the list's middle.[19]

The second point is that although cash is clearly used to finance terrorism, the amount of cash used is quite small. In 2022 the US government published a report on terrorist financing, abbreviated TF. To prevent terrorism, banks and other financial institutions are required to file suspicious activity reports, or SARs, when something doesn't look or smell right about a transaction or customer. The government TF report states:

> Most of the suspicious transactions identified for suspected TF are outbound transfers made by U.S. persons seeking to provide funds to terrorist groups active outside of the United States. The low value of most person-to-person transactions associated with terrorism (one assessment found most SARs involved suspicious transactions less than $800) and the sheer size and scope of finance flowing through the U.S. give terrorist organizations and their financiers the opportunity to blend in with normal financial activity.[20]

The key number in this quote is $800. Cutting off this low level of TF would mean prohibiting a significant portion of US cash transactions.

Even terrorist incidents that occur within the United States often don't use large amounts of money to sow terror. One of the largest domestic terrorist incidents was the bombing of the Alfred P. Murrah Federal Building in Oklahoma City in 1995. A massive homemade bomb hidden in a rental truck killed 168 people, injured over 500, and destroyed or damaged 300 buildings.[21]

The detailed timeline leading up to the bombing shows exactly how the bomb was constructed and that much of the money the terrorists spent was cash. However, the total amount of cash needed was quite small and not noteworthy until after the fact.[22]

For example, the key ingredient in the bomb was two tons of ammonium nitrate fertilizer. In 1995, this commonly available fertilizer cost about $170 per ton. The bombers stole explosives from a Kansas quarry, which meant they spent no money to trigger the bomb. One of the most expensive items they purchased was $900 worth of racing fuel to make the bomb more destructive. Even if the terrorists used only credit or debit cards, the low cost of the items used would not have triggered warnings by officials monitoring suspicious transaction spending.[23]

Another domestic terrorism act was the Boston Marathon Bombing. The bombing killed three people and injured hundreds of others. In the hunt for the suspects the entire Boston area was locked down for an entire day. I live in Boston and vividly remember the bombing. My son was running the marathon course and I was waiting to cheer him on when the race was suddenly stopped and everyone was sent home.

Although the economic damage to the city and people's lives ran into the millions of dollars, the bombs used to terrorize the city were exceptionally cheap to make. The Boston bombers built two explosive devices using kitchen pressure cookers, fireworks, nails, and ball bearings. They then hid the bombs in cheap backpacks. The most expensive items used were the pressure cookers, which at the time cost slightly more than $100 each.[24]

An analysis of terrorism in Europe also found most attacks were quite inexpensive to carry out. The research found "most of them cost less than USD 10,000". This figure clearly shows that even a severe legal cash restriction has minor effects on the financing of terrorists and activists.[25]

Terrorism doesn't require using bombs. Mass shootings at schools, shopping malls, and concerts happen with increasing frequency around the world with many people killed and wounded each year.[26]

The cost to purchase guns and ammunition used in these attacks is quite low. A store specializing in hunting and fishing gear located near my home is selling semiautomatic weapons starting at just $300. They also sell bullets in bulk at less than $1 per round.

The equipment needed to carry out terrorism and mass shootings does not need to be expensive. It takes very little money to wreak havoc on a large number of people's lives. Given terrorism can be done so cheaply, eliminating cash will not make countries safer.

Additionally, requiring people to fill in government forms reporting when large amounts of cash trades hands will not stop terrorism, because many of these despicable acts are done with only small amounts of money.

ORGANIZED CRIME

Organized crime takes many forms. Drug traffickers send cocaine, heroin, and hallucinogens around the world. Human traffickers move sex workers, slaves, and illegal migrants. Counterfeiters make illegal and inferior copies of pharmaceuticals, luxury goods, and intellectual property, like movies. Pirates, long associated with the age of sailing ships, still attack vessels on the seas. There is a flourishing trade in wildlife, ancient artifacts, illegally harvested trees, and even human organs.

Organized crime generates large amounts of money. The United Nations estimated in the early 2000s that proceeds from organized crime each year were about 1.5% of global GDP. Much of this crime occurs with participants using paper money.[27]

The Global Initiative Against Transnational Organized Crime is a Swiss-based organization that has created a detailed country-by-country database tracking the extent of organized crime. The Global Initiative summarizes the extent of organized crime using an index that ranges from 10, which means organized crime permeates all aspects of society, to 1, which means almost no organized crime exists. The index is based on the amount of ten types of criminal activities, such as human trafficking and heroin trading, plus the reach in a country of four types of criminal groups, like mafias. Currently, among the world's roughly 200 countries the average score is 4.9. Comparing the organized crime index with Bank for International Settlement data shows the same findings as Tables 15.1 and 15.2. Many countries have the same amount of organized crime but very different cash use.[28]

Let me give you four examples. Both China and Saudi Arabia have an identical 6.0 crime index score. This means both have more organized crime than the average country. Although they have the same amount of organized crime, their use of electronic payments is quite different. China rarely uses paper money, with cashless payments equal to over 80% of GDP, but Saudi Arabia, with cashless payments under 10% of GDP, does use paper money.

India and the United States have the same crime index of 5.5, but India is much more cash intensive than the United States. Korea and Germany also have the same crime index of 4.9, but Germany is more cash intensive than Korea. Near the bottom of the list are Belgium and Switzerland. Belgium is a more cashless society than Switzerland, but the two countries have the same organized crime index value of 4.3.

CONCLUSION

Corruption, terrorism, and organized crime are major societal problems. All three are associated in people's minds with cash, which is why many people advocate for banning paper money. The data and anecdotes presented in this chapter make a strong case that switching to a cashless economy will not reduce these three problems.

Bribes can be paid by giving jewelry, liquor, banquets, expensive trips, or even a promise of job after someone leaves public office. Cash isn't needed to corrupt officials. Although large-value notes like the €500 are associated with terrorism, much terrorist activity is done on the cheap. There does not seem to be any reduction in terrorism since the European central bank's decision to withdraw the €500 note from circulation. Cash is not causing corruption, terrorism, or organized crime. Although cash is linked in the public's mind to these problems, the data show eliminating paper money will not eliminate crime.

The main point of this chapter is simple; corruption, organized crime, and terrorism will continue to flourish in a cashless society. Eliminating cash will not suddenly result in less crime, less corruption, or less terror. Instead, problems will shift into new and unexpected directions.

CHAPTER SIXTEEN

DOES ELIMINATING CASH REDUCE TAX EVASION?

D o some people and businesses use cash to avoid paying taxes? Of course they do, because using paper money makes it difficult for tax authorities to know about transactions. Some research suggests cash businesses hide about half their revenue. Tax evasion is a key reason paper currency opponents give for eliminating cash.[1]

However, before throwing cash away it is important to look deeper into the relationship between cash and tax evasion. Even if cash businesses hide half their revenue, there are few all-cash businesses remaining and most are quite small. Economies around the world are dominated by giant corporations that are not using cash to hide their operations. Instead dishonest companies use other methods, like creating ghost companies that provide fake invoices and receipts to falsely boost costs and eliminate profits.[2]

Opponents of paper currency believe eliminating cash will stop people from cheating on their taxes. This chapter lays out three types of evidence that the existence of cash is not the cause of tax cheating. First, India eliminated all high-denomination paper money notes in 2016. Overnight 86% of paper currency disappeared. The result was massive economic disruption, but India saw neither a short-term nor a long-term boost in tax collections.

Second, data are available on tax evasion and cash use for roughly a dozen of the world's largest economies. These data show no relationship between changes in cash use and tax evasion. Third, estimates of US tax evasion show federal tax receipts would be 15% higher if everyone were completely honest. However, analyzing this 15% gap suggests at most one-quarter is explained by cash use. This means in the best-case scenario eliminating cash would boost US tax receipts by less than 4%.

Tax evasion is a lot like students cheating on tests and exams. Although most students are honest, a small but persistent minority are not. As a teacher I notice that every time I close off one way of cheating, dishonest students come up with another method. Tax cheaters are just like my dishonest students. Eliminate paper money and tax scofflaws will find another way to cheat.

The simplest example of people searching for new ways to cheat the tax collector was the creation of Bitcoin, the popular cryptocurrency. Bitcoin is an international currency whose first users believed transactions were anonymous. Research into who used Bitcoin and why during its first decade of existence found approximately one-quarter of all users and about half of all transactions with this cryptocurrency were for illegal purposes, such as buying illicit drugs. Early users thought income earned in Bitcoins was untraceable by tax authorities and undetectable by law enforcement.[3]

Tax avoidance is not a modern invention that started with cryptocurrencies. Instead, tax avoidance is so much a part of human history we almost overlook it. In previous generations a significant part of government revenue came from taxing imports like liquor, silks, cigarettes, and other valuables. The English word for avoiding import taxes is to *smuggle*, and the remnants of people's attempts at avoiding these taxes live on in many place names. Within an easy drive of my home I can swim at Smugglers Beach on Cape Cod, ski at Smugglers Notch in Vermont, or stay in a scenic inn at Smuggler's Cove in Maine.

Today, smuggling is no longer high on the list of tax authority concerns because relatively little revenue comes from imports and much more comes from income taxes, sales taxes, and value added taxes, or VAT. No matter where taxes come from, tax avoidance is a societal problem. Although no one wants to pay taxes, governments have to generate revenue to provide for roads, schools, airports, defense, and other public goods society demands.

While people hate paying taxes and have a long history of avoiding them, will eliminating cash significantly boost tax receipts? It appears without cash, people who want to cheat on their taxes, just like my students, will find another way to cheat. The following sections dive into the details of why eliminating paper money will not curb tax evasion.

INDIA'S 2016 ELIMINATION OF MOST CASH

What happens if a country tries to go cashless and eliminates all large denomination notes? Does government revenue rise and tax evasion fall? India tried this experiment, called *demonetization*, in 2016. A detailed analysis of what happened did "not detect any systematic impact of demonetization on either the number of tax filers or tax revenues."[4]

India has a relatively large amount of tax evasion. Some pundits say tax evasion, not cricket, is India's national sport.[5]

The government of India has created advertising campaigns, web pages, and even comic books designed to foster a culture of paying taxes. Even with these efforts the largest country in the world has relatively few taxpayers, with the government estimating slightly more than 80 million people pay income taxes out of a population of around 1.4 billion. That's less than 6%![6]

In early November 2016 the Indian government demonetized in an attempt to curtail black markets, reduce illegal activities, and limit tax evasion. It announced the two highest currency denominations, the 500 and 1,000 rupee notes, would be withdrawn from circulation at the end of December 2016 and become worthless. Overnight this edict destroyed 86% of all paper money in India. People were given just seven weeks to bring their money to banks and either deposit it into an account or trade old notes in for newer notes.

The government's goal was to force people to declare all their hidden paper money, what Indians call *black wealth*, or lose it. The theory was people hoarding large amounts of ill-gotten cash would prefer to give up some of the money to taxes rather than losing it all. The policy also tried to force people working in the informal cash economy who did not pay taxes to join the formal banked economy and start paying taxes.

This sudden demonetization policy sparked economic pandemonium and even deaths. However, what it didn't do was boost tax revenue. The detailed analysis did not detect any impact on the number of tax filers or amount of tax revenue, and found over 99% of the newly banned money was successfully converted. This meant almost no one holding their black wealth in cash lost money during the switch.[7]

Figure 16.1   India's federal government gross tax revenue.

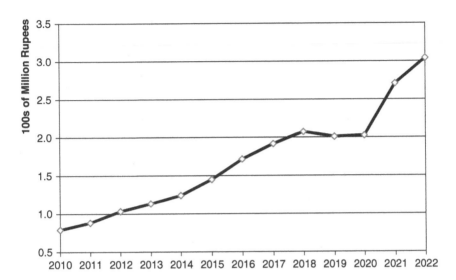

It doesn't take sophisticated economic analysis to see banning cash had no impact. Figure 16.1 shows the Indian government's gross tax revenue over time.[8]

Starting in 2010 India saw steadily increasing tax revenue because the economy grew, the population increased, and inflation rose. If banning cash boosted tax revenue then the amount the government collected should jump dramatically higher starting in 2017. Instead, 2017 and 2018 followed the same steadily increasing pattern seen before cash was banned. Then starting in 2019 tax receipts fell because of a significant cut in corporate tax rates.[9]

THE TAX GAP AROUND THE WORLD

If cash use causes tax evasion, then, as people use more electronic payments and less cash, tax evasion should fall. This section looks at changes over time in roughly a dozen economically large countries and finds no relationship between tax evasion and a country becoming cashless.

Government officials and academics boil the amount of cheating on taxes down into a single concept called the *tax gap*. The tax gap is the difference between how much money the government would collect if everyone were honest and paid on time versus the actual amount paid. The bigger the tax gap, the less revenue the government gets.

The tax gap is presented in both percentage terms and absolute dollars. For example, the latest US tax gap figure is 15%. The Internal Revenue Service, or IRS, estimates it collected 85% of the taxes owed the federal government and missed collecting 15%, which is over a half-trillion dollars.[10]

The tax gap varies widely from country to country. Is the tax gap associated with cash use? High-quality data on the tax gap and cashless payments are available only for 13 countries. Among the 13, countries like Italy and Turkey have large tax gaps and countries like Switzerland and Canada have small tax gaps. The researchers who created the tax gap data do not mention cash or currency use as a determinant of higher or lower compliance. Instead they say, "The problem is that the irresponsible policies of numerous governments do not prompt taxpayers to comply with the tax law regulations."[11]

What happened to tax compliance in these 13 countries as the number of cashless transactions changed over a two-year period? Italy and Turkey both started out with the largest tax gaps and over two years both countries saw more cashless transactions. Although citizens in both countries did more cashless transactions, their country's tax gaps moved in opposite directions. The Italian tax gap shrank while the Turkish tax gap grew!

The German case is even harder for people who want to get rid of cash to explain. Over a two-year period the typical German made six fewer cashless transactions per year. Even though Germans were using cash more often, their tax gap shrank, which means compliance went up.

About half the countries (Turkey, France, Australia, Japan, Switzerland, and Canada) increased the average number of cashless transactions but at the same time experienced a larger tax gap. The world has over 200 countries and high-quality data on the tax gap and cashless transactions cover slightly more than a dozen. However, the data that do exist suggest there is no relationship between changes in cashless transactions and the tax gap.[12]

US TAX GAP

As mentioned previously, the IRS estimates they miss collecting about 15% of all taxes owed the federal government, or about a half-trillion dollars. Opponents of paper money are outraged by the 15% figure because this shifts the burden of paying for government services onto the backs of honest taxpayers, giving cheaters a free or reduced-price ride. Opponents of paper money believe cash users "conveniently" forget to report paper money income.

This book doesn't argue that cash users don't cheat on their taxes. Of course some people use cash to cheat. Instead, I show that switching everyone to electronic methods will not result in the IRS seeing a dramatic increase in tax collection, based on two observations.

First, over the last half-century the United States has steadily moved away from using cash. If cash causes tax avoidance then over this time the tax gap should have shrunk. Eric Toder investigated tax gap changes since the 1970s and found "the size of the estimated tax gap in relation to taxes owed has been remarkably stable over time."[13] A stable tax gap combined with a steady decline in cash use suggests eliminating cash will not reduce the tax gap.

Second, even if using electronic payments would reduce the amount of tax evasion, the bump in tax collections would not be very large. The IRS's own research indicates at most one-quarter of the US tax gap is attributable to income hidden by using cash.

Underreporting income is a key way to avoid taxation. Using paper currency is only one of many ways of hiding income from the government. Other ways that people hide income are by using cryptocurrency, paying in gold coins, or asking for preloaded debit or gift cards.[14]

Additionally, many people underreport their income even when it is paid electronically and every detail of the transaction is reported to the government. For example, each month millions of retired workers are sent Social Security, pension, and annuity payments. These are electronic, not cash payments. At the end of the year the Social Security administration, pension, and annuity providers tell the IRS the exact amount of taxable and nontaxable income for every recipient. The latest IRS report shows $13 billion of the tax gap happened because of people underreporting these forms of retirement income, even though the government knows every detail.[15]

The US government does not blame cash payments as a major reason for underpayments. A detailed analysis of the tax gap mentions cash payments only twice.[16] First are tips for waiters, bartenders, and other service workers.[17]

The IRS states:

Tip income is concentrated in a few industries and occupations and represents a relatively small amount of overall wages, salaries, and tips. However, since a significant portion of tip income is paid in cash by customers, tip income is subject to less information reporting than most wages and salaries. The lack of complete information reporting and the cash nature of many tips suggest that tip income has a lower compliance rate than other wages and salaries and is harder to detect during an audit.[18]

The IRS estimates total underreporting of all cash wages, salaries, and tips represents just 1% of the tax gap. Eliminating cash will reduce this kind of tax avoidance, but given this represents only 1% of the tax gap the government will not see a significant boost in revenue.

The other area where "taxpayers are intentionally noncompliant or conduct business in cash with poor or nonexistent record keeping" has much greater impact. The IRS calls this "items subject to little or no information reporting." The area includes self-employed income, farm income, royalties, and rents. Together the government estimates this entire category is responsible for about one-quarter of the tax gap, which is about $125 billion. That billion-dollar figure sounds huge, but it is only 2% of federal government spending.

Assuming cash is entirely responsible for all tax avoidance in the area of little or no information reporting, IRS data suggest eliminating cash still leaves about three-quarters of the tax gap outstanding!

ELECTRONIC TAX FILING

The goal of many governments around the world is to make payments and common tasks completely electronic. Governments want to do this to boost tax payments and reduce the opportunities for government officials to take bribes. A simple experiment was tried in Tajikistan, a country where one-third of all businesses were expected to pay a bribe when interacting with government officials and most businesses were required to interact face-to-face with the same tax officials monthly.

The experiment randomly selected businesses in the capital city and allowed every one of these business to file and pay their taxes electronically, instead of visiting the tax officials' offices.[19] The results were startling: "we are unable to detect any average effect on the total amount of tax collected by the administration or on bribe payments."

Although the total paid in taxes did not change, who paid taxes did. The Tajikistan tax authorities created a score for each business's likelihood of tax evasion. Firms that were considered low risk paid less in taxes when e-filing; it appeared the tax officials coerced them in face-to-face meetings to overpay because tax officials had quotas to meet. However, firms considered likely to evade taxes paid significantly higher taxes; tax officials in face-to-face meetings had let them underpay in exchange for bribes.

The Tajikistan experiment is a warning to governments that believe switching to electronic payments and filing methods will make the tax gap shrink or even vanish. Switching to electronic payments in Tajikistan redistributed who paid the tax but did not boost the total amount collected.

INFLATION TAX

Not many people realize governments around the world still earn money when cash is used to evade paying taxes. Governments do not earn as much as when businesses and citizens pay their fair share, but they still earn something.

Governments indirectly tax cash holdings and transactions by using inflation. Inflation is a government tax on people and businesses holding paper money.

Let's assume there is a drug lord holding $100 million in cash and the country has an inflation rate of 10%. The drug lord thinks they are paying nothing in taxes to the government, but they are wrong. At the beginning of the year the drug lord's cash pile purchases $100 million worth of goods and services. However, after one year of 10% inflation the typical item in the country now costs more. This results in the drug lord's cash stash only purchasing $90 million worth of goods and services.

Where did the missing $10 million go? Inflation is a complex subject but, stripping it down to its essential component, that money was taken by the government. Inflation happens when a government creates too much money in the economy. Prices rise because too much money is chasing too few goods and services.

Let's make this inflation argument clearer by a simple example. Let's assume there is a small island nation that issues its own money. The government wants to build a new airport but doesn't want to raise taxes to pay for the construction so it issues an extra $1 billion in money to pay the construction company. The construction company uses the money to pay workers and buy supplies. The spending causes prices to rise, making existing money holdings worth less. When the inflation cycle is done the government has a new airport and citizens paid for it by seeing the money they held devalued.

Examples like this happen in the real world. In 2006 the African country of Zimbabwe owed the International Monetary Fund (IMF) $221 million. Zimbabwe's leaders did not like the IMF's loan conditions requiring the government to enact more liberal economic policies. To pay off the loan the government secretly printed 21 trillion in Zimbabwean currency and used that money to buy US$221 million. The US dollars were given to the IMF to eliminate the country's debt. Printing all this money, however, started a rapid rise in prices. By summer 2008 Zimbabwe was experiencing an annual 2.2 million percent rate of inflation. At this rate all prices were doubling about every three weeks. Zimbabwe got rid of the external debt, but citizens ended up with paper currency that was worthless.

While the United States and many other major economies do not have very high inflation, there are some countries that do. In high-inflation countries, holding cash, even overnight, can be extremely costly. For example, in January 2023 Turkey had an official annual inflation rate of over 60%.[20] When an economy has a 60% annual inflation rate, holding cash for one year means losing over half its value, and holding cash for just one week means losing over 1%.

In high-inflation countries businesses quickly learn they must keep all cash balances overnight in banks to avoid inflation destroying the cash's value. Putting money in the bank earns interest, which counteracts the rise in prices. But cash businesses that are hiding sales and illegal businesses, which break the law, don't deposit money in banks. Some of their profits are lost to inflation. Their losses are the government's gain. This shows even when people and businesses use cash to evade taxation, governments still earn something.

CAN TAX EVASION BE REDUCED WITHOUT GETTING RID OF PAPER MONEY?

The previous sections provide evidence that eliminating cash does not boost tax collections. I want to end this chapter by showing where paper money and electronic payments coexist, tax evasion can be reduced without getting rid of paper money but instead by increasing monitoring.

Tax evasion has both costs and benefits. The more someone cheats the more likely they are to get caught. However, the more someone cheats the more benefit they receive. It is like speeding while driving a car. People who drive just a little bit over the speed limit are rarely stopped by the police, but typically don't get to their destination much sooner. People driving twice the legal speed limit are frequently pulled over, but if they are not stopped they arrive much earlier. Governments can exploit the trade-off between these costs and benefits without getting rid of cash by increasing monitoring and asking businesses to estimate some payments.

The previous section showed tax authorities believe waiters, bartenders, and service workers who receive cash tips are significantly underreporting their income. I agree with this belief. As a business school professor

I sometimes get access to private business data in exchange for providing advice. A large local restaurant once provided full access to their point-of-sale database. The database had details on every order: the server's name, number of patrons, dishes ordered, drinks purchased, meal cost, how the patron paid, and the amount they tipped.

About half of credit or debit card customers gave a 15% tip and half gave a 20% tip for an average tip of 17.5%. The average cash tip was zero, which does not mean people paying cash are stingy. Instead, it means cash tips were not reported.

Restaurants send workers and the tax authorities a form each year showing total wages plus actual tips earned. Before the advent of computerized point-of-sale systems it was hard to estimate missing tips. Today data from these systems could enable restaurant and bar owners to send out annual forms containing boxes for both actual tips from electronic payers and estimated tips from cash users.

CONCLUSION

Tax evasion is widespread in the world. There is even a short documentary film called *Tax Evasion: A Greek National Sport*. It is not happening only in Greece. Writers have claimed it is also the national sport of India, China, Germany, and Bulgaria, to name a few countries.[21]

To prevent tax evasion some people recommend eliminating cash. This chapter shows shifting to a cash-free economy will not do much to boost the amount of taxes collected.[22] Shifting to a cashless economy will not boost tax collections because cash is not causing people to be dishonest. Dishonest taxpayers use cash because it is convenient and untraceable. However, eliminating cash will result in the dishonest simply searching for another convenient and untraceable form of money because dishonest people will find a way to cheat.

Using cash doesn't turn honest taxpayers into dishonest tax cheats. People and businesses in the United States have paid income and corporate taxes for over a century. During most of that time cash was the primary means of payment. The US government was able to raise enough in taxes to fund major wars, build massive amounts of infrastructure, pay for the public education of millions, and build a social safety net long before electronic payments were created.[23]

When citizens feel their taxes are used wisely to support effective programs and efforts they will pay their fair share whether cash or electronic means are used. When people feel government officials are corrupt, self-serving, pushing narrow agendas, or using taxes to punish groups, then cheating will be widespread no matter what means of payments are used.

SECTION VI

CONTROL

How much control and information do we want to give governments, businesses, and high technology companies over our money? I am sure every person reading this book will have different answers. Nevertheless, it is important to describe some of the key facts so that everyone can make an informed decision.

Shifting to electronic means gives a few people, businesses, or states incredible power to control who spends or when spending can happen. Earlier, Chapter 11 talked about efforts to bring billions of unbanked people into the modern economy by providing mobile payments, using cell phones to buy and sell, and store money. Mobile payments seem like a wonderful and effective tool to eradicate poverty and improve the lives of families living in marginal conditions. However, as the first chapter in this section (Chapter 17) points out, governments around the world have shut down mobile phone networks for long periods of time, rendering mobile payments useless and trapping money inside an insurmountable wall.

Chapter 18 points out that even when paper money exists, governments and businesses can make accepting paper money so onerous and so difficult that they can effectively block paper money transactions. These difficulties are illustrated with a story of how I tried to pay my US federal taxes in cash.

Chapter 19 investigates who is pushing for a cashless economy and why they are pushing so hard. By understanding the motivations of the various actors it is possible to reduce their incentives and increase cash use.

Chapter 20 offers ideas for increasing cash use. Some are simple, like telling others about the advantages of paper money. Some are more complex, like requiring people to use cash when making sports bets, purchasing tobacco products, or doing other activities that in the past were considered sinful activities. Implementing even a few of the ideas will ensure cash continues to be a useful tool.

CHAPTER SEVENTEEN

CASH PREVENTS GOVERNMENT CONTROL

D o you like making choices? This chapter starts out with two questions and then provides information so you can make your own decisions about the answers. First, how much control and information do we want to give governments over what we purchase? The second question is tougher to answer. In every nation there are rabble-rousers, malcontents, opposition figures, and others who are on society's edges. In modern society money is power. Do we want to give governments the ability to take away troublemakers' and fringe actors' ability to spend money?

The next sections show governments are already using their power to control spending. Currently, this control is limited to a small number of cases but if cash is eliminated there is no guarantee that control will stay limited.

SHUTTING OFF BANK ACCOUNTS

The majority of cashless transactions happen using a bank account. Yes, people swipe phones, tap cards, and even use biometrics to pay for purchases but supporting most of that technology is an account at a financial institution. What happens when that bank account is suddenly closed or locked, which is called being *debanked*? A debanked customer loses the ability to spend money in a cashless society.

Banks closing customer accounts started attracting widespread attention in 2023 because of a high-profile case that happened in the United Kingdom. Nigel Farage, an English politician who pushed very hard for the United Kingdom to leave the European Union, claimed he was debanked. Mr. Farage stated his bank account was closed because of his political activity.[1]

Farage's bank was forced to reveal their internal documents leading to the decision. The bank decided the former Brexit Party leader's views were "at odds with our position as an inclusive organization." Reporters covering the story then found British banks were closing "well over 1,000 [accounts] for every business day of the week." Debanking occurred with little or no explanation and sometimes with no warning, effectively cutting off the debanked person, even a very public and wealthy figure like Farage, from making purchases.[2]

Being debanked for political reasons also happened in another large democracy. At the end of the COVID pandemic, truck drivers in Canada started protesting and demanding an end to pandemic restrictions, like being forced to get vaccinated. The protests were noisy and annoying, primarily in Ottawa, which is Canada's capital city. Demonstrators drove their vehicles slowly in circles while honking their horns. Over time, the number of demonstrators steadily grew in size. Soon the sheer number of truckers began causing gridlock in Ottawa, especially around the Parliament. Canada's prime minister decided that protests, which paralyzed traffic, were a threat to national security and invoked temporary emergency powers.

The emergency powers enabled policemen to write down all the protestors' vehicle license plate numbers and after looking up the names and addresses of the drivers the government had their bank accounts frozen. The government then started arresting people, who had no ability to post bail because they were debanked. Freezing accounts stopped the protests but sent a chilling message that even engaging in legal protests can be dangerous to protestors' financial health.[3]

This example of a government taking away troublemakers' ability to spend money happened in democratic Canada. What will happen in more authoritarian countries?

Another example of large numbers of people suddenly not being able to access their money happened in 2021 when Russia invaded Ukraine. Russian travelers who were outside Russia suddenly found their credit cards did not work and had no access to their bank accounts. Overnight, Western sanctions shut off all Russian access to money when outside of that country. The denial of access affected all Russians, both supporters and critics of the war.

Being debanked doesn't just happen in England, Canada, or to Russian travelers. It is happening frequently enough in the United States that the *New York Times* ran an entire series of articles outlining the problem. The newspaper even offered an entire article of helpful tips for reducing the chances readers suddenly get locked out of their own accounts.[4]

Debanking is happening around the world because government rules make it very risky for both banks and their employees to allow an account with even a hint of suspicious financial activity to continue operating. If a bank does not alert the authorities and later the authorities discover a pattern of problem transactions, the government levies stiff fines and penalties. Bank employees in the United States can face up to five years in jail and the fine is up to $5,000 for each violation; each day the problem continues constitutes a separate violation.[5]

Governments are using banks as their eyes and ears to prevent money laundering, financial scams, and human sex trafficking. However, in an attempt to reduce these crimes, innocent customers are routinely debanked. The *New York Times* pointed out examples of people being debanked for getting large international wire payments from Nigeria, depositing varying amounts of cash rounded to the nearest $1,000, or working in a strip club.

Whatever the reason for being debanked, having cash on hand when your credit, debit, and ATM cards suddenly stop working is useful protection that ensures a bank's often seemingly capricious decision doesn't ruin your financial life.

DIGITAL CURRENCY

Debanking becomes even easier with a new idea called *central bank digital currencies*, or CBDCs for short. Decentralized cryptocurrencies like Bitcoin and Ethereum have become important financial tools. However, because no country or individual controls decentralized cryptocurrencies, many states are investigating creating their own cryptocurrency and some have rolled these currencies out.

One of the first large-scale rollouts is happening in China. China's paper currency is called either the *yuan* or *renminbi*. In 2021 the central bank of China started issuing a digital version of the country's money, which is called either the *e-CNY* or *e-RMB*. In response to this, US politicians have been pressuring the Federal Reserve to create a US "central bank digital currency, so we remain competitive globally."[6]

Cryptocurrencies are the ultimate electronic money because there is no paper version of the money. One problem with government digital currency is that it gives the state incredible powers over who can use and not use money. Imagine for a moment paper money disappears and everyone uses a state-run digital currency. Not only does the state have a complete record of every purchase but also the state has the ability to shut off a person's access to their money.

Some researchers think the ability to have a record of every purchase is a positive. In a discussion of the eCedi, the first African digital currency backed by the central bank of Ghana, one group of researchers state, "Some of the key benefits of CBDCs identified in the literature include increased control over money issuance by the central bank and greater insight into how people spend their money."[7]

I am skeptical that governments will stay benign while tracking spending. The state does not care what most citizens purchase and who they purchase it from. However, all governments have real and perceived enemies. Tracking spending or preventing purchases is a straightforward method of controlling opponents. Moreover, history is full of mass movements to control various real and perceived vices. For example, a century ago the United States instituted prohibition, which outlawed alcohol sales. When governments start tracking spending, will it lead to government control of the types of spending allowed?

CBDCs provide countries with an unprecedented method of economic control. Chapter 13 discussed negative interest rates, which punishes those saving money because every day that money is held a small amount is taken away. With a CBDC there is no limit to the level of negative interest rates when the economy falls into a recession.

Let's assume all money is held in a CBDC. Instead of paper money, your wallet contains electronic money like e-dollars, e-euros, or e-yen. If a government wants people to spend money to kick-start the economy out of a recession or depression, they can simply announce "all digital currency in your e-wallet expires in one year." This is effectively a minus 100% interest rate and presents people with a use-it-or-lose-it situation.

Keeping paper money around provides a simple check that prevents central bankers from being able to implement these kinds of extreme measures.

GOVERNMENT CONTROL OF THE UNBANKED

Another important aspect of government control is how governments, particularly in the developing world, can control the poor. Banks with imposing facades and spacious lobbies are a hallmark of rich major cities. However, relatively few of the world's eight billion people have access to these fancy financial institutions.

The World Bank, an international organization seeking to reduce poverty, tracks banking system use. As shown in Chapter 11, three-quarters of the population didn't have a bank account among the ten poorest countries, like Egypt, Pakistan, and Afghanistan. In rich countries almost everyone is banked. Among the ten richest countries on the list – places like Sweden, Germany, and Denmark – less than 1% of the population was unbanked.

The World Bank was quite broad in defining people who were financially included. For example, if someone used their mobile phone to send or receive money anytime in the past year they were considered as being part of the banking system. Also, people who had any kind of financial accounts, such as having money in a postal savings account, were also considered banked.

The percent unbanked is likely higher because data show about 10% of the world's accounts were inactive. Inactive means the account holder did not make a deposit or withdrawal to the account in the past year.[8]

The World Bank estimates roughly one-quarter (24%) of the world's population is unbanked. The world has about eight billion people; this means almost two billion are unbanked. Governments, international agencies, and many companies are making a big effort to help. However, banks do not want to open permanent branches to serve many of these people who live in rural, poor areas where it is unprofitable to open a physical branch.

The current solution is to provide the unbanked with ways to send and receive money on their mobile phones or via the internet. Mobile phones are ubiquitous in society. The World Bank pointed out that starting about 2015 "the poorest households are more likely to have access to mobile phones than to toilets or clean water."[9]

The widespread availability of phones has resulted in an explosion in mobile payments, where people use their phone to pay bills and send money to friends and family. Their rapid growth has dramatically boosted bank account ownership around the world.

The World Bank estimates that in 2011 just about half the people in the world over the age of 15 had an account either at a financial institution or with a mobile money service provider. A decade later the figure was over three-fourths of all people.

Mobile phone use for financial transactions is also increasing in the US. The Survey of Consumer Payment Choice found large jumps in just one year. "Forty-six percent of consumers made at least one mobile payment in the 12 months ending in October, up from 38 percent in October 2019."[10]

Even with the explosion in mobile payments, the world needs to keep using cash for two reasons. First, governments can and do shut down mobile phones and the internet. If all of your money is tied to a mobile payment and banking system and the government shuts down the network and internet, you are effectively broke no matter how much money is in your mobile phone account.

In summer 2024 there were widespread antigovernment protests in Bangladesh. Many people were angry about the difficulty of finding a job. To quell protests the police were mobilized, a curfew was instituted, and broadband and the mobile internet were shut down for almost a dozen days. This didn't prevent the government from collapsing, but people dependent on mobile money, cashless payments, or cryptocurrency were out of luck during a tumultuous time. After the old government leaders fled the country, one of the new government's first acts was to bring banks back online.[11]

Government shutdown of communications happens in other countries. Mobile payments and banking are exploding in Africa, especially in Nigeria, Africa's most populous country with over 200 million people. Unfortunately, the Nigerian government and people are faced with periodic attacks from militant Islamist and jihadist rebels.

One way the Nigerian government has tried to thwart the militants is by shutting down the communication networks. In 2021 the government shut down all cell services in Zamfara State, which is about the size of the Netherlands. The shutdown was designed to prevent rebels who had staged a mass kidnapping from making ransom calls. The government said the shutdown would last two weeks. However, the two-week shutdown ended up lasting months and spread from Zamfara to other neighboring provinces, affecting about ten million people. This made mobile banking and payments impossible for millions of people for a long period of time.[12]

A year later the Nigerian government blocked 73 million mobile phones in a security lockdown. Each person in Nigeria is assigned a national identity number. The government blocked any phone that was not tied to a national identity number.[13]

Other large African countries have shut down communications. In 2011 Egypt shut down the cell service and the internet during the Arab Spring. Ethiopia shut down cell and internet service for two years in the war-torn Tigray region.[14]

How widespread is communication shutdown? In 2023 the governments in five countries (Uganda, Turkmenistan, Iraq, Senegal, and Guinea) shut down communication networks across the entire country for more than a week. When the cell network is turned off for national security, mobile payments do not work and citizens are denied access to their money. Keeping cash in use is important when governments have the ability to shut off cell phone networks.

CURRENCY TRANSACTION REPORTS

This chapter has pointed out future problems like issues with CBDCs. Before ending let's focus on the present. Governments already have tools that move people away from cash and into electronic payments. Right now in the United States any cash transaction of $10,000 or more that involves a business must be reported to the federal government. This limit was set in 1970, when the rule was enshrined in the Bank Secrecy Act. Individuals or corporations that attempt to spend, deposit, or withdraw more than $10,000 are allowed to make these transactions. However, when this happens at a financial institution or business, like a car dealership, then the business must fill in a currency transaction report (CTR) and report details to the federal government.

The Treasury Department periodically analyzes the time and effort it takes to file these reports. In 2019 about 16 million CTRs were filed.

Although many financial institutions have automated much of the process, the government estimated it took over two million hours to fill in the reports at a cost of more than $50 million. These are huge figures for just the labor to fill and review paperwork in a single year.[15]

The CTR limit of $10,000 strangles the use of cash above this limit because filling in the report and explaining where the money comes from takes time. CTR limits have a chilling effect on cash use but no real impact on safety and security. Chapters 14 and 15 on crime, corruption, and terrorism suggest that in the half-century that US banks and businesses have been filling in CTR reports they appear to have little or no effect on making US society safer.

However, these chapters did not specifically check if the massive number of CTRs actually reduced criminal activity. In 2018 the Treasury Department's Inspector General checked. The Inspector General's scathing report titled "The Internal Revenue Service's Bank Secrecy Act Program Has Minimal Impact on Compliance" summarizes the ineffectiveness of CTRs.[16]

Given that the US government admits CTRs are not useful in reducing crime and it costs a small fortune to fill them in, it is time to rethink the need for the entire program. Rules that simply create paperwork and ensure a bureaucracy is employed are not helpful to a smoothly functioning society.

CONCLUSION

The experiences in this chapter are not theoretical. Many of us have temporarily experienced what it is like to be debanked. This happens when the bank suddenly locks your credit, debit, ATM, or phone account.

I once flew into Italy and spotted in the airport's baggage claim area a machine selling bus tickets to my hotel. The machine didn't take cash, only debit and credit cards. I tried buying a ticket but the machine rejected my first card. My backup card also failed. I do not know why but inserting both cards triggered a fraud alert and led two different banks to shut down the cards "for my personal safety." Luckily, I had cash and was able to get to my hotel room, where via email and text messages I was able to convince both banks to turn my cards back on. Nevertheless, for a short period of time, until I was able to convince both banks that no thief had my cards, I was effectively debanked. It is an unnerving experience to have no access to your bank accounts while in a foreign country and wonder how to pay for food, lodging, and transportation.

For innocent tourists, being debanked or temporarily losing access to funds is often a minor inconvenience. However, when governments debank people or shut down large swaths of the mobile phone networks in an attempt to restore peace, the resulting problems are an order of magnitude greater than what I experienced in that airport baggage area. A simple method of reducing the impact of debanking and a forced shutdown of telecommunications is to ensure cash stays in use in all parts of society.

CHAPTER EIGHTEEN

CAN BUSINESSES AND GOVERN-MENTS REFUSE TO TAKE CASH?

C an stores, restaurants, and even the government refuse to take your cash? The front of every piece of US currency states, "This note is legal tender for all debts public and private." Moreover, the statement that US currency is legal tender has been enshrined in federal law in various forms since the late 1800s. Doesn't this statement on every piece of currency and the various federal laws mean all kinds of organizations must accept US paper money?[1]

This might surprise you but the answer is no! It is perfectly legal for many places to refuse cash transactions. The question might have seemed hypothetical a few decades ago, but today many places have stopped accepting cash and only allow electronic payments.

Most airlines stopped accepting cash for in-flight purchases of food and beverages about 2010. Many toll roads and bridges no longer accept cash. Concession stands at almost all pro sports stadiums in the United States are cashless, which means people without credit or debit cards have a hard time getting a hot dog or a beer while watching a game. My office is across the street from Major League Baseball's Fenway Park whose policy is. "Fenway Park has transitioned to a fully cashless environment. For convenience and to improve speed of service, concession stands throughout the ballpark will only accept credit cards or touchless payment with smartphones."[2]

Even some large restaurant chains embrace the practice. A high-end US salad restaurant named Sweetgreen, with about 100 locations, stopped accepting cash in many of its stores for almost two years before reversing its policy.[3]

Even the US government doesn't really want to use its own money. Each year millions of people file federal income tax forms. Although the majority either get a refund or owe nothing, a substantial number owe the US government money. When I owed roughly $1,000 in taxes, I tried paying the IRS (Internal Revenue Service) with paper money. It was possible, but as the end of the chapter shows, it was not easy.

I advocate for national laws guaranteeing the acceptance of cash by all types of stores, transport, medical care, and other places people spend money. However, until these laws are universally passed, let's look at why some merchants refuse cash.

Business owners often tell me they don't want to accept cash because it increases the chance of stores being robbed and the temptation for employees to steal money. Although these are legitimate business concerns, when stores switch to electronic methods these kinds of crimes still happen; they just happen in different ways. For example, when someone uses a stolen credit card to buy something and the purchase is disputed, the store loses the money as well as the item purchased.

ARE THERE LAWS FORCING BUSINESSES TO TAKE CASH?

The ability for a store to refuse cash is stated on the US central bank website, which states: "There is no federal statute mandating that a private business, a person, or an organization must accept currency or coins as payment for goods or services. Private businesses are free to develop their own policies on whether to accept cash unless there is a state law that says otherwise."[4]

Let's take a look at that last sentence. The state of Massachusetts was one of the first places in 1978 to put a law on its books requiring all retail establishments to accept cash payments. The rule is simple and clear: "No retail establishment offering goods and services for sale shall discriminate against a cash buyer." In addition to Massachusetts there are about 15 other states from Arizona to Maine with legislation requiring some face-to-face businesses to accept cash.[5]

There are also city laws and ordinances that require retailers to accept cash. The cities of Chicago, New York City, Philadelphia, San Francisco, and Washington all have these laws. Philadelphia requires not only retail stores but also vending machines in the city to accept cash.[6] Beyond these state and city rules, legislation called the *Payment Choice Act* has been introduced into Congress a number of times to make cash acceptance a national law.[7]

These rules sound wonderful, but there are limits to their usefulness. First, they typically only cover retail establishments, which are usually stores.

This means the regulations don't cover restaurants, doctors, dentists, busses, taxis, motels, parking lots, phones, gyms, or a host of other types of businesses. These laws ensure cash can buy a bag of potato chips and soda at the local convenience store, but do not cover other important types of transactions like purchasing a cooked meal from a restaurant.[8]

Second, although the laws ensure cash is accepted, the rules say nothing about making cash convenient. The building where I teach has a food court selling sandwiches, soup, and snacks to go. To save costs the university eliminated human cashiers and installed a self-service checkout that only accepts electronic payments. Beside the checkout is a small sign that tells customers they can use cash, but need to find an employee to accept the money. The university switched to cashless payments to reduce staff, so finding an employee is tough.

Third, some organizations get around the laws by providing machines that accept cash and put it on a debit card. These machines are nicknamed *reverse ATMs*. For example, as mentioned, many sports stadiums do not accept cash for food, drink, and souvenirs at the concession stands. To use cash at Fenway Park, one of baseball's oldest stadiums, you have to find a cash-to-debit card machine located in the concourse before standing in line at the concession stand, which significantly adds to the hassle factor.

Another problem with reverse ATMs is that many charge a fee to provide a card and also a fee to reload cards. Yankee Stadium, another famous baseball park, charges a $3.50 convenience fee for their reverse ATMs, making going out to a sporting event an even more expensive experience for cash payers.[9]

Fourth, the penalty for not accepting cash is often small. Massachusetts's primary penalty for not accepting cash is a $500 fine set in 1978. Inflation since the law was enacted has steadily eroded this amount's deterrence.

The last problem is the most important issue. As mentioned every piece of cash states it is "legal tender for all debts public and private." This statement means the only circumstance when a business must accept the bill is when a person owes that company a debt. If no debt has been incurred, they are not legally required to take US currency. Businesses can legally reject cash if they tell a customer before any debt is incurred.

Imagine it is very late at night and your car needs gasoline. Many gas stations do not take large bills late at night. If the gas station requires customers to pay for gas before pumping it into their car, they have the legal right to refuse $50 and $100 bills. They do not have to accept large bills because until the customer has put gas into the car, the customer does not owe the station owner anything. However, if the customer is allowed to pump gasoline into the car first and then pay, the owner must accept all types of US bills because the customer has a debt to pay.

The same issue arises on airplanes. If you want to buy a drink, the airline doesn't have to accept cash as long as it requires you to pay for the drink up-front. Until you have drunk your beverage, you owe no debt to the airline. This is why airlines announce before doing drink service they don't accept cash onboard and airline staff ask for a credit or debit card before handing over the beverage.

TRYING TO PAY THE IRS WITH CASH

Businesses are not the only group using methods to discourage or prevent individuals from paying with cash. The US government makes it extremely difficult for people to pay the IRS their federal income tax with paper money. In the spirit of research, I decided to see just how hard the process was.

When I told friends and colleagues of my wish to pay the IRS in cash many burst out laughing. Others had comments ranging from "can you really do that?" to "why would anyone even try?" I explained that for years when teaching about money I noted the legal tender statement on the front of every piece of US currency. This statement seemed ironic because I couldn't figure out how to pay income taxes with paper currency.

A student found where the instructions for paying the government with paper money were buried, so I gave it a try. The five-step set of instructions hinted that paying cash directly is a time-consuming process and cash payers needed to start a month or two before taxes are due.[10]

Based on the instructions I completed my taxes early. I called the IRS office to schedule an appointment to see when and where I could pay. The IRS phone operator was cheerful, helpful, and tried her very best to dissuade me from paying in cash. She even offered to talk me through the steps to pay online.

The IRS has plenty of suggested alternatives to paying in cash. One method is using cash to "Buy a prepaid credit card and pay online." This sounds easy but turns out to have a lot of hidden fees. For example, as pointed out previously Walmart, one of the largest US retailers, offers a reloadable basic debit card. The card costs $1 to buy, $6 per month in fees, and $3 to load with cash at Walmart's registers and more elsewhere. Once the card is loaded with money, the businesses the IRS uses to accept debit card payments charge about $2.50 extra for each payment, which are limited to two per year. That is a minimum of $12.50 in extra fees to convert paper money into something the IRS wants to handle.

Another method the IRS offers is partnering with national chains, like CVS, Walgreens, 7-Eleven, and Family Dollar, to accept cash on its behalf. Their service fees are less, either $1.50 or $2.50 per payment. However, the steps needed to navigate these chains' online instructions before showing up at a retailer seemed almost as difficult as filling in the tax forms.

More important, these national chains have a $500 limit per payment and a $1,000 maximum amount accepted per year. This made the method unpractical for me and for most people who owe the IRS money because most people who owe the tax authority money owe more than $1,000.

A third choice the IRS offered was to use a credit or debit card. However, this method charged about 2.5% more for the convenience and didn't involve using cash at all.

After I declined all of the alternative payment offers, the IRS operator admitted there was an appointment available a few days later at the downtown Boston taxpayer assistance center. She mentioned I was lucky because the operator's schedule showed many in-person centers booked until May, long after taxes were due on April 15th.

In line with my research and to verify any difficulty or delay was due to IRS policies, I went to the bank for exact change in crisp new bills. My goal was not to cause pain to the tax authorities, like people who try to pay using wheelbarrows full of coins. I wanted a slim packet of high-denomination bills to make the counting as fast and error free as possible.

The day of my appointment I arrived at the downtown federal government building and went through a very rigorous airport-style screening where armed guards asked me to remove my belt, watch, coat, and hat. The lady behind me in line also had to take off her shoes.

Inside the IRS office the receptionist was polite and again suggested all the ways to pay without cash. After I declined, he asked me to take a seat in the waiting area filled with people clutching paperwork. He palmed his face with his hand as I walked away and shook his head – not a positive sign for my quest.

After I waited 30 minutes, another polite IRS employee came out and told me they could not accept cash that day because no courier was scheduled. She said current IRS rules require that a courier immediately take all cash to the bank because "holding cash was not safe" in the office. I found this amusing given the federal office building was swarming with armed guards and required extensive screening to enter.

They arranged for me to come back a week later when another cash payer was showing up and a courier was scheduled. This time I had more success. It took another 30 minutes with an IRS employee, but they were able to complete a multipart carbon form and give me a handwritten receipt saying my taxes were paid.

Paying the IRS with cash is possible, but it turned out to be onerous and time-consuming. When I asked various IRS employees about the number of other people who paid in cash they used phrases like "only a handful" or "just a few." The process discouraged me from trying to pay with cash again.

The front of every piece of US currency states the piece of paper is "legal tender for all debts public and private" and income taxes are most people's biggest public debt. However, making it so hard to pay in cash shows even the government discourages the use of their own paper money.

At this point most readers are probably shaking their heads wondering why anyone would go through the trouble of ever paying their taxes in cash. The answer is that some people and businesses have no choice. Currently, many states have legalized marijuana sales. However, the federal government considers selling marijuana illegal. Because federal rules control banks, the marijuana industry is a cash-only business. Marijuana dispensaries are big businesses in many states and they have to pay taxes to the federal government just like any other business, even though that same government considers their business dealings illegal. The easiest way for them to pay is with cash.

I talked with the CEO of a large chain of marijuana dispensaries, which has paid the IRS millions of dollars, all in cash. While she experiences similar problems to the ones I outlined, she also pointed out businesses have an additional hurdle that individuals do not encounter.

The IRS has strict laws prohibiting businesses from paying employment taxes in cash. Employment taxes entitle workers to Social Security and Medicare. The IRS's website clearly states, "Federal tax deposits must be made by electronic funds transfers (EFT)." People who pay in cash are subject to a "failure to deposit penalty," which applies to employers that don't make employment tax deposits in the right way.[11]

The penalty is up to 10% of the payment due, plus interest. The penalty might be waived if the business can prove to the IRS that no bank will give it an account, but barring that exception the IRS refuses to take cash for payment of a business's public debt to the federal government.

In my mind the "failure to deposit penalty" is clearly a case in which the federal government breaks its own promise that paper money is legal tender. I propose a simple remedy to all these problems in the next section.

WHY DOES THE IRS NOT WANT CASH?

Some business managers tell me cash is inefficient. Although I am not convinced of this fact, this might be a key reason why the government doesn't want tax payments in cash. Every year the US tax authority publishes the *IRS Data Book*, containing the key statistical tables tracking the number of returns, amount of refunds, and money collected.

One important measure of efficiency tracked in the book is the cost to the government of collecting $100 in revenue. The agency has dramatically improved its collections efficiency. Over the last half-century, the cost to collect $100 in taxes dropped by almost half without adjusting for inflation and by a factor of ten after adjustment.[12]

Minimizing the number of cash payers, who take time and effort, helps boost efficiency. But efficiency is not the only criteria by which the tax authorities should be judged. Governments wanting high compliance rates should make it as easy as possible to pay taxes.

There is a simple solution that enables the IRS to be efficient and ensures people can use legal tender to pay. The Code of Federal Regulations, which governs the IRS and other agencies, allows authorized banks to accept tax payments. The law doesn't specify what types of payments can be accepted. The law is quite broad and allows the Secretary of the Treasury to specify "the manner, times, and conditions" by which banks can collect the tax.[13]

This means if procedures existed, cash payers could walk into major banks, hand the teller paper money, and have the bank inform the IRS the amount paid. By using banks the IRS could avoid handling cash and cash payers could avoid dealing directly with the IRS. If these procedures existed then my experience, which started by getting cash at a major bank, delivering paper money to the IRS, only to see the money go right back to the bank, could have been much simpler.

Allowing people to pay their taxes in banks using cash would reduce the IRS's burden, ensure the federal government is not breaking the promise it makes that is enshrined on every piece of paper money, and ensure cash's continued usefulness.

CONCLUSION

Can stores, restaurants, and even the government refuse to take your cash? Many times the answer is yes. Even when there are rules and laws requiring a business or government agency to accept cash, there is no requirement, as I experienced with the IRS, that the process has to be easy.

So what is the answer to this problem? Chapter 20 suggests every country enact a rule requiring all government agencies and medium and large-sized companies to take cash. If cash is legal tender, we should be able to use it anywhere.

CHAPTER NINETEEN

WHO IS PUSHING THE WORLD TO GO CASHLESS?

If cash is so great and provides so much resilience, why doesn't everyone realize this? The answer is simple. A few groups that benefit greatly when cash disappears have become very effective at convincing all of us that getting rid of cash is best for society. The rest of this chapter talks about some of the different groups benefiting from a cashless society.

The chapter's key point is what is good for each of these groups is not necessarily good for creating a resilient society. As an example, going cashless makes a company like American Express much better off. However, making this company and its shareholders better off results in the entire economy becoming more brittle and prone to disruption any time one of the legs supporting the cashless economy collapses.

Electronic payments are not necessarily the natural outcome of living in the computer age. The push to a cashless society has not always existed. In the mid-1980s, a decade after Apple Computer started selling its first personal computer, the Bank for International Settlements surveyed how payments were made in major countries. The report stated, "However, there is little evidence that retailers and personal customers are dissatisfied with the instruments available under existing payments systems, and the banks might have to overcome considerable resistance for the launch of new instruments to be completely successful."[1] Since that report was issued banks and other financial groups, like credit card companies, have become very successful in convincing many retailers and individuals to give up cash.

It is important to point out there is a small countermovement touting the benefits of cash. One example of a trade association lobbying for more cash use is the International Currency Association, which runs a website called "Cash Matters," dedicated to pointing out the usefulness of cash.[2]

Another trade group promoting cash is ESTA, which is an association of European cash management companies. There are also more narrowly focused associations promoting cash such as those backed just by businesses that build and service cash machines and ATMs. The pro-cash and the pro-cashless groups discussed next are not disinterested parties. They are all seeking a share of the profits that come from facilitating payments.[3]

CREDIT AND DEBIT CARD COMPANY INCENTIVES

Some of the largest beneficiaries of a cashless society are credit and debit card companies. These organizations want to move customers away from cash and toward electronic payments because every time someone swipes, taps, or uses a mobile payment linked to a card they make money. Although they only make a small amount on every transaction, these cards are used billions of times each year.

To give you an idea of how profitable these cards are let's look at American Express, nicknamed Amex. This company is the third largest credit card company in the United States. In their annual report American Express shows their average US card member spent $24,000 in 2023 using their Amex card. The company kept an average cut, called the discount rate, of 2.3% of that spending and passed the rest on to merchants.

It is not only merchants who pay the company. Many American Express customers pay a wide variety of annual fees for the privilege of having a card. Some cards, which offered relatively few benefits, were free, like Amex's Blue card. However, others like the Amex's Gold, Platinum, or Black cards charge hefty annual fees, but provide customers with rewards. American Express reports the average annual fee paid across all their cards was almost $100.[4]

Combining just the discount rate and annual fees shows merchants and US cardholders gave American Express over $600 a year per card, just to avoid using cash. Amex also earns money from interest on loans to credit card customers who don't pay off their bill each month, and charges late fees when people don't pay on time.

American Express faces significant costs to earn that money. The company has spent billions building a massive computer and communications infrastructure to handle cashless payments. Each year the company has to pay about 75,000 employees, many to handle customer problems. Plus, the company incurs bad debts, because not every customer pays their bill. There are also large costs to handle fraud, advertising, taxes, and a host of other expenses.

Even with these charges American Express is a very profitable company. It earned over $8 billion in profits in 2023. Dividing this $8 billion figure by the roughly 140 million active American Express cards shows each card provided the company with an average of over $60 in profit. That is a nice business to be in, which is one reason why so many credit card companies are trying to convince people to use their products.

Visa and Mastercard are two other companies doing electronic payments. Neither issues cards; instead, banks issue cards with the Visa and Mastercard logos on them. These two companies provide the backend systems that do the actual transactions, which move money from the buyer's bank account to the seller's. Because Visa and Mastercard provide only the backend systems, these companies don't earn annual card fees or interest on credit card balances like American Express.

Instead, Visa, MasterCard, and other payment processors primarily earn money on something called the *interchange fee*. This fee, which is not very large, is their charge for acting as an intermediary and is discussed in more detail in Chapter 10, on pricing. Visa and Mastercard's annual reports show they make about 8¢ profit on each transaction that goes through their respective systems. Eight cents doesn't sound like much, but 8¢ times billions of transactions translates into large profits. Mastercard's annual profits were over $11 billion and Visa's profits were over $17 billion. Add in American Express' profits of $8 billion and these three companies' annual profits were over $36 billion, or more than $100 for every person living in the United States.

All of these companies are proud of what they do and are clear about their intention to push for a cashless society. In one of Visa's annual reports the company states, "Visa's mission is to accelerate the electronification of commerce." Although not many people ever say or write "electronification," its meaning is clear: replacing paper money with electronic payments.[5]

CREDIT AND DEBIT CARD COMPANY GROWTH

Large profits create a simple incentive for credit and debit card companies. The more people swipe, tap, or use mobile payments the more money they earn. More important, credit card companies are a classic example of a high fixed cost, but very low marginal cost industry. High fixed costs mean it costs credit and debit card companies a lot of money to create their cashless networks. High fixed cost industries are hard for competitors to break into because few companies have the financial and people resources. This reduces competition. Low marginal costs mean once these networks are in place it costs the company almost nothing to process one more transaction. Once the network is paid for, then each additional transaction is almost pure profit.

To provide an idea of how large these companies are, Table 19.1 shows some key facts about five of the world's six major credit and debit card

Table 19.1   Key Data on Five Major Credit Card Companies in 2022

	Visa	Mastercard	American Express	JCB	Diners Club Discover	Total
Payments volume (trillions US$)	$11.7	$6.6	$1.5	$0.3	$0.2	**$20.3**
Number of transactions (billions)	260	150	10	6	4	**430**
Average transaction size (US$)	$45	$44	$154	$52	$61	**$47**
Number of cards (billions)	4.2	2.7	0.1	0.2	.08	**7.2**

companies.[6] For those readers not familiar with JCB, this is Japan's largest credit card organization.

Table 19.1 actually underestimates the size of credit and debit card transactions for two reasons. First, China's UnionPay, which is a state-operated enterprise, is not part of the table because it does not publicly reveal statistics. Estimates suggest UnionPay has over 9 billion cards in circulation, making it the world's biggest cashless payment company.[7] Second, there are many other companies that issue credit or debit cards. This table only covers five of the biggest.

The top row of Table 19.1 shows that customers used these five companies in 2022 to make over $20 trillion of payments. World gross domestic product (GDP) in that year was about $100 trillion. That means credit and debit card payments from these big players were one-fifth of the world's annual output.

The second row of Table 19.1 shows these five companies reported processing over 400 billion transactions. The world's population then was about 8 billion people. This means these five companies handled 50 cashless transactions for every person alive in the world in just that year!

The third line of Table 19.1 shows not only are there a huge number of transactions, but the average transaction size is not trivial. The smallest, at $44, was made by the typical Mastercard user. The largest, at $154, was by an American Express customer.

The bottom line of Table 19.1 shows these five companies have distributed over seven billion cards. Plus, China's UnionPay has distributed billions of cards. This means if cards were evenly distributed, and they are not, there would be more than one credit or debit card for every person in the world.

Not only are the numbers large, the total payments flowing through these five major cashless payment companies' networks are growing dramatically over time. In 2006 these five companies processed about $4.3 trillion of payments. By 2022 these five handled over $20 trillion. In less than two decades the amount of money flowing through these companies increased by almost a factor of five times!

SMALLER CREDIT CARD COMPANIES

This book focuses on giant credit card companies, like Visa and Mastercard, because they are ubiquitous. However, there are many businesses beyond these giants that issue credit cards. Every five years the US government runs a business census designed to capture all companies. The census does not track profits; instead it tracks revenue, which is money coming in. The latest census found over 600 credit card issuing establishments had almost $130 billion of revenue from interchange, overdraft, and annual fees.[8] Based on census data, over 40% of the US credit card issuing market is held by smaller companies and brands not shown in Table 19.1.

Many of these smaller credit card companies issue private label cards that are used for specialized tasks or only in one store. One of the most famous private label credit cards was created by Sears, which was one of the biggest retailers before going bankrupt. It started offering customers credit before World War I and its cards were ubiquitous among middle-class families. Sears transitioned this private card to the mass market by creating the general purpose Discover Card in the mid-1980s.

Today, other large retailers still offer private credit cards that work only in their stores or gasoline stations. Macy's, a large department store based in New York, offers customers two types of credit cards: a store card that only works in Macy's and one cobranded with American Express, which works anywhere Amex cards are accepted. Together these cards are extremely profitable. Macy's annual report shows one-third of their annual profit came from customers using these two credit cards. Only two-thirds of their profit came from their core business of selling clothes, shoes, cosmetics, and housewares.[9] All these profits are the reason credit card companies push for more customers.

BANKS' INCENTIVES

Banks also want to move customers away from cash and toward electronic money and payments for three reasons. First, like the credit and debit card companies previously discussed, banks make money when their customers swipe, insert, or use mobile payments tied to a bank's card.

Banks, however, earn money a different way than companies like Visa and Mastercard, which get a cut of every transaction. Let's use Citi, a large New York–focused bank, as an example. In 2021, Citi reported their worldwide credit card division had a profit of $6.9 billion.[10]

However, Citi didn't make all this money from charging merchants or customers annual fees for using their cards. In a separate section of Citi's annual report labeled "Commissions and Fees" Citi shows they earned over $10 billion in interchange and other credit card fees, but gave back over $10 billion in rewards to customers and merchants. Roughly whatever Citi earned on credit card transactions was rebated back.[11]

So how did Citi earn its money? It earned much of it by making loans to customers who didn't pay off their balance in full each month. Citi reports that at the end of 2021 the total credit line on all their cards was a bit over $700 billion. This means if everyone with a Citi credit card charged each card to the limit, Citi would be on the hook for $700 billion.

Many of Citi's credit card customers didn't max out their cards and many pay off their balances each month. However, some customers don't pay off their bill each month. This automatically generates an unsecured loan from the bank. Citi reports they loaned out about $152 billion to these credit card customers. This means Citi card holders carried balances from month-to-month of about one-fifth their credit limit.[12]

These unsecured loans charge high interest rates. Government reports show the average US interest rate on credit card loans was 15%. That high interest rate on unpaid balances brought in billions in profits to Citi.

Beyond the large amount of money earned by charging interest, Citi and other large credit card issuers earn money from fees when people charge more than their credit limit or take a cash advance.[13]

The second reason banks want a cashless society is that it forces everyone to become part of the financial system and a bank customer. As discussed previously there are many people around the world who don't use banks and have little or no ties to financial institutions.

Bringing these customers into the formal financial sector is good business for banks. It raises revenue because bank accounts cost money, doing transactions costs money, and if a customer makes a financial mistake such as spending more than what is in their account the bank can level punitive charges.

Let's take Bank of America, another major US bank, as an example. Its 2021 annual report shows that it earned $3.7 billion in just consumer service fees on checking, savings, and other deposit accounts.[14] The bank's annual report claims it services approximately 67 million consumer and small business clients. That works out to about $55 in fees a year for each client. Although $55 doesn't seem like much, for poor people it can represent a financial hardship.

The third reason for going cashless is that banks want to lower their costs. Accepting cash and distributing cash is more expensive for banks because cash is labor intensive compared to doing things electronically. ATMs need to be refilled with cash periodically. Coins are heavy to move. Tellers need to be hired to count cash and distribute it to customers that don't want to use ATMs. Security teams need to be hired to guard cash.

Plus, these costs vary depending on the local crime rate. In areas with high crime, banks are more heavily fortified than in low-crime areas. I live in a low-crime neighborhood. On my way to work I often watch my bank getting its cash delivery. An armored car pulls up to the front door and typically two workers get out. One pushes a hand truck with money and the other lightly armed person guards the process. This is a very different experience than what happens in high-crime areas. I was once in a high-end shopping mall in Cape Town, South Africa, which at the time had a very high crime rate. A team pulled up to refill the ATMs in the mall. The refilling exercise was quite thrilling. It was like watching a Hollywood war movie with a large team of extremely heavily armed, muscled men fanning out ahead and behind the person pushing the hand truck with money.

A cashless society reduces a bank's costs because after a system is set up, electronic transactions are far cheaper and faster than handling cash. A cashless system enables banks to handle more transactions with fewer employees. Last, in a cashless society banks do not have to pay to physically move money around.

GOVERNMENT'S INCENTIVE

It is not only banks and credit card companies that want a cashless world. Strange as it might seem many governments don't like cash. This is strange because many governments around the world print their own money. You would think the organization that creates cash would support it. Unfortunately, many people in government would like to do away with paper money because a cashless society is easier to tax and police. Being cashless enables government to trace funds used for terrorism and illegal activities after the fact.

Governments have been making it harder over time to make large cash payments. In May 2016 the European central bank announced it was stopping the production and issuance of the €500 banknote.

In July 1969, the US government eliminated its four largest bills in circulation: the $500, $1,000, $5,000, and $10,000 notes. This left the $100 bill as the largest note in circulation in the United States. Because of inflation the value of the $100 bill has been steadily falling over time, making it less useful for facilitating large transactions.

Large cash transactions also now need to be reported to government authorities, reducing the desire of people and businesses to handle cash. Both the United States and Canada require any business that receives a cash payment over $10,000 to promptly file a form with the government providing details on who brought in the cash, who received the cash, and the purpose of the transaction.[15]

Another reason governments want to eliminate cash is to reduce the number of under-the-table and off-book transactions. This tries to ensure that taxes are collected for all economic activities, instead of just some.

All societies have both formal and informal sectors. The formal sector reports all transactions to the government, pays taxes, and follows government regulations. The informal sector does not. The informal sector is a cash-based economy with no governmental oversight. Large supermarket chains are part of the formal sector, but farmers selling fruit and vegetables along the roadside are part of the informal sector. Parts of the informal sector are carrying out illegal activities such as prostitution, gambling, or selling drugs. Other parts, like hiring teenagers to babysit or mow a lawn, are legal but are done informally because of the high burden of reporting these activities to the government.

By eliminating cash, governments are trying to reduce the size of the informal sector. This theoretically boosts government taxes and reduces illegal activity, but does not appear to have any impact in practice. It also boosts reported GDP, because the government now has more accurate data on economic activity.

However, eliminating the informal sector does not necessarily improve society's welfare because all activities are now monitored and covered by government rules. For example, when my children were little I used to occasionally hire the teenager next door to babysit so my wife and I could go out. It was an informal transaction. At the end of the night I would give her cash for her efforts.

This transaction was illegal first because it was undeclared income. The government expected me to report paying her and she was expected to pay taxes on her earnings. More important, babysitting broke child labor laws. In my state 14- and 15-year-olds cannot work weeknights, from 7 p.m. to 7 a.m., during months when school is in session.[16]

The child labor laws were put in place to eliminate children working in sweat shops, factories, and mines. However, the laws are rigid and make no exceptions for the type of duties. They don't allow the teenager next door to be paid to sit in my home and do their homework while my children sleep. Being forced to file the paperwork with the government every time I needed a babysitter would have eliminated my desire to hire the teenager next door.

HIGH TECHNOLOGY'S INCENTIVE

The third group pushing society to use electronic payments is high-technology computer companies. There are many large computer companies that are built around the idea of cashless payments. Companies like Amazon, Apple, and Google want us wedded to our phones and computers. Being cashless helps these companies grow.

Many people use Amazon for shopping. There is no way to directly hand Amazon currency to pay for a purchase. Amazon has a web page that tells customers how to pay for purchases with cash, but the method is convoluted. First, you need to go to a store or supermarket that sells Amazon gift cards and accepts cash. With cash you buy an Amazon gift card. Then you log in to your online account and add the gift card to your balance. You now have the ability to spend money up to the amount of the gift card.[17]

This workaround has three problems. First, Amazon's current rules only give customers the ability to add between $5 and $500, making larger purchases problematic. Second, customers must be computer literate, able to navigate a complex sequence of steps, have access to a smartphone or computer, and have an internet connection. Not everyone in society has these skills. Last, if too much money was added it is very difficult to get the extra money back in cash.

High-tech companies have a long history of not wanting cash. In 2010 Apple Computer released the iPad. The iPad was one of the first tablet computers and was an extremely popular item when released. A disabled woman living on a fixed income named Diane Campbell walked into Apple's Palo Alto, California, store and tried to buy an iPad with cash. She was refused by the manager and told only debit or credit cards were allowed in Apple stores. It took Apple a while, but after a spate of bad press they reversed their policy and finally allowed Ms. Campbell and others to pay cash for Apple products.[18]

Beyond wanting to make payment processing easier, these companies also want a piece of the profits earned by making cashless payments. Apple Computer is a very successful company. Their products like the iPhone are sold worldwide. Since 2014 they have encouraged customers to use their mobile wallet called *Apple Pay*. The idea is simple: instead of carrying around cash or credit cards a user pays by simply waving their phone at the register when checking out. Apple's marketing trumpets it as "faster and easier than using cards or cash" plus it is "safer than touching buttons and exchanging cash."

When Apple introduced this product it was able to convince some of the United States' largest banks like JP Morgan Chase and Bank of America to give Apple 0.15% of every credit card transaction their customers made with Apple Pay. That amount doesn't sound like much. It is only 15¢ on a $100 purchase.

Apple does not break out in its financial reports how much money it earns from Apple Pay. However, PYMNTS.com estimates in 2021 people spent $90 billion using this app. If that figure is accurate then Apple earned $135 million in 2021 just by being one in a long chain of intermediaries that takes a small cut of a purchase when people check out. Beyond those millions of dollars, Apple also gains valuable information on where its customers shop and how much they spend.[19]

It is not just high-technology companies selling actual products that are encouraging the shift to a cashless economy but also companies selling virtual products. One example is Roblox, an online game platform that builds a virtual world aimed at youngsters. Players create their own avatars and spend virtual money to clothe and accessorize their virtual counterparts. This virtual money is training children to reject paper money, which is useless online.[20]

RETAILERS' INCENTIVE

Some retailers, especially those merchants that sell things that are discretionary or impulse purchase items, are in favor of a cashless economy. However, some are not. As Chapter 7 showed, people spend more when using credit or debit cards than they do when paying with cash. By accepting electronic payments retailers can boost sales.

Because the electronic payments industry takes a relatively large cut or payment from each sale a number of merchants have a cash-only policy or, when legal, add an extra charge to cashless payments. An increasing number of merchants simply have signs encouraging the use of cash. Typically, these merchants are selling items or services that are viewed as necessities. My favorite bagel and coffee shop in New York City imposes a surcharge on credit or debit card purchases. The owner likely sees no major boost in sales using cashless payments for two reasons. First, the shop is within a block of two different banks with ATMs, ensuring customers can easily get cash. More important, there is little in the shop that people view as an impulse purchase. Although the exact order varies, most people standing in line order a drink and a bagel sandwich. The cost per person of each order is small and roughly the same so it is easy to plan ahead and carry enough cash.

Conversely, I enjoy shopping at Costco, which is a large warehouse store filled with both necessities and splurge items. Costco sells everything from unbranded milk, eggs and bread to designer watches and diamond rings. Costco makes it interesting to shop because it has a treasure hunt atmosphere. The company says this on their website:

> One of the most exciting things about shopping in our warehouses is you never know the kind of incredible deals you'll find from one visit to the next! Costco members know the trick to getting the best value on exclusive or one-time-buy merchandise: Visit often![21]

Because of the treasure hunt atmosphere I never know ahead of time how much I will spend when walking into the store. Having the ability to make electronic payments is useful for Costco because it encourages me to splurge when I don't have enough cash in my wallet to pay for items.

FINANCIAL TECHNOLOGY INCENTIVES

Over the past decades a large number of financial technology, or fintech, companies have sprung up. These companies are providing a variety of alternatives to using cash, credit, or debit cards. Several automate moving money directly from one person to another. Examples of these companies are well-known names like PayPal, AliPay, and Zelle.

Other examples of fintech companies are those that offer buy now and pay in installment plans. Examples are companies like Klarna and AfterPay.

AfterPay was bought by Square, another fintech company. In their last annual report before being purchased, they pushed ideas like financial inclusion and being fair to everyone. The reality is that they take a large cut from each merchant's sale, simply by guaranteeing the merchants their funds and letting customers pay over two months instead of instantly.

CONCLUSION

This chapter reviewed the reasons why powerful organizations are pushing society toward cashless payments. However, what is best for banks, credit card companies, technology companies, and even some governments is not necessarily what is best in the long run for society. These groups are focused on boosting their profits and ensuring their survival in the competitive business world, not making individuals better off.

Before ending I want to tell the story about the demise of electric street cars in Los Angeles (LA), California. This historical episode, when powerful groups tried to eliminate a public good, has many parallels to the forces seeking to eliminate cash use today.

Los Angeles (LA), California, is a spread-out metropolis both today and a century ago. A century ago it had a vibrant public transportation network in the form of electric street cars that ran on train tracks powered via overhead wires. In the 1930s LA had over 1,000 miles of electric street car routes, operated by two companies.

The street cars faced many of the same complaints people make today about using cash. Many people felt the street cars were not convenient, they were slow, and they were unhealthy when jammed with people. No matter how people felt, many still used street cars. Use shot up dramatically during World War II when gasoline was rationed and it was difficult to buy or repair a car because automobile plants shifted to producing military vehicles.

The end of the war marked the end of the line for street cars for three reasons. First, the war effort transformed the oil, tire, and car industries into behemoths. These industries wanted new outlets for the goods produced in the massive factories they built during the war. Second, civilians and returning soldiers were tired of rationing and other war privations. They wanted to spend money on things like cars, which promised freedom. Last, the heavy use during the war meant the street car system needed a major capital upgrade that would cost much money.

Combined, these factors made the short-term decision easy; in the mid-1940s most of LA's street car system was sold to a company called National City Lines. National City was partly owned by the car maker General Motors, the oil companies Standard Oil of California and Philips Petroleum, plus the Firestone tire company. These powerful forces had no incentive to maintain the system so National City started ripping up LA's electric street car tracks.

The street car system was replaced with buses built by General Motors that ran on oil from companies like Standard Oil of California and used Firestone tires. There is a long-running academic debate over whether self-serving corporate interests purposely killed the street car system or it would have died on its own. Either way, starting in the mid-1940s commuters had only two choices: drive their own cars or take the public bus.[22]

Today, Los Angeles roads and highways are choked with traffic. It often takes hours in a car or bus to cross the city. As long ago as 1990 a local newspaper wrote how people were putting refrigerators, desks, and televisions in their cars to handle being stuck in horrendous traffic.[23]

Destroying the old electric street car system temporarily made things better, but today the crush of traffic has made things much worse. To fight this congestion, the city is slowly rebuilding public transport. There are now four light rail lines, the new name for electric street cars, and two subways. Many are along the same routes the electric trolleys traveled prior to being dismantled. The difference is that rebuilding LA's public transport is now costing the public billions because the old system was completely dismantled.

Like the powerful forces facing the LA street cars almost a century ago, powerful forces and organizations want to eliminate cash. These powerful organizations are not evil. They are simply trying to boost their revenue or reduce their costs. Nevertheless, if they succeed, society will likely spend large amounts to revive paper money once the problems of an entirely electronic payment world are understood.

CHAPTER TWENTY

CONCLUSION

WHAT TO DO TO ENSURE CASH DOES NOT DISAPPEAR

The goal of this book is to convince you to use cash more often. Feel free to continue using electronic forms of payments. Just don't overlook cash. Paper money is not simply for keeping a stash around for emergencies. As Chapter 3 pointed out, if everyone stops using cash to pay for goods and services, then emergency stashes will be useless because no business or government agency will have the ability to accept paper money when needed. In national defense terms, frequently using cash ensures it will work in emergencies.

This chapter concludes with some simple ideas to ensure cash still has a place in society. The first part focuses on what individuals can do, and the second part focuses on policy ideas that need more collective action. For example, one way to combat the trend toward electronic payments is to require a few select industries, like those that deal with selling "sin" products like marijuana, liquor, or lottery tickets, to accept only cash. Another idea is to bring back larger denomination bills to make larger cash transactions simpler and faster.

The ideas in this chapter are not meant to be all-inclusive. They are primarily designed to start discussion and provide some simple methods to ensure paper money does not become an extinct item found only in museums. Implementing some of these ideas will ensure cash stays as a vital part of society.

INDIVIDUAL ACTIONS

There are a number of actions individuals can do to ensure paper money continues to be used in society.

Boosting your use of paper money is the most important action anyone can do. To ensure this happens, jot down every time you actually use cash. People track their calories, steps walked, and even minutes of sleep. Tracking cash use is even simpler and just as important.

It is easy to get in the habit. When faced with small and medium purchases, try to avoid using electronic payments like credit cards. For example, pay for restaurant meals and takeout food only with paper money. Some people like using credit cards because it is easier to return purchases. Given it is almost impossible to ask for money back after eating food, pay with paper money at restaurants. The waitstaff will appreciate this because they take cash tips home that very day. Tips given via electronic payment are often held back until payday.

Second, make sure you always carry some paper money in a wallet, purse, or pocket. It is impossible to spend cash if you only have electronic means of payment at your disposal. The goal is not to carry so much you become a target for pickpockets, purse snatchers, and muggers, but enough to make purchases when needed.

Third, financial planners suggest everyone should have some emergency savings. Instead of keeping all your emergency savings in a bank, keep some of it in cash at home. This way when a natural disaster strikes or some other calamity happens, like a widespread power failure, you will still be able to purchase goods and services.

You don't need to keep a huge amount of cash at home. The goal is not to make your home a target for thieves. However, it should be enough money to cover regular spending for a few weeks, plus enough extra to get yourself and any family members out of harm's way.

Fourth, the next time you are thinking of giving someone a gift card, give cash instead. Cash is more useful for birthdays, weddings, and other special occasions than a gift card, which ties the recipient to a specific company and type of purchase.

Last, be an evangelist. Tell other people about the various reasons to use cash. You don't need to promote every reason given in this book. Instead, use the ones that resonate most deeply for you. Like many things in life, small differences matter. Making small changes so that you use cash more often has a profound impact when millions also make these same small changes.

COLLECTIVE ADVOCACY

Although individuals can do things to promote the use of cash, there is also a need for more collective action, especially at the country level. We need both nonprofit and government agencies to act as advocates for using cash. For example, Spain has a cash advocacy group called *Plataforma Denaria* and another European organization is called *Cash Essentials*, which provides news, reports, and blog articles on the future of cash. The United States needs a similar organization.

The US government also needs to become involved. There are numerous agencies that advocate for particular groups. For example, the Small Business Administration is a government agency devoted to starting and growing small businesses. We need government agencies that act as cash advocates. Three potential agencies come to mind. First, the Bureau of Printing and Engraving is a logical choice because they print paper money. Second is the Federal Reserve System's Cash Product Office, which is responsible for distributing paper money. Last is the Consumer and Financial Protection Bureau, which is charged with protecting citizens from predatory financial services and already does research into debit cards, credit cards, and buy-now-pay-later services. It does not matter which of these agencies takes the leadership role in promoting cash. It is only important that governments promote their own currency.

BUREAUCRATIC FIXES – ATMS

As people slow down their use of cash, banks are closing locations and removing ATMs. Figure 20.1 shows the number of US banks and branches peaked in 2008 at about 90,000 and has been steadily falling since. From a bank's perspective, branch locations and other physical locations like ATMs are expensive. Each needs periodic restocking with cash, staff to handle customers, maintenance workers to clean the floors, and security people to guard or check the premises. Because a bank's goal is to maximize profits, getting rid of branches and ATMs makes sense.

However, from a societal perspective, bank locations and ATMs are crucial for maintaining cash. If these physical locations disappear it will be harder to get and deposit currency when needed.

Figure 20.1 Number of banks and bank branches in the United States.

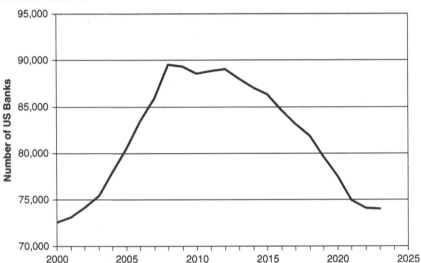

Banks are heavily regulated because the industry's quest for profits leads to periodic banking panics and collapses. Regulators can easily write new rules that ensure banks keep a minimum number of branches and ATMs in service within a geographic area.

Banks will lobby heavily against the concept of regulations requiring a minimum number of branches or ATMs. However, there is a long history of government mandates that fix societal issues against industry wishes. The auto industry lobbied heavily against seat belt and air bag mandates. Home builders have pushed back against rules requiring smoke detectors, energy-efficient windows, and low-water-use plumbing products. Utilities have railed against clean air and clean water rules. All of these regulations have made life safer and better for millions. Rules that ensure the infrastructure needed to move, use, and store cash will also help society.

It is not only ATMs that are a problem, but also reverse ATMs. As I mentioned, reverse ATMs are machines that take in cash and spit out a preloaded debit card for use in cashless venues. Many of these reverse ATMs charge fees to procure a card and fees to reload a card with money. At a minimum, fees for reverse ATMs should be outlawed. However, legislators should think more broadly and require reverse ATMs to refund unused amounts in cash.

INFLATION ADJUSTMENT FOR CURRENCY TRANSACTION REPORTS

As mentioned in Chapter 17, any cash transaction of $10,000 or more in the United States must be reported to the federal government with a currency transaction report (CTR). The CTR limit of $10,000 strangles the use of cash above this limit because filling in the report and explaining where the money comes from takes time.

The CTR's limit was set in 1970 and has not been adjusted since. Inflation, however, has steadily eroded the value of the US dollar. From 1970 to 2023, consumer prices have increased by over eight times. Ten thousand dollars from 1970 adjusted for inflation was over $80,000 when this book was written so the CTR limit could be increased tenfold.

The United States updates income tax brackets and Social Security payments for inflation. It is time to update money laundering reporting limits for inflation and reduce the paperwork burden. The CTR limit should be raised from $10,000 to $100,000. This will reset the limit to roughly the level it was when Congress first passed the law mandating the forms. There is precedence for reducing the burden caused by CTR forms; in the 1990s Congress directed the US Treasury to reduce the number of CTRs by 30%.[1]

Although raising the limit is a useful first step, Congress should also add an automatic inflation-adjustment clause to the laws mandating CTR forms so that future inflation does not result again in the current situation in which millions of CTR forms are filled in but not examined.

BRING BACK LARGE BILLS

Central banks and government treasury departments around the world have removed large denomination bills from circulation. In 2000, Canada started removing the $1,000 Canadian bill from circulation. There were fewer than four million of these bills in circulation when it started. The Bank of Canada stated when announcing this decision that it felt removal "will have little impact on Canada's currency system and its ability to meet the needs of businesses and individuals." Then in 2021 the Bank stopped considering the $1,000 bill as legal tender. This meant it was no longer an official means of settling debts.

The European central bank, which coordinates the printing of euros by 19 countries, stopped producing the €500 banknote in 2019. Recall from Chapter 15 that this banknote was allegedly nicknamed by criminals the "Bin Laden." Bin Laden, the mastermind behind the September 11, 2001, attacks in the United States, supposedly funded his network using high-value euro notes. Eliminating this note was designed to hamper cash transactions by organized crime and terrorists.[2]

The European central bank, however, continues to keep the €500 banknote as legal tender and only takes the bills out of circulation when they come back into the banking system. This means large numbers of these bills are still in use. In 2021 about 381 million €500 banknotes were still in circulation, down from a peak of 522 million in 2018.[3]

Recently, some prominent economists have suggested countries should move to a cashless society, with actions like eliminating the $100 bill. Kenneth Rogoff, a Harvard professor who was also chief economist of the International Monetary Fund, wrote in the *Wall Street Journal* that going cashless reduces crime. Rogoff's idea was that going cashless ensures tax cheats, drug lords, gangs, and terrorists cannot easily fund their activities. If only small bills are allowed, then people making illegal payments need briefcases stacked with huge numbers of small denomination bills like $5s and $10s. This is much more difficult than discreetly using a small envelope filled with a few very high-value notes.[4]

This book has argued that the linkage between cash and crime was either weak or nonexistent. If crime is not substantially affected by the availability of cash, then governments need to bring back higher value notes like the US$500 bills and European €500 notes. In a disaster it is much easier to tuck a few large bills into your clothes than to lug wads of small currency. Higher denominations like $500 bills will enable larger transactions when cashless methods are unavailable.

It is relatively easy to see how large denomination bills make it easy to transport a large amount of money. The Federal Reserve Bank of Chicago has a money museum as part of its outreach to the general public. One of my favorite attractions at this museum is the money cube. The cube contains $1 million, all in $1 bills. The cube is huge at about four feet to each side. Because each dollar bill weighs 1 gram the money inside the cube weighs over a ton.[5]

The opposite of the giant cube was one of Las Vegas's most famous attractions for decades. Binion's Horseshoe Casino had a small wall of $1 million comprised of one hundred $10,000 bills. Tourists stood next to the wall to have their picture taken alongside a "million dollars." Cash in the United States is bundled into small bricks called a *strap*, which easily fit into most purses or jacket pockets. No matter what the denomination, a strap in the United States contains 100 notes. Binion's Casino display needed just one strap of $10,000 bills to create their $1 million display. The Chicago Fed's museum needed 10,000 straps for their cube.

Binion's Casino display was a tourist attraction because the US government eliminated large denomination bills in 1969. Until 1969 it was possible to go to a major bank and get $500, $1,000, $5,000, and $10,000 bills. Today, these bills are primarily found in the hands of collectors. Their scarcity boosts their actual price well beyond the face value of the bill. When Binion's Casino sold the million dollar collection, a coin dealer estimated each bill was worth about double its face value.

Figure 20.2 shows how much the $500 bill has been worth over time. In 1969, when the $500 bill was taken out of circulation it purchased $500. However, inflation has steadily eroded the value of the $500 bill. When this book was written, the $500 bill had experienced a reduction in purchasing power of 10 times.[6]

Figure 20.2 shows that if the $500 bill were brought back in 2020, it would purchase less than what the $100 bill purchased in 1967 when the large denomination bills were taken out of circulation. If $100 bills did not cause problems for society in 1967, why would a $500 bill be problematic today, when it is worth less?

Figure 20.2   How much a US$500 bill purchases.

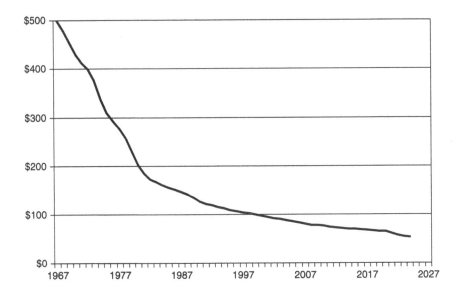

One simple idea is to automatically produce new higher denomination bills whenever total inflation crosses a predetermined level. For example, each time cumulative inflation hits 100%, the government could automatically produce a new high denomination bill whose value is double the value of the previous highest piece of currency in circulation.

LEGISLATION DESIGNED TO ENSURE STORES TAKE CASH

For public officials interested in laws that will have an impact on helping cash regain its allure, there is one set of laws to pass and another to repeal. We need to pass laws that prevent industries from being cashless.

Each piece of currency states the "note is legal tender." However, as the US Federal Reserve points out, "There is, however, no Federal statute mandating that a private business, a person, or an organization must accept currency or coins as payment for goods or services. Private businesses are free to develop their own policies on whether to accept cash unless there is a state law which says otherwise."[7]

Preventing customers from paying with cash is unethical because not all people have access to credit or debit cards. Nor does everyone want to be formally connected to the financial sector. Laws that prevent this have already been passed in cities like Philadelphia and states like Massachusetts. However, the laws that have been passed have a large loophole that businesses are exploiting. Massachusetts passed its laws decades ago, but the law deals only with "retail establishments," and the exact definition of a retail establishment is unclear.

Restaurants, bars, busses, planes, parking garages, gyms, and a host of other types of businesses are not subject to the law and can legally refuse cash. The laws mandating accepting cash need to be broadly based and not just focused on convenience stores or supermarkets. The present definition means many key establishments that people use in daily life are not covered. You can buy meat and vegetables at a supermarket with cash, but if you don't have a kitchen and only have cash, you can't go to a restaurant that is cashless. Transportations like buses, taxis, trains, and planes are not covered. This means cash-only customers can be forced to walk.

Communications are not covered. The ability to communicate is now considered a right in some places. California provides free cell phones to the homeless and people living in extreme poverty. What about those that are just getting by? A retail law can shut out a portion of society from getting phone service. People might be too rich to get free phone service, but too poor to have a credit card.

Major entertainment venues like professional sports stadiums are not covered and most are now cashless. This is surprising because many sports stadiums were built or subsidized using taxpayer money. This means poor people are taxed once to support homes for professional sports and then taxed a second time by having to use a reverse ATM to buy tickets to see a game.

The set of laws that need to be repealed are those that prevent cash discount programs.[8] In October 2011, the Durbin amendment of the Dodd-Frank Act allowed merchants to offer their customers a discount on cash transactions. The specific language in the Durbin amendment was that merchants could, if they wished, add a credit card surcharge. Credit card customers would then pay more and cash customers would pay less.

Electronic payment businesses hated the Durbin amendment because it cut into their profits. They have been able to convince ten states and one territory to effectively strip the Durbin amendment of its power. It is now illegal to have a cash discount program in California, Colorado, Connecticut, Florida, Kansas, Maine, Massachusetts, New York, Oklahoma, Texas, and Puerto Rico. These states passed laws prohibiting merchants from adding any credit card surcharges. By barring surcharges, they blocked the Durbin amendment's goal of making it easier to use cash. Rolling back legislation in these ten states is another step in making cash more widely accepted.

SIN PURCHASES

Another thing policymakers and politicians can do to ensure cash remains a useful tool in society is to mandate "sin" purchases be made only with cash. Allowing electronic payments results in a frictionless purchase experience. This makes sin purchases easier. If we want to reduce the amount and frequency of sin purchases, these industries should be cash only.

For example, as discussed in Chapter 18, many US states now allow residents to legally purchase marijuana. Federal law, however, stills considers marijuana an illegal substance. And because federal laws control how banks operate, the large interstate banks do not accept cash from or maintain accounts for marijuana businesses. This mismatch between federal and state laws means right now marijuana businesses in places like California, Colorado, and Massachusetts are forced to be all-cash businesses.

Marijuana use was and still is something that large parts of society want to control. That is why for years it was illegal across the entire United States and is still illegal in many countries around the world. There are many different ways of controlling its use.[9] The simplest is preventing the industry from accepting electronic payments. The marijuana industry should continue to be a cash-only business for purchases. Being cash only reduces demand for marijuana first because it makes purchasing the product less convenient. Second, it ensures customers can only purchase the product when they have enough ready cash on hand. Drugs cannot be charged on credit cards and paid off later.

The marijuana industry has found a loophole for the cash-only mandate. In some dispensaries there are cashless ATMs.[10] A patron puts their ATM card into the machine. No cash is dispensed. Instead, the money is moved directly to the cannabis dispensary's account and the patron is charged a "cash withdrawal fee." This disguised cash withdrawal circumvents banks' hesitation to handle marijuana-related transactions. Fixing this loophole is easy. The marijuana industry is heavily regulated and all types of ATMs can simply be banned inside or within 100 feet of these stores.

Although this section advocates that marijuana purchases should be cash only, the regulations that prohibit these businesses from having bank accounts in federally chartered banks should be scrapped because they hurt the ability for cash to be easily recycled through the economy. Allowing banks to accept large cash deposits from dispensaries will boost banks' capacity to handle cash and will ensure paper money is readily available for other businesses.

OTHER SIN OR VICE PURCHASES

Similar to marijuana, society's views toward many other sin or vice products have changed. When I was young, the only legal form of gambling where I lived was betting on horse or dog races. Today, there is a casino a few miles from my home, sports betting is available legally on my phone, and most convenience stores I pass sell lottery tickets.

However, although society has become more permissive toward marijuana and gambling, over time it has become less permissive toward tobacco. Decades ago Hollywood movies showed tough actors sneering at audiences with a cigarette clinched between their teeth and glamorous starlets dangling cigarettes daintily between their fingers. Today, cigarettes, cigars, and other forms of tobacco are rarely, if ever, seen in block-buster movies.

One way states are trying to curtail the use of tobacco is by enforcing age restrictions. A few years ago I was in a very remote part of Montana and stopped in to the only business that existed for many miles. This tiny business combined the local post office, grocery store, and restaurant. While I ate and chatted with the owner another person came in and asked to buy a pack of cigarettes.

There was something odd about how the buyer asked and looked. The owner refused to let them purchase the cigarettes unless the buyer showed identification, which they didn't have. It was clear the owner was trying to throw the person out of the store without physically touching them. I was confused until the owner explained the buyer was underage and part of a government sting operation that was trying to entrap her. If she was caught selling cigarettes to a minor, the state's health department would shut down the business, even though it was the area's only establishment. Sting operations are one way to reduce tobacco purchases, though they are not particularly effective, especially in rural areas where there are few strangers and everyone is personally known to the only shopkeeper.

A simpler way to reduce cigarette and other tobacco purchases is to require these purchases be cash only. If society wants to cut back on the amount people smoke, these sales should require using paper money, just like marijuana sales. Forcing people to get cash before buying tobacco products and preventing them from purchasing when they don't have enough money is another method of reducing demand.

It doesn't have to be just marijuana or tobacco. Anything society wants to regulate can be made into a cash-only business to reduce demand. For example, gambling is another potential area where some politicians want to restrict sales. One way to reduce gambling is to ensure all bets can only be made with cash. In 2020, the United Kingdom banned the ability to make online bets using a credit card and Australia is proposing a similar ban.[11] Other possible purchases to control are liquor store sales or the sale of "magic mushrooms" formally called *psilocybin*, a recreational drug. In general, any activity that society classifies as a vice or sin that people want to reduce can be shifted to cash only, which introduces friction and slows down purchases.

YEAR-END BONUSES

The ideas discussed so far ensure cash is accepted as a means of payment at some retail establishments. Another approach to ensuring cash is used is to provide it to more people. In the past and even today some people are paid their wages in cash. Yes, it is legal to pay workers in cash! In 2021, the American Payroll Association ran a survey that found 96% of people got direct deposit and most of the rest received paper checks. The survey's choices didn't even include a category for "cash."[12]

I don't recommend society go back to paying everyone in cash all the time. I enjoy the freedom of not having to go into the office on payday. However, one simple way to ensure cash is injected into society is to pay year-end bonuses in cash. Regular paychecks would continue to be directly deposited into bank accounts.

If you are thinking about this idea there will likely be resistance from the payroll department because every bonus will end in a slightly different amount. My last paycheck ended in $7.39. To keep things simple, give everyone the same amount in cash bonuses, say $200, and provide the rest of the bonus via direct deposit or whatever standard method people are paid in your organization. This saves the payroll department from counting lots of coins and small bills at the end of the year, when they want to be out celebrating, but still gets cash into people's hands.

MILITARY PAY

One reason to keep paper money around is for national defense reasons. Cash provides a backup that works when enemies are engaging in either cyber or physical attacks on the country's banking system. To boost national defense, cash should be used in society, especially in areas near key military bases. It is hard to convince members of the military to fight when the government is not able to pay their wages.

Many members of the military live paycheck-to-paycheck. Military members in this situation cannot wait a few extra weeks while the government rebuilds the financial infrastructure after either a physical or cyberattack.

The paycheck-to-paycheck problem is seen by the number of payday lenders and pawn shops located near military bases. The problem is also seen with some lower-ranking members of the military living off food stamps and some taking second jobs. Many military commanders are concerned about pay because a soldier worrying about having their home repossessed or their family going hungry is not concentrating on their job of defending the country.

Congress has set up a system in which the pay for members of the military automatically rises at the same rate as pay in the civilian world. Military pay raises in 2020 and 2021 were about 3%, which is about a week and a half of pay. One way to bolster national defense is to change how people in the military receive their raise.[13]

Instead of boosting the pay for every member of the armed forces by a small amount each week, keep pay the same and give soldiers an extra pay period in cash. Currently the military gets paid every two weeks for a total of 26 payments. A simple idea is to give the military 27 payments, where the 27th payment is done in cash.

The military used to pay people in cash. Ensuring it still has the ability to make cash payments boosts national defense. Paying soldiers in cash is a bit like target practice. Every now and then people have to be recertified to make sure they still have excellent skills.

To make the policy practical, the bonus pay in cash would only happen for US forces stationed stateside in major metropolitan areas that have banks or several stores relatively close to bases. It makes no sense to provide cash pay to crews underwater in submarines, fighters in war zones, or service people who are in remote jungles or Arctic bases.

Because the goal is to ensure cash is used in the economy, the optimal time to provide the cash payments is right before major holidays associated with gift giving. For example, for the US military the optimal time would be to distribute the pay between Thanksgiving and Christmas. Other countries would have different time frames.

The goal of the policy is to ensure the military has some experience with paying workers in cash again. Electronic payments have their use. The military spends billions on wages and benefits each year. It is not practical in today's economy to move that amount of cash around. However, a small slice once a year is a prudent idea that will boost national defense in preparation for the next war.

MANDATORY PREPAREDNESS FOR FINANCIAL COMPANIES

Society mandates all kinds of preparedness drills. Schoolchildren have fire drills multiple times a year where they must march outside and wait for the fire department's signal that all is okay before returning to their classrooms. We do this even though relatively few fires occur in school buildings.

Corporations test computer and communications systems regularly to ensure they work during adverse conditions. Some companies periodically shut off their electrical power to ensure backup systems automatically turn on and engage. The military does training drills to ensure both officers and enlisted personnel are ready to defend a country. These drills are done because emergencies don't wait for a convenient time. Instead they typically happen with little or no warning.

Countries should prepare the same way to ensure paper money can be used as a backup when electronic measures fail. Large banks and financial companies used to settle their debts by having runners carry paper money, stocks, and bonds between financial houses. The prudent thing today is to require banks to regain the ability to settle debts and trades using paper money.

I am not suggesting something outrageous. Instead, once a quarter all major banks and financial institutions need to be able to send paper money to each other and receive it. The amounts being sent do not need to be large; anything over the money-laundering limits works. In simple terms large banks need to prove to government regulators four times a year they have the systems in place to send and receive cash. Proving this by moving $15,000 or $20,000 at a time to and from peer institutions ensures if widespread use of cash is needed, there are established procedures to handle the situation.

THE END

This book combined data, stories, and personal anecdotes to convince you that paper money is not dead, but something that everyone in society should use more often. Convincing people is not easy.

While I was writing this book my mother told me about going shopping and trying to make a small purchase. The Visa credit card which she used all the time was rejected. It had expired. She told me it was lucky the store was willing to take her backup American Express card. Many local shops don't accept American Express because it charges merchants higher fees than Visa. I casually asked what would have happened if the shop didn't take the American Express card? Glumly, she said, "I would have gone without the item."

I asked, "Did you have any cash in your wallet?" Her response was "Oh, I completely forgot about all the cash I had in my purse. I should have used that instead." This story encapsulates why once people start using electronic methods, changing their payment habits is so hard. When people stop using cash, they forget it exists and all the benefits of cash disappear.

Cash provides society, you, and vulnerable individuals with many powerful benefits outlined in this book. It is fine to use some electronic means of payments. I occasionally do. But don't forget to also use cash. If everyone stops using cash, its benefits disappear. Reviving paper money once people understand what is lost will be much more costly for society than reviving things like phonograph records. Make a conscious decision to use cash in your life. Doing so will provide both personal benefits and benefits to many others in society.

A well-known credit card once ran an advertising campaign that with a slight twist neatly summarizes this book. "Cash . . . Don't leave home without it!"[14]

ACKNOWLEDGMENTS

Although my name is the only one on the cover, this book has benefitted from the efforts of many people. First is my Grandmother Betty to whom this book is dedicated. Grandma's use of cash and her amazing stories had a profound influence on my life. The book is also dedicated to my wife, Kim, who is a tireless cheerleader for the ideas that cash is important and convinced me this book needed to be written. Kim read every chapter numerous times and offered important suggestions. Without her efforts this book would not have been completed.

My children also provided incredible help. Thank you to Christine for improving the book's title, Natalie for helping create the book proposal, Rebecca for proofing numerous chapters, and Joshua and Benjamin for being amazing sounding boards.

Debra Agliano, Frank Agliano, and Sue Kahn each read an early draft of the entire book and provided detailed feedback on how to make the book much more readable.

There were three professors who graciously read or listened to my arguments. They are not responsible for any mistakes. Professor Peter-John Gordon of the University of West Indies, Professor H. Sami Karaca, and Professor Tal Gross of Boston University's Questrom School of Business.

There were quite a few people who reached out with their stories, ideas, and concerns about the disappearance of cash. In particular I want to mention Mitchell Smith for his ideas, especially about automatically producing higher denomination bills when inflation makes lower-valued bills worth less; Rosa Cazares, who pointed out the problems businesses that work in cash have when dealing with the tax authorities; and Andrew Gold, who discussed cryptocurrencies.

I want to thank two science writers. Emeritus Professor Douglas Starr at Boston University, who codirected the Graduate Program in Science Journalism for 29 years, was kind enough to share his wisdom which helped me polish the book proposal. Jeff Grabmeier, Senior Director of Research Communications at The Ohio State University, taught me how to connect to the media and how to write for a wide audience.

Many of the ideas in this book were polished by talking to people in the press all over the world. A wide variety of media professionals helped me connect with these reporters: Paul Alexander, Questrom's CMO, and his assistant Katie Gauthier; Jill Totenberg, head of The Totenberg Group; many people in The Belfort Group, especially Madison Sherriff, Steve Sisto, Shannon Light, and Drew Vaughan; and Philip McGowan and William Weaver of Finn Partners.

The faculty and staff at Boston University's Questrom School of Business have created a wonderful and supportive environment where thoughts outside the mainstream like "bringing back cash" are encouraged. It is impossible to name everyone but I want to single out Dean Susan Fournier, Dean J. P. Matychak, and Dean Paul Carlile, plus three of my department chairs, Michael Salinger, Jim Rebitzer, and Keith Marzilli Ericson.

Many people at Wiley made this book possible. Bill Falloon took a chance on my proposal and convinced Wiley to publish this book, Judith Newlin edited the book, Susan Geraghty copyedited my words, and

Vithusha Rameshan smoothly handled the entire production process. Most all, I want to thank Delainey Henson who guided this book through every step of Wiley's publication process.

Last the staff at The Boston Federal Reserve's "Survey of Consumer Payment Choice:" Scott Schuh, Joanna Stavins, Kevin Foster, Oz Shy, and Claire Greene all deserve special mention because their path-breaking work opened my eyes to the problems of a cashless world.

NOTES

CHAPTER 1

1. One in five admit to dropping their phone into the toilet (Bialik and Orth 2023).
2. Urban and Valdes (2022).
3. For typewriters see Free (2018) and for fountain pens see Kelly (2019).
4. Zagorsky (2000).

CHAPTER 2

1. Prasad (2021).
2. The reasons were first written about by Keynes (1936) with additional reasons found in Barnett et al. (1992).
3. Data from Federal Reserve Bank of Atlanta (2023).
4. The rejection letter is at https://historical.ha.com/itm/explorers/space-exploration/ neil-armstrong-1974-diners-club-typed-signed-rejection-letter-with-returned-signed-1500-check-directly-from-the-armstro/a/6209-50146.s#6209-11028.
5. Bech et al. (2018).
6. The ratio is a good but not a perfect indicator because GDP measures how much a country produces. A better denominator tracks how much a country spends. Production and spending are only the same if people do not save

money and if imports and exports match. Nevertheless, this ratio still provides a good indicator of which countries use or do not use cash.

7. Eschelbach (2022).

8. De Nederlandsche Bank (2021).

9. *The CIA World Factbook* shows in 2020 there were 154 mobile phones for every 100 people in Japan, and Sweden had 128 mobile phones for every 100 people. CIA data show 95% of Swedes use the internet, compared with 90% of Japanese.

10. Zagorsky (2021).

11. Kinosian and Renteria (2024).

12. The survey has thousands of respondents fill in a diary over three consecutive days in October. Some respondents mark down their spending at the beginning of the month, others the middle, and the rest at the end. Respondents record details about the amount and method of payment for every transaction. Respondents are also asked to count the amount of cash they are holding at the beginning and end of each day to determine their exact cash use.

13. The payments study is at https://www.federalreserve.gov/paymentsystems/fr-payments-study.htm.

14. Inflation increased only 37% during those years.

15. Carlton (2023).

16. Zagorsky (2024a).

17. Zagorsky (2024b).

CHAPTER 3

1. Data on US currency in circulation come from the Federal Reserve's "H.6 Statistical Release." https://www.federalreserve.gov/releases/h6. The inflation adjustment used the CPI-U.

2. The US Consumer Expenditure Survey (https://http://www.bls.gov/cex) shows single-person households earned about $61,000 a year. The amount in Figure 3.1 of $7,000 cash per person figure is about 11% of these earnings, or about six weeks.

3. Porter and Judson (1996).

4. The armored car industry is NAICS Code 561613. Before 1998 the SIC system combined armored car employment with private detectives. Data for the "County Business Patterns" are found at https://www.census.gov/programs-surveys/cbp.html.

5. Inflation adjustment was done for 2020. The Bank for International Settlements tracks the amount of foreign exchange traded via surveys done every three years. The 2001 survey was the first survey to include the euro and showed the top five currencies traded were the US dollar (45%), euro (19%), Japanese yen (12%), British pound (6.5%), and Swiss franc (3%). See https://www.bis.org/statistics/rpfx19.htm.

6. The euro growth is remarkable because even though more countries adopted the euro after its introduction, the figures are adjusted for the extra population using the currency. Additionally, euro data in the table start two years after all the other currencies because the currency did not launch coins and banknotes until New Year's Day 2002.

CHAPTER 4

1. Figure 4.1 is a modification of one found in Federal Deposit Insurance Corporation (2007).

2. For an illustration of how Amex works see American Express (2020), section 4.2, p. 10.

3. Federal Communications Commission (2024). "Table 6.12: Telephone Service and Internet Access Rates in Low-Income Households." https://docs.fcc.gov/public/attachments/DOC-401168A1.pdf.

4. Eaton reports published from 2009 to 2018 are found at https://www.eaton.com/us/en-us/products/backup-power-ups-surge-it-power-distribution/backup-power-ups/blackout-and-power-outage-tracker.html.

5. The expectation is that a provider will file a form OE-417, called the "Electric Emergency Incident and Disturbance Report." Data are found at https://www.eia.gov/electricity/monthly.

6. Analysis of credit card transactions shows they take 0.00649 kWh for each transaction. To print each banknote it takes about 0.08 kWh (Laboure 2021).

7. Paper money lifespan information comes from https://www.federalreserve.gov/faqs/how-long-is-the-life-span-of-us-paper-money.htm.

8. The repo market provides cash loans to banks and other financial institutions. Institutions temporarily needing cash provide US Treasury bills as collateral to lenders. When the lender gets the Treasury bills they electronically move money to the borrower. When the borrower does not need the money anymore they repurchase their certificates from the lender for a slightly higher

amount than the money they were loaned, giving the lender a profit or interest on the deal (Wallerstein 2023).

9. Financial Crimes Enforcement Network (2024).
10. Arctic Wolf (2023).

CHAPTER 5

1. Apple operating temperatures are found at https://support.apple.com/en-us/HT201678.
2. North Bay (2018).
3. Baker et al. (2023).
4. Data are at https://www.ncei.noaa.gov/access/billions.
5. The government also goes to great efforts to make sure the data are reliable and comprehensive. The data cover all types of disasters from hurricanes to floods, wildfires, and winter storms, all of which destroy electrical and communications infrastructure, causing failure of electronic payments. The total cost of each event includes both losses covered and not covered by insurance. The losses include damage to buildings, roads, and infrastructure, as well as items destroyed within buildings when a major disaster strikes (Ross and Lott 2003).
6. The Atlas is found at https://library.wmo.int/index.php?lvl=notice_display&id=21930 and is maintained by the Centre for Research on the Epidemiology of Disasters. There are drawbacks to the Centre's data. For example, if a typhoon wreaks havoc on five countries, the database contains five different entries for the storm. It also has no hard cut-offs for what defines a disaster. https://public.wmo.int/en/media/press-release/weather-related-disasters-increase-over-past-50-years-causing-more-damage-fewer.
7. Areddy (2021b).
8. Barrett (2021).
9. Reuters has a timeline for the first five weeks after the storm at https://www.reuters.com/article/usa-puertorico-power-timeline/timeline-the-long-power-restoration-process-in-puerto-rico-idINL2N1N51KV.
10. White and Hayes (2018).
11. EIA power outages are found at https://www.oe.netl.doe.gov/oe417_annual_summary.aspx.
12. Daugherty (2012).
13. USDA Forest Service (2013).

14. Cal Fire (2024).
15. Turco et al. (2019).
16. Frost et al. (2022).
17. Bateman (2022).
18. National Reserve Bank of Tonga (2016).
19. National Reserve Bank of Tonga (2022).
20. Wallace (2022).
21. Wetzel (2022).
22. Miyake et al. (2012)
23. Wallace (2022).
24. State of Hawaii (2023).

CHAPTER 6

1. The idea of bombing a country back to the Stone Age is attributed to US General Curtis LeMay in the mid-1960s. However, the phrase likely appeared first as an attempt at humor by columnist Art Buchwald.
2. Tobias (2022).
3. The e-hryvnia is explained at https://bank.gov.ua/en/payments/e-hryvnia.
4. Data from Carnegie Endowment's FinCyber Project (2024) discussed later in this chapter.
5. McCoy (2014).
6. Cybersecurity and Infrastructure Security Agency (2020).
7. Federal Deposit Insurance Corporation (2021).
8. FinCyber Project (2024).
9. Rothbard (2002), pp. 59–62.
10. Newman (1957) and Newman (1958).
11. Hatfield (2015).
12. Rhodes (2012).
13. Examples of forged money created by the Nazis are found online at the Bank of England's museum, www.bankofengland.co.uk/museum.
14. Ibrahim (1992).
15. Sanger (2021).
16. Wahlquist and Lu (2022).
17. Hochman (2022), p. 45.
18. Hammer (2018).

19. A history of these notes can be found at https://www.federalreservehistory.org/essays/gold-reserve-act.
20. Bilger (2020).
21. Lacker (2004).
22. Gore (2020).
23. Isidore (2018).
24. Vanderford (2022).
25. CFA Institute (2019).
26. Page 21, paragraph 79 of United Nations (1998).
27. Waller (2021).
28. Swedish Civil Contingencies Agency (2022).

CHAPTER 7

1. Zellermayer (1996).
2. About 40% people earning $100,000 a year in the United States live paycheck to paycheck ("New Reality Check," 2022).
3. Page 4 of American Express (2021).
4. Simmons (2016).
5. Feinberg (1986), Hirschman (1979), and Williams (2014).
6. Prelec and Simester (2001).
7. Banker et al. (2021).
8. Prelec and Loewenstein (2018) and Rick (2018).
9. Kahneman et al. (1990) and Thaler (1980).
10. Kamleitner and Erki (2013).
11. Greene and Stavins (2020), p. 13.
12. Table 3 of Bhutta et al. (2020) shows the median transaction account in 2019, which includes checking, savings, and money market accounts, held $5,300.
13. Consumer Financial Protection Bureau (2021).
14. The average from 2003 to 2022 of all credit card balances that are 90 days or more late is 9.36%. Bankruptcy court statistics are available at https://www.uscourts.gov/statistics-reports/analysis-reports/bankruptcy-filings-statistics and https://www.newyorkfed.org/medialibrary/interactives/householdcredit/data/xls/hhd_c_report_2022q3.xlsx.
15. Prelec and Simester (2001).

CHAPTER 8

1. Rates for credit card plans where accounts are assessed. Interest rates are from the Federal Reserve's Consumer Credit Series G19. https://www.federalreserve.gov/releases/g19/current/default.htm.
2. Bhutta et al. (2020), Table 5.
3. Consumer Financial Protection Bureau (2023b), Figure 12.
4. Soman (2003).
5. Thomas et al. (2011).
6. Park et al. (2021).
7. Willingham (2017).
8. Carraher et al. (1988).
9. Brazilian street children selling candy on the street have better addition and subtraction skills than comparable aged children attending public school (Saxe 1988), Tables 4 and 5.
10. Nouchi (2016).
11. Wolfe (2023).
12. See Section 5.5.2 in Visa (2024).
13. Consumer Finance Protection Bureau (2022).

CHAPTER 9

1. Fanelli et al. (2022).
2. Armangue (2021).
3. Details on Santa Cruz are in History.com Editors (2024). Springsteen's first album was entitled "Greetings from Asbury Park, N.J." Ukraine's music banning is written about by Olson (2022).
4. Federal Trade Commission (2014) and Lauer (2020).
5. de Montjoye et al. (2015).
6. For example, Venmo, an electronic payment app, can share all your payment activity with "Anyone on the Internet," "Just your Friends," or "No One." Most users don't change the default sharing setting.
7. Kapner (2024).
8. Gervis (2020).

9. Data are based on five NEFE surveys: 2010, 2014, 2016, 2018, and 2021. Data are from https://www.nefe.org/.

10. The reason questions were not asked in the 2010 survey but started in 2014. The overall average shows 35% believed some or all aspects of their finances should be private, 29% stated they knew their partner or spouse would disapprove, 23% were embarrassed or fearful, 18% guessed their spouse or partner would disapprove, and 28% proved other reasons. The total adds up to more than 100% because some respondents provided more than one reason.

11. The 2020 US Census showed there are about 258 million people aged 18 and over. Multiplying this figure by the percentage who ever comingled their finances (64%), by the percentage who ever hid cash (20%), and then by those who believe some aspects of their finances should be private (35%) gives 11.6 million people.

12. Ashraf (2009), Boltz et al. (2019), and Castilla (2019).

13. Data are from https://www.cdc.gov/violenceprevention/intimatepartnerviolence/fastfact.html.

14. Gray (2006).

15. Rossi et al. (1996).

16. Duhigg (2012).

17. Duhigg (2014), Chapter 7.

18. United Nations (2021).

19. Lieber and Siegel Bernard (2022).

20. The Philadelphia Federal Reserve tracks the number of credit card accounts at the largest financial institutions. In the second quarter of 2022 there were 454 million credit card accounts (https://www.philadelphiafed.org/surveys-and-data/large-bank-credit-card-and-mortgage-data). The Census Bureau found in the 2020 Census 258 million people aged 18 and older (https://www.census.gov/library/stories/2021/08/united-states-adult-population-grew-faster-than-nations-total-population-from-2010-to-2020.html).

CHAPTER 10

1. Spending data from the BLS's Consumer Expenditure Surveys are at https://www.bls.gov/cex.

2. Office of Management and Budget (2024).

3. PayPal (2023), p. 108 for total payment volume and p. 134 for net revenues.

4. American Express (2020), Mastercard (2022), and Visa (2024).
5. FMI (2024).
6. https://www.federalreserve.gov/paymentsystems/regii-average-interchange-fee.htm.
7. Since Vigna's (2021) article, discount fees have not changed much. On April 20, 2024, they hit $128.45; one month later on May 20, 2024, they were $1.91. Fees from YCharts (https://ycharts.com/indicators/bitcoin_average_transaction_fee).
8. Sammut-Bonnici and Channon (2014).
9. Cuban's company website is https://costplusdrugs.com. Calculations from Costco's annual report.
10. The "Cost of Collection" is published by the British Retail Consortium at https://brc.org.uk/media/597229/brc-payment-survey-2019-full-report.pdf. The 2023 survey is located at https://www.brc.org.uk/media/683937/payment-survey-2023.pdf. Type into a search engine "Cost of Collection British Retail Consortium." The 2008 survey is located at https://www.esta-cash.eu/wp-content/uploads/2017/11/c7772fad153c9399314798e60d009910 87d060dc-5a1d85f6893d2-British-Retail-Consortium-%E2%80%9CThe-Cost-of-Collection%E2%80%9D.pdf.
11. Arango and Taylor (2008), pp. 15–23.
12. Quaden (2006), pp. 41–47.
13. Felt et al. (2021), pp. 37–77.
14. Supreme Court of the United States (2018).
15. American Express (2022).
16. Mohammed (2017).
17. Valentino-Devries et al. (2012).
18. Michaels and Pacheco (2024).
19. An example of an item pricing law is one enacted by Massachusetts (2024) in "General Laws Part I Title XV Chapter 94 Section 184C." https://malegislature.gov/Laws/GeneralLaws/PartI/TitleXV/Chapter94/Section184c1.

CHAPTER 11

1. The 2021 percentage was 1.7% and the average amount was $25.13. Figures calculated by the author and adjusted using the SCP's individual weights.
2. See https://www.gofundme.com/c/pricing.
3. Colpaert and Ferdman (2019).

4. Agarwal et al. (2023) , Felt et al. (2021), and Schuh et al. (2010).
5. Data on the unbanked come from Federal Deposit Insurance Corporation (2022). Alternative estimates come from the Federal Reserve's "Survey of Household Economics and Decision-Making" nicknamed SHED. SHED found 6% did not have a bank account, slightly higher than the FDIC figures. A further 13% had a bank account, but used alternative financial services, like check-cashing outlets. For a review of the unbanked see Boel and Zimmerman (2022).
6. Target's fees for Mastercard and American Express cards are the same. https://www.target.com/c/american-express-mastercard-and-visa-gift-cards/-/N-x7n3r.
7. One electronic bill payment service for the unbanked is MoneyGram. https://www.moneygram.com/mgo/us/en/paybills.
8. Data from https://www.worldbank.org/en/topic/financialinclusion/overview.
9. AT&T did not break out the write-offs or charge offs for their wireless division. Data on Verizon and T-Mobile are from their 2021 annual reports. Lifeline data at https://www.fcc.gov/lifeline-consumers. Verizon, p. 83 (https://www.verizon.com/about/sites/default/files/2021-Annual-Report-on-Form-10-K.pdf). T-Mobile, p. 56 (https://s29.q4cdn.com/310188824/files/doc_financials/2021/ar/TMUS-2021-Annual-Report.pdf).

CHAPTER 12

1. The 2019 figure was 272 million people (United Nations 2019).
2. See https://www.americanexpress.com/en-us/company/legal/cardmember-agreements.
3. Islam (2024).
4. US rules are found in the Code of Federal Regulations Title 31, "Money and Finance: Treasury" Part 1020 – Rules for Banks. https://www.ecfr.gov/current/title-31/subtitle-B/chapter-X/part-1020.
5. Banks can create accounts using the next of kin's address to help those in hospitals or nursing homes and have their children manage their financial affairs.
6. HUD does an annual count of the homeless every January. Reports are found at https://www.huduser.gov/portal/datasets/ahar.html. Transients are calculated every 10 years as part of the decennial census. Because of COVID there are no figures for 2020. In 2010 the number of transients was 118,486 (McNally 2012).

7. For immigrants's impact on Social Security see Gross et al. (2013). Illegal immigration data are found on the Department of Homeland Security's website: https://www.dhs.gov/immigration-statistics/population-estimates/unauthorized-resident.
8. Kugel (2024).
9. Amex fees are at https://www.americanexpress.com/us/customer-service/faq.foreign-transaction-fees.html.
10. World Trade Organization (2024).
11. Bank of America fees are at https://locators.bankofamerica.com/international.html.
12. Cui (2024).
13. Utrecht to Tilburg.
14. International Monetary Fund (2023).
15. Gray (2021).
16. Egypt Independent (2022) and IMF (2024).
17. Raszewski (2022).
18. Examples of black markets in the 1980s are found in Shachmurove (1999).

CHAPTER 13

1. Rose (2023).
2. Homer and Sylla (2005).
3. Bank of Japan (2024).
4. Central banks are interested in creating their own digital currencies because this is another way to eliminate the brake of paper money (Ozili 2023).
5. A summary of bank failures is found at https://www.fdic.gov/bank/historical/bank/index.html.
6. Federal Deposit Insurance Corporation (2019).
7. Quote from https://www.fdic.gov/consumers/banking/facts/priority.html.
8. Consumer Financial Protection Bureau (2023a).
9. This equation is named after Irving Fisher (1867–1947), a famous Yale University economist.
10. Figure 13.1 uses Federal Reserve Bank of St. Louis's FRED database series GS5 and FII5.

CHAPTER 14

1. The United Nations Crime Trends Survey is located at https://dataunodc. un.org/dp-crime-corruption-offences.
2. The network is located at https://www.ftc.gov/enforcement/consumer-sentinel-network.
3. "An Old Swindle Revived" (1898).
4. Leonhardt (2019).
5. The 1990 census shows there were roughly 160 million adults, and in 2022 there were about 255 million adults: https://www2.census.gov/library/publications/decennial/1990/cp-1/cp-1-1.pdf and https://www.census.gov/data/tables/2022/demo/age-and-sex/2022-age-sex-composition.html.
6. Calculations by the author using National Crime Victimization Survey data files stored at the University of Michigan's ICPSR (https://www.icpsr.umich.edu/web/NACJD/series/95) and adjusted for inflation using the CPI to 2023 dollars.
7. "Fair Credit Billing Act" is 15 U.S.C. §§ 1666-1666j. Federal Trade Commission Legal Library. https://www.ftc.gov/legal-library/browse/statutes/fair-credit-billing-act.
8. The law calls this kind of theft a *billing error*. In particular, the law considers a billing error to be "a reflection on a statement of an extension of credit which was not made to the obligor."
9. Kugel (2024).
10. Pressler (2015).
11. Nilson (2021).
12. Reports are at https://www.federalreserve.gov/paymentsystems/regii-data-collections.htm.
13. Debit cards are covered under Congress's Electronic Fund Transfer Act. Federal Trade Commission Legal Library, "Electronic Fund Transfer Act," 15 U.S.C. §§ 1693-1693r. https://www.ftc.gov/legal-library/browse/statutes/electronic-fund-transfer-act.
14. See the FTC's "Lost or Stolen Credit, ATM, and Debit Cards" at https://consumer.ftc.gov/articles/lost-or-stolen-credit-atm-debit-cards.
15. US Senate (2022).
16. Sutton and Linn (1976).

17. Data are averages from 2013 to 2019 because after 2019 the Commission combined credit card and financial institution crimes (www.ussc.gov/research/datafiles/commission-datafiles).
18. The federal punishments for bank robbery are laid out in US Code Chapter 18 § 2113 Parts (a), (d), and (e).
19. Baertlein (2017).

CHAPTER 15

1. Kidwell (2016).
2. Ngcobo et al. (2022).
3. Jolly (2022).
4. Nigeria's police once published hints on how to deal with these traffic stops (BBC 2019b). Tanzania even has surveys that track the amount of money paid in bribes and how often truck drivers had to pay (https://www.tralac.org/images/docs/6827/policy-briefroad-blocks-along-central-and-dar-corridor.pdf).
5. Qian and Wen (2015).
6. Nelson (2014).
7. Uretsky (2016).
8. Vrushi (2020).
9. Barnes et al. (2022).
10. Data come from Transparency International (2023) and are annual averages of 2012 to 2020. A prior index that existed from 1995 to 2011 is not comparable to the later data series.
11. Cashless payments as a percentage of GDP is from Table CT8E at https://data.bis.org. Use of payment services/instruments: value of cashless payments as a ratio to GDP. Extracted from http://stats.bis.org:8089/statx/srs/table/CT8e.
12. Cashless payments per person is from Table CT5 at https://data.bis.org. Use of payment services/instruments: volume of cashless payments. Extracted from http://stats.bis.org:8089/statx/srs/table/CT5.
13. Correlation between cashless payments as a percent of GDP and corruption is zero. The correlation between number of cashless payments and corruption is +0.75.
14. See https://www.riksbank.se/en-gb/about-the-riksbank/history/historical-timeline/1600-1699/first-banknotes-in-europe/.
15. Annex Table 1.1 in Development Services Group (2022).

16. Ewing (2016).
17. The Global Terrorism Database is located at https://www.start.umd.edu/gtd.
18. Data are the annual averages of 2012 to 2020.
19. The correlation is actually negative, which means more terrorism is associated with higher levels of being cashless. The correlation of the average number of terrorist attacks and number of cashless transactions is −0.28 and the correlation between attacks and cashless transactions as a percent of GDP is −0.19.
20. Page 16 in Department of the Treasury (2022).
21. The FBI has a summary of the Oklahoma City Bombing at https://www.fbi.gov/history/famous-cases/oklahoma-city-bombing.
22. Frontline (2014).
23. Hocking (2005).
24. ABC News (2013).
25. Schneider (2017).
26. The Gun Violence Archive tracks US mass shootings at https://www.gunviolencearchive.org.
27. United Nations (2011).
28. The organized crime index for 2021 is found at https://ocindex.net.

CHAPTER 16

1. See Hess (2021), Morse et al. (2009), and Rogoff (2016).
2. Carrillo et al. (2023).
3. Foley et al. (2019).
4. Lahiri (2020).
5. Dhara and Thomas (2011).
6. Comic books are found at https://incometaxindia.gov.in/Pages/comic-books.aspx. The number of taxpayers in the United States is about 50% with about 160 million tax forms filed out of 330 million people (Internal Revenue Service, 2023; see Table 2).
7. Lahiri (2020).
8. Tax revenue from www.indiabudget.gov.in.
9. BBC News (2019a).
10. Tax gaps are found at www.irs.gov/newsroom/the-tax-gap.
11. Raczkowski and Mróz (2018).

12. The correlation of the difference in the tax gap from 2013 to 2015 and the difference in average number of cashless transactions is −0.01.
13. Toder (2007).
14. Neate (2017).
15. Internal Revenue Service (2022, Table 5). https://www.irs.gov/pub/irs-pdf/p1415.pdf.
16. Internal Revenue Service (2022, Sections 4.2.1.1 and 4.2.1.2.1).
17. Employees who did not report tips are also not paying as much as they should in Social Security and Medicare taxes. This leads to these employees shortchanging themselves when they retire because their reported income is lower. However, the IRS does not think these extra taxes are significant and the loss "estimate is less than one-half billion dollars."
18. Internal Revenue Service (2022), p. 18.
19. Okunogbe and Pouliquen (2022).
20. Turkish Statistical Institute (2023).
21. The 2018 movie is directed by Kelly Sarri. See Dhara and Thomas (2011), Richter (2012), Smatrakalev (2012), and Tong (2010).
22. Rogoff (2016).
23. The 16th Amendment, ratified in 1913, established Congress's right to impose a federal income tax. Corporate tax rates are found in Taylor (2003).

CHAPTER 17

1. Farage (2023).
2. Brignall (2023) and "Key Points from Coutts' Dossier on Nigel Farage" (2023).
3. Vieira (2022).
4. Lieber (2023), Lieber and Siegel Bernard (2023), and Siegel Bernard and Lieber (2023).
5. Penalties are found at https://www.fincen.gov/penalties.
6. Waters (2022).
7. Duho et al. (2022).
8. World Bank data are at https://www.worldbank.org/en/publication/global findex.
9. World Bank (2016).
10. Foster et al. (2021).
11. Zami (2024).
12. Bamidele (2021) and Princewill (2021)

13. Iruoma and Nwafor (2022).
14. Richtel (2011) and Zelalem (2022).
15. Financial Crimes Enforcement Network (2020).
16. Treasury Inspector General (2018).

CHAPTER 18

1. What is legal tender varies depending on the country and sometimes the location. For example the Bank of England states, "What's classed as legal tender varies throughout the UK. In England and Wales, it's Royal Mint coins and Bank of England notes. In Scotland and Northern Ireland it's only Royal Mint coins and not banknotes." https://www.bankofengland.co.uk/explainers/what-is-legal-tender.
2. See "Cashless Environment" at https://www.mlb.com/redsox/ballpark/information/guide (retrieved May 28, 2024).
3. Zraick (2019).
4. The statement is found at https://www.federalreserve.gov/faqs/currency_12772.htm.
5. The law is Commonwealth of Massachusetts (2024). The states are Arizona, Colorado, Connecticut, Delaware, District of Columbia, Idaho, Maine, Massachusetts, Michigan, Mississippi, New Jersey, New York, North Dakota, Oklahoma, Pennsylvania, and Rhode Island.
6. City of Philadelphia (2024).
7. House of Representatives (2023).
8. The North American Industry Classification System (NAICS) is the standard used by the US federal government to classify businesses. Retail are businesses that begin with codes 44 or 45. Other common sectors like accommodation and food services (codes starting with 72) or health care (codes starting with 62) are not considered by the federal government as retail establishments. https://www.census.gov/naics/?58967?yearbck=2022.
9. Adedoyin (2024).
10. Instructions are at https://www.irs.gov/payments/what-to-expect-when-you-pay-cash-at-an-irs-office.
11. Depositing and reporting employment tax instructions are found at https://www.irs.gov/businesses/small-businesses-self-employed/depositing-and-reporting-employment-taxes. The failure to deposit penalty is at https://www.irs.gov/payments/failure-to-deposit-penalty.

12. In 1972 it cost the IRS $0.49 per $100 collected. In 2022 the cost not adjusted for inflation was $0.29.
13. U.S. Code Title 26, Subtitle F, Chapter 64, Subchapter A, Section 6302–Mode or time of tax collection. https://www.law.cornell.edu/uscode/text/26/6302.

CHAPTER 19

1. Bank for International Settlements (1985).
2. See https://www.cashmatters.org.
3. Examples of these trade groups are the ATM Industry Association (www.atmia .com) and the National ATM Council (www.natmc.org).
4. Table 5 of American Express's 2023 annual report shows the average card fee was $92.
5. Statement from p. 6 of Visa's 2015 annual 10-K report. https://www.sec.gov/ Archives/edgar/data/1403161/000140316115000013/v093015.htm.
6. Data for the table comes from Visa's 2022 annual 10-K report. https://www.sec .gov/ix?doc=/Archives/edgar/data/1403161/000140316123000099/v-20230930.htm.
7. Li (2022).
8. NAICS code 522210 are credit card issuers. https://data.census.gov/cedsci/ table?q=522210&tid=ECNCRFIN2017.EC1752CRFIN.
9. Macy's 2021 annual report, p. 28. https://www.macysinc.com/investors/sec-filings/all-sec-filings/content/0001564590-22-011726/0001564590-22-011726.pdf.
10. Citi 2021 annual report, p. 18. https://www.citigroup.com/citi/investor/quar-terly/2022/ar21_en.pdf.
11. Ibid, p. 162.
12. Ibid, p. 68. On p. 289 total credit lines on cards for Citi in 2021 were over $700 billion.
13. FRED time series TERMCBCCALLNS.
14. Bank of America 2021 annual report, p. 76. https://investor.bankofamerica. com/annual-reports-and-proxy-statements.
15. In the United States the IRS form is 8300 (https://www.irs.gov/pub/irs-pdf/ f8300.pdf). In Canada the form is FINTRAC's Large Cash Transaction Report (https://fintrac-canafe.canada.ca/reporting-declaration/form/LCTR-eng.pdf).
16. Work hours restrictions are found at https://www.mass.gov/service-details/ work-hours-restrictions-for-minors.

17. See https://www.amazon.com/cash.
18. ABC News (2010).
19. Webster (2021).
20. Needleman and Donaldson (2022).
21. See https://customerservice.costco.com/app/answers/detail/a_id/716/~/why-does-costco-have-a-treasure-hunt-atmosphere%3F.
22. St. Clair (2020) suggests corporate interests killed it, and Slater (1997) suggests it would have died on its own.
23. Bailey (1990).

CHAPTER 20

1. The Money Laundering Suppression Act (MLSA) of 1994, Public Law 103-325.
2. Ewing (2016).
3. Circulation of euro banknotes is found at https://www.ecb.europa.eu/stats/policy_and_exchange_rates/banknotes+coins/circulation/html/index.en.html.
4. Rogoff (2014) and Rogoff and McAndrews (2017).
5. A video of the cube is found at https://www.chicagofed.org/education/money-museum/videos/million-dollar-cube.
6. The graph was created by adjusting $500 for changes in the US Consumer Price Index (CPI-U) found at www.bls.gov.
7. The statement is found at https://www.federalreserve.gov/faqs/currency_12772.htm.
8. Briglevics and Shy (2014) argue that a lot of merchants don't want to offer discount programs to steer credit card users toward debit cards, but they don't investigate why merchants don't offer cash discounts.
9. One method to reduce consumption of sinful products is to boost taxes on purchases. However, when taxes are raised to high levels then bootlegging and illegal production take over (Schmacker and Smed 2023).
10. Kary (2022).
11. Rowland (2023) and U.K. Gambling Commission (2020).
12. The survey is found at https://www.nationalpayrollweek.com/npw-survey.
13. Basic pay in the military is tied to Employment Cost Index changes, which is a quarterly survey of private and public sector employees run by the Bureau of Labor Statistics. Pay raises are found at https://militarypay.defense.gov/Pay/Basic-Pay/AnnualPayRaise.
14. American Express started running their "Don't leave home without it" advertising campaign in 1975.

BIBLIOGRAPHY

ABC News. "Apple Reverses Its No-Cash Payment Policy for iPads." May 20, 2010. https://abc7news.com/archive/7451437.

ABC News. "Feds Race to Trace Boston Marathon Pressure Cooker Bomb." April 17, 2013. https://abcnews.go.com/Blotter/feds-race-trace-boston-marathon-pressure-cooker-bomb/story?id=18976352.

Adedoyin, Oyin. "Want to Pay Cash? That'll Cost You Extra." *Wall Street Journal.* June 6, 2024. https://www.wsj.com/personal-finance/paying-cash-fees-reverse-atm-744d1bd6.

Agarwal, Sumit, Andrea Presbitero, Andre Silva, and Carlo Wix. "Who Pays for Your Rewards? Redistribution in the Credit Card Market." Finance and Economics Discussion Series 2023–007. Board of Governors of the Federal Reserve System. 2023. https://doi.org/10.17016/FEDS.2023.007.

American Express. "Merchant Reference Guide." October 2020. https://www.americanexpress.com/content/dam/amex/us/merchant/merchant-channel/USA_RefGuide_Oct2020-FINAL.pdf.

American Express. "Annual Report/10-K." 2021. https://s26.q4cdn.com/747928648/files/doc_financials/2021/ar/Final-Annual-Report-03-18-22.pdf.

American Express. "Merchant Reference Guide, Section 3.2: Treatment of the American Express Brand." October 2022. https://www.americanexpress.com/content/dam/amex/us/merchant/new-merchant-regulations/Reference-Guide_EN_US.pdf.

Anaza, Nwamaka A., Delancy H. S. Bennett, Yana Andonova, and Emeka Anaza. "DPS 2.0: On the Road to a Cashless Society." *Marketing Letters* 33, no. 4 (2022): 693–704.

Apple Computer. "If Your iPhone or iPad Gets Too Hot or Too Cold." August 1, 2024. https://support.apple.com/en-us/HT201678.

Arango, Carlos, and Varya Taylor. "Merchants' Costs of Accepting Means of Payment: Is Cash the Least Costly?" *Bank of Canada Review* (Winter 2008–2009): 15–23. https://www.bankofcanada.ca/wp-content/uploads/2010/06/arango_taylor.pdf.

Areddy, James. "China Flooding Exposed Risks in Beijing's Plan to Launch Digital Currency." *Wall Street Journal.* October 19, 2021a. https://www.wsj.com/articles/china-flooding-exposed-risks-in-beijings-plan-to-launch-digital-currency-11634654928.

Areddy, James. "Floods Expose Digital Currency Risks." *Wall Street Journal.* October 20, 2021b.

Armangue, Bernat. "Under Taliban, Thriving Afghan Music Scene Heads to Silence." Associated Press. 2021. https://apnews.com/article/entertainment-middle-east-music-arts-and-entertainment-afghanistan-a2ac1095df0568387d6cee15eb82a3b5.

Arctic Wolf. "10 Major Retail Industry Cyber Attack." June 8, 2023. https://arcticwolf.com/resources/blog/10-major-retail-industry-cyber-attacks.

Ashraf, Nava. "Spousal Control and Intra-Household Decision Making: An Experimental Study in the Philippines." *American Economic Review* 99, no. 4 (2009): 1245–77. https://doi.org/10.1257/aer.99.4.1245.

Baertlein, Lisa. "Chipotle Says Hackers Hit Most in Data Breach." Reuters. May 30, 2017. https://www.reuters.com/article/idUSKBN18M2BY.

Bailey, Andrew. "Banknotes in Circulation – Still Rising. What Does This Mean for the Future of Cash?" *Banknote 2009 Conference.* Bank for International Settlements. December 9, 2009. https://www.bis.org/review/r091214e.pdf.

Bailey, Eric. "Gadgets to Cope with Gridlock: Commuters Are Filling Their Cars with Devices from Portable Fax Machines to TVs to Take Advantage of Their Time on the Road." *Los Angeles Times.* May 17, 1990. https://www.latimes.com/archives/la-xpm-1990-05-17-mn-278-story.html.

Baker, Mike, Sergio Olmos, and Eileen Sullivan. "Maui Sent an Evacuation Alert. Why Did So Few People Get It?" *New York Times.* September 3, 2023. https://www.nytimes.com/2023/09/03/us/maui-wildfires-emergency-alerts.html.

Bamidele, Damilare. "Calls and Internet to Be Restored in Zamfara as Govt Suspends Telecoms Shutdown." Technext. November 29, 2021. https://technext24 .com/2021/11/29/calls-and-internet-to-be-restored-in-zamfara-as-govt-suspends-telecoms-shutdown.

Bank for International Settlements. "Payment Systems in Eleven Developed Countries." February 1985. https://www.bis.org/cpmi/publ/d01b.pdf.

Bank for International Settlements. "Annual Report 2021/2022." 2022.

Bank of Japan. "Statement on Monetary Policy." January 23, 2024. https://www.boj .or.jp/en/mopo/mpmdeci/mpr_2024/k240123a.pdf. (Effective rates are found at https://fred.stlouisfed.org/series/IRSTCI01JPM156N.)

Banker, Sachin, Derek Dunfield, Alex Huang, and Drazen Prelec. "Neural Mechanisms of Credit Card Spending." *Scientific Reports* 11, no. 4070 (2021). https://doi.org/10.1038/s41598-021-83488-3.

Barnes, Julian, Michael Forsythe, David Kirkpatrick, and Jason Horowitz. "U.S. Officials Say Superyacht Could Be Putin's." *New York Times.* March 11, 2022. https:// www.nytimes.com/2022/03/11/us/politics/putin-yacht-russia-ukraine.html.

Barnett, William A., Douglas Fisher, and Apostolos Serletis. "Consumer Theory and the Demand for Money." *Journal of Economic Literature* 30, no. 4 (1992): 2086–119. http://www.jstor.org/stable/2727974.

Barrett, Eamon. "China's Latest Floods Put Its Climate-Friendly 'Sponge Cities' to the Test." *Fortune.* August 7, 2021. https://fortune.com/2021/08/07/sponge-city-concept-zhengzhou-flooding-china-climate-change/.

Bateman, Tom. "Tonga Is Finally Back Online. Here's Why It Took 5 Weeks to Fix Its Volcano-Damaged Internet Cable." *Euro News.* February 23, 2022. https:// www.euronews.com/next/2022/02/23/tonga-is-finally-back-online-here-s-why-it-took-5-weeks-to-fix-its-volcano-damaged-interne.

BBC News. "India Delivers Surprise Corporate Tax Cuts to Boost Economy." September 20, 2019a. https://www.bbc.com/news/business-49764964.

BBC News. "Nigeria Police Publish Tips on How to Survive Their Checkpoints," May 9, 2019b. https://www.bbc.com/news/world-africa-48214438.

Bech, Morten, Umar Faruqui, Frederik Ougaard, and Cristina Picillo. Payments Are a-Changin' but Cash Still Rules." *BIS Quarterly Review* (2018): 67–80. https://www.bis.org/publ/qtrpdf/r_qt1803g.pdf.

Bhutta, Neil, Jesse Bricker, Andrew Chang, Lisa Dettling, Sarena Goodman, and Joanne Hsu. "Changes in U.S. Family Finances from 2016 to 2019: Evidence from the Survey of consumer Finances." *Federal Reserve Bulletin* 106 (2020): 1–2.

Bialik, Carl, and Taylor Orth, "Toilet Talk: Polling Americans' Potty Preferences." *YouGov* 7 (2023). https://today.yougov.com/society/articles/45245-toilet-talk-polling-americans-potty-preferences.

Bilger, Mark. "Cyber-Security Risks of Fedwire." *Journal of Digital Forensics, Security and Law* 14, no. 4 (2020). https://doi.org/10.15394/jdfsl.2019.1590.

Boel, Paola, and Peter Zimmerman. "Unbanked in America: A Review of the Literature." *Federal Reserve Bank of Cleveland, Economic Commentary* 2022-07. 2022. https://doi.org/10.26509/frbc-ec-202207.

Boltz, Marie, Karine Marazyan, and Paola Villar. "Income Hiding and Informal Redistribution: A Lab-in-the-Field Experiment in Senegal." *Journal of Development Economics* 137 (2019): 78–92. https://doi.org/10.1016/j.jdeveco.2018.11.004.

Briglevics, Tamas, and Oz Shy. "Why Don't Most Merchants Use Price Discounts to Steer Consumer Payment Choice?". *Review of Industrial Organization* 44, no. 4 (2014): 367–92. https://doi.org/10.1007/s11151-014-9419-y.

Brignall, Miles. "UK Banks Are Closing More Than 1,000 Accounts Every Day." *The Guardian.* July 30, 2023. https://www.theguardian.com/business/2023/jul/30/uk-banks-closing-more-than-1000-accounts-every-day.

Cal Fire. "Wildfire Statistics." 2024. https://www.fire.ca.gov/our-impact/statistics.

Carlton, Jim. "The Number of ATMs Has Declined as People Rely Less on Cash." *Wall Street Journal.* March 3, 2023. https://www.wsj.com/articles/the-number-of-atms-has-declined-as-people-rely-less-on-cash-81268fa2.

Carraher, Terezinha Nunes, Judith Sowder, Larry Sowder, and Analúcia Dias Schliemann. "Using Money to Teach About the Decimal System." *The Arithmetic Teacher* 36, no. 4 (1988): 42–43. http://www.jstor.org.ezproxy.bu.edu/stable/41194381.

Carrel, Paul, and John Revill. "Swiss Franc Remains in Demand as Safe Haven Says Swiss National Bank's Maechler." *Reuters.* November 11, 2021. https://www.reuters.com/business/swiss-franc-remains-demand-safe-haven-says-swiss-national-banks-maechler-2021-11-11/.

Carrillo, Paul, Dave Donaldson, Dina Pomeranz, and Monica Singhal. "Ghosting the Tax Authority: Fake Firms and Tax Fraud in Ecuador." *American Economic Review: Insights* 5, no. 4 (2023): 427–44. https://doi.org/10.1257/aeri.20220321.

Castilla, Carolina. "What's Yours Is Mine, and What's Mine Is Mine: Field Experiment on Income Concealing Between Spouses in India." *Journal of Development Economics* 137 (2019): 125–40. https://doi.org/10.1016/j.jdeveco.2018.11.009.

Central Intelligence Agency. *The CIA World Factbook.* 2024. https://www.cia.gov/the-world-factbook/.

CFA Institute. "Flash Crashes." 2019. Accessed October 29, 2024. https://www.cfainstitute.org/en/advocacy/issues/flash-crashes.

City of Philadelphia. "Code - Chapter 9-1132: Cash Payments in Retail Establishment." 2024. https://www.phila.gov/documents/regulations-on-cash-payments-in-retail-establishments.

Colpaert, Pieter, and Roberto Ferdman. "This App Lets You Give Money to Homeless People from Your Phone." *Vice Media.* May 6, 2019. https://www.vice.com/en/article/wjvavy/this-app-lets-you-give-money-to-homeless-people-from-your-phone.

Commonwealth of Massachusetts. "General Laws, Part III, Title IV, Chapter 255d, Section 10a." 2024. https://malegislature.gov/Laws/GeneralLaws/PartIII/TitleIV/Chapter255D/Section10A.

Consumer Financial Protection Bureau. *"The Consumer Credit Card Market."* September 2021. https://files.consumerfinance.gov/f/documents/cfpb_consumer-credit-card-market-report_2021.pdf.

Consumer Financial Protection Bureau "CFPB Moves to Reduce Junk Fees Charged by Debt Collectors." June 29, 2022. https://www.consumerfinance.gov/about-us/newsroom/cfpb-moves-to-reduce-junk-fees-charged-by-debt-collectors.

Consumer Financial Protection Bureau. "CFPB Finds that Billions of Dollars Stored on Popular Payment Apps May Lack Federal Insurance." June 1, 2023a. https://www.consumerfinance.gov/about-us/newsroom/cfpb-finds-billions-of-dollars-stored-on-popular-payment-apps-may-lack-federal-insurance/.

Consumer Financial Protection Bureau. "The Consumer Credit Card Market." 2023b. https://files.consumerfinance.gov/f/documents/cfpb_consumer-credit-card-market-report_2023.pdf.

Cui, Judy. "China Travel: Cashless-Society Shift Hits Foreign Tourists Who Really Want to Open Wallets and Spend." *South China Morning Post.* February 12, 2024. https://www.scmp.com/economy/china-economy/article/3251523/china-travel-cashless-society-shift-hits-foreign-tourists-who-really-want-open-wallets-and-spend.

Cybersecurity and Infrastructure Security Agency. "Fastcash 2.0: North Korea's Beagleboyz Robbing Banks." August 26, 2020. https://www.cisa.gov/sites/default/files/publications/AA20-239A_FASTCash2.0_508.pdf.

Daugherty, Greg. "Hurricane Sandy Proves Cash Is Still King in Emergencies." *Consumer Reports.* November 5, 2012. https://www.consumerreports.org/cro/news/2012/11/hurricane-sandy-proves-cash-is-still-king-in-emergencies/index.htm.

De Nederlandsche Bank. *Knowledge and Appreciation of Euro Banknotes in the Netherlands: 2021 Survey.* Panteia, 2021.

Department of the Treasury. "2022 National Terrorist Financing Risk Assessment." February 2022. https://home.treasury.gov/system/files/136/2022-National-Terrorist-Financing-Risk-Assessment.pdf.

Development Services Group. "Statistical Information Country Reports on Terrorism 2021." US State Department. 2022. https://www.state.gov/wp-content/uploads/2023/02/2021_Statistical_Annex_Final-508-compliant.pdf.

Dhara, Tushar, and Cherian Thomas. "In India, Tax Evasion Is a National Sport." Bloomberg. July 28, 2011. https://www.bloomberg.com/news/articles/2011-07-28/in-india-tax-evasion-is-a-national-sport.

Duhigg, Charles. "How Companies Learn Your Secrets." *New York Times Magazine.* February 19, 2012. https://www.nytimes.com/2012/02/19/magazine/shopping-habits.html.

Duhigg, Charles. *The Power of Habit: Why We Do What We Do in Life and Business.* Random House, 2014.

Duho, King, Stephen Abankwah, Gabriel Azu, Duke Agbozo, Vincent Duho, and John Atigodey. "Central Bank Digital Currency in Ghana, the E-Cedi: Disruptions, Opportunities and Risks." *Dataking Policy Brief 006.* 2022. https://ssrn.com/abstract=4113179.

Eaton. "Blackout and Power Outage Tracker." Accessed July 19, 2024. https://www.eaton.com/us/en-us/products/backup-power-ups-surge-it-power-distribution/backup-power-ups/blackout-and-power-outage-tracker.html.

Egypt Independent. "CBE Restricts Misuse of Credit and Debit Cards Abroad." *Egypt Independent.* December 23, 2022. https://egyptindependent.com/cbe-restricts-misuse-of-credit-snd-debit-cards-abroad.

Eschelbach, Martina, Kerstin Lorek, Julien Novotny, Annett Pietrowiak, and Volker Seile. "Payment Behaviour in Germany in 2021." 2022. https://www.bundesbank.de/resource/blob/894118/6c67bcce826d5ab16a837bbea31a1aa9/mL/zahlungsverhalten-in-deutschland-2021-data.pdf.

European Central Bank. "*Study on the Payment Attitudes of Consumers in the Euro Area (Space).*" 2024.

European Environment Agency. "Forest Fires in Europe." November 18, 2021. https://www.eea.europa.eu/en/analysis/indicators/forest-fires-in-europe.

Ewing, Jack. "Europe to Remove 500-Euro Bill, the 'Bin Laden' Bank Note Criminals Love." *New York Times.* May 4, 2016. https://www.nytimes.com/2016/05/05/business/international/ecb-to-remove-500-bill-the-bin-laden-bank-note-criminals.html.

Fanelli, James, Ben Foldy, and Dustin Volz. "A Crucial Clue in the $4.5 Billion Bitcoin Heist." *Wall Street Journal.* February 15, 2022.

Farage, Nigel. "I Blame EU Rules for My Banking Travails, Which Britain Has Madly Adopted." *The Telegraph.* July 13, 2023. https://www.telegraph.co.uk/news/2023/07/15/i-blame-eu-rules-for-my-banking-travails-which-britain-has.

Federal Communications Commission. "Universal Service Monitoring Report 2023." March 14, 2024. https://docs.fcc.gov/public/attachments/DOC-401168A1.pdf.

Federal Deposit Insurance Corporation. "Credit Card Activities Manual." 2007. https://www.fdic.gov/regulations/examinations/credit_card/pdf_version.

Federal Deposit Insurance Corporation. "Failed Bank Information: Information for First Bank of Beverly Hills, Calabasas, CA." 2019. https://www.fdic.gov/resources/resolutions/bank-failures/failed-bank-list/beverlyhills.html.

Federal Deposit Insurance Corporation. "Rules and Regulations." *Federal Register* 86, no. 223 (November 23, 2021): 66425. https://www.fdic.gov/news/board-matters/2021/2021-11-17-notational-fr.pdf.

Federal Deposit Insurance Corporation. "*2021 FDIC National Survey of Unbanked and Under-Banked Households.*" 2022. https://www.fdic.gov/analysis/household-survey/2021report.pdf.

Federal Deposit Insurance Corporation. "Bankfind Suite's Historical Bank Data." 2024. https://banks.data.fdic.gov/explore/historical.

Federal Reserve Bank of Atlanta. "Survey and Diary of Consumer Payment Choice." 2023. https://www.atlantafed.org/banking-and-payments/consumer-payments/survey-and-diary-of-consumer-payment-choice.

Federal Reserve Board of Governors. "Federal Reserve Payments Study." 2022. https://www.federalreserve.gov/paymentsystems/fr-payments-study.htm.

Federal Trade Commission. "Data Brokers: A Call for Transparency and Accountability." May 2014, https://www.ftc.gov/system/files/documents/reports/data-brokers-call-transparency-accountability-report-federal-trade-commission-may-2014/140527databrokerreport.pdf.

Feinberg, Richard A. "Credit Cards as Spending Facilitating Stimuli: A Conditioning Interpretation." *Journal of Consumer Research* 13, no. 3 (1986): 348–56. http://www.jstor.org.ezproxy.bu.edu/stable/2489426.

Felt, Marie-Helene, Fumiko Hayashi, Joanna Stavins, and Angelika Welte. "Distributional Effects of Payment Card Pricing and Merchant Cost Pass-Through in Canada and the United States." Bank of Canada. 2021.

Financial Crimes Enforcement Network. "Report 112-Currency Transaction Report, *Federal Register* 85, no. 94 (May 14, 2020). https://www.govinfo.gov/content/pkg/FR-2020-05-14/pdf/2020-10310.pdf.

Financial Crimes Enforcement Network. "*Sar Filings by Industry.*" 2024. https://www.fincen.gov/reports/sar-stats/sar-filings-industry.

FinCyber Project. "Timeline of Cyber Incidents Involving Financial Institutions." Carnegie Endowment for International Peace. 2024. https://carnegieendowment.org/features/fincyber-timeline?lang=en.

FMI. "Annual Financial Review: Grocery Store Chains Net Profit." 2024. https://www.fmi.org/our-research/supermarket-facts/grocery-store-chains-net-profit.

Foley, Sean, Jonathan Karlsen, and Talis Putnins. "Sex, Drugs, and Bitcoin: How Much Illegal Activity Is Financed Through Cryptocurrencies?" *Review of Financial Studies* 32, no. 5 (2019): 1798–853. https://doi.org/10.1093/rfs/hhz015.

Foster, Kevin, Claire Greene, and Joanna Stavins. "The 2020 Survey of Consumer Payment Choice." no. 21-1. Atlanta Federal Reserve. 2011. https://www.atlantafed.org/-/media/documents/banking/consumer-payments/survey-of-consumer-payment-choice/2020/2020-survey-of-consumer-payment-choice.pdf.

Free, Cathy. "Sales Are Booming at Manhattan Typewriter Store, Mostly Thanks to Young People (and Tom Hanks)." *Washington Post.* September 24, 2018. https://www.washingtonpost.com/dc-md-va/2018/09/24/sales-are-booming-manhattan-typewriter-store-mostly-thanks-young-people-tom-hanks/.

Frontline. "McVeigh Chronology." PBS. 2014. https://www.pbs.org/wgbh/pages/frontline/documents/mcveigh/mcveigh2.html.

Frost, Natasha, Mitra Taj, and Eric Nagourney. "Tonga Shrouded by Ash and Mystery after Powerful Volcano Erupts." *New York Times.* January 16, 2022. https://www.nytimes.com/2022/01/16/world/asia/tonga-tsunami-peru.html.

Garcia, Raffi, and Jyothsna Harithsa. "Gender and Racial Behavior in Consumer Payment Methods Under Economic Uncertainty." *AEA Papers and Proceedings* 114 (2024): 174–79.

Gervis, Zoya. "Most Couples Admit to 'Cheating' on Their Partners with Food." *New York Post.* February 11, 2020. https://nypost.com/2020/02/11/most-couples-admit-to-cheating-on-their-partners-with-food.

Gore, Leada. "Nashville Bomb AT&T Outage Latest Updates: Some Walmart Stores in Alabama Cash Only, No Returns." Alabama Media Group. December 26, 2020. https://www.al.com/news/2020/12/nashville-bomb-att-outage-latest-updates-some-walmart-stores-in-alabama-cash-only-no-returns.html.

Goss, Stephen, Alice Wade, J. Patrick Skirvin, Michael Morris, K. Mark Bye, and Danielle Huston. "Effects of Unauthorized Immigration on the Actuarial Status of the Social Security Trust Funds." *Social Security Administration Notes* 151 (2013). https://www.ssa.gov/oact/NOTES/pdf_notes/note151.pdf.

Gray, Geoffrey. "Tough Love." *New York Time Magazine*. 2016. https://nymag.com/relationships/features/16463.

Gray, Simon. "Recognizing Reality—Unification of Official and Parallel Market Exchange Rates." *IMF Working Paper No. 2021/025* (2021): 45.

Greene, Claire, and Joanna Stavins. "The 2020 Diary of Consumer Payment Choice." Federal Reserve Bank of Atlanta. 2020. https://www.atlantafed.org/-/media/documents/banking/consumer-payments/diary-of-consumer-payment-choice/2020/2020-diary-of-consumer-payment-choice.pdf.

Goss, Stephen, Alice Wade, J. Patrick Skirvin, Michael Morris, K. Mark Bye, and Danielle Huston. "Effects of Unauthorized Immigration on the Actuarial Status of the Social Security Trust Funds." *Social Security Administration*, 151 (April 2013). https://www.ssa.gov/oact/NOTES/pdf_notes/note151.pdf.

Hammer, Joshua. "The Billion-Dollar Bank Job." *New York Times Magazine*. May 6, 2018, p. 43.

Hatfield, Stuart. "Faking It: British Counterfeiting During the American Revolution." *Journal of the American Revolution* (2015). https://allthingsliberty.com/2015/10/faking-it-british-counterfeiting-during-the-american-revolution.

Hayashi, Fumiko, and William Keeton. "Measuring the Costs of Retail Payment Methods." *Federal Reserve Bank of Kansas City Economic Review* 97, no. 2 (2012): 37–77.

Hess, Ryan. "Cash and Tax Evasion." PhD thesis, University of Texas Austin. 2021. http://dx.doi.org/10.26153/tsw/13636.

Hirschman, Elizabeth. "Differences in Consumer Purchase Behavior by Credit Card Payment System." *Journal of Consumer Research* 6, no. 1 (1979): 58–66.

History.com Editors. "Rock 'n' Roll Is Banned in Santa Cruz, California." May 31, 2024. https://www.history.com/this-day-in-history/rock-and-roll-is-banned-in-santa-cruz-california.

Hochman, Brian. *The Listeners: A History of Wiretapping in the United States*. Harvard University Press, 2022.

Hocking, Martin. "11 - Ammonia, Nitric Acid and Their Derivatives." In *Handbook of Chemical Technology and Pollution Control* (Vol. 3), ed. Martin Hocking. Academic Press, 2005, 321–64.

Homer, Sidney, and Richard Sylla. *A History of Interest Rates*. Wiley Finance, 2005.

House of Representatives. "H.R. Bill 4128 - Payment Choice Act of 2023, 118th Congress (2023–2024)." 2023. https://www.congress.gov/bill/118th-congress/house-bill/4128.

Ibrahim, Youssef. "Fake-Money Flood Is Aimed at Crippling Iraq's Economy." *New York Times*. May 27, 1992, Section A, p. 1.

Internal Revenue Service. *Federal Tax Compliance Research: Tax Gap Estimates for Tax Years 2014-2016* (Vol. 1415, Rev. 08-2022). Author, 2022. https://www.irs .gov/pub/irs-pdf/p1415.pdf.

Internal Revenue Service. *Data Book, 2022* (Vol. 55–B). Author, 2023. https:// www.irs.gov/pub/irs-pdf/p55b.pdf.

International Monetary Fund. "Annual Report on Exchange Arrangements and Exchange Restrictions." July 2023. https://www.imf.org/en/Publications/ Annual-Report-on-Exchange-Arrangements-and-Exchange-Restrictions.

International Monetary Fund. "Staff Country Reports: Arab Republic of Egypt." *Country Report No. 2024/098* (March 19, 2024), Fig. 3, p. 7. https://www.imf .org/en/Publications/CR/Issues/2024/04/26/Arab-Republic-of-Egypt-First- and-Second-Reviews-Under-the-Extended-Arrangement-Under-the-548335.

Iruoma, Kelechukwu, and Justice Nwafor. "Nigeria Blocks 73 Million Mobile Phones in Security Clampdown." *Reuters* 2022. https://news.trust.org/ item/20220420123542-btwyo.

Isidore, Chris. "Machines Are Driving Wall Street's Wild Ride, Not Humans." CNN. February 6, 2018. https://money.cnn.com/2018/02/06/investing/wall- street-computers-program-trading/index.html.

Islam, Syful. "Bangladesh Banks in Liquidity Crisis, Hit by Forced Merger Plan." *Nikkei Asia*. May 15, 2024. https://asia.nikkei.com/Business/Finance/ Bangladesh-banks-in-liquidity-crisis-hit-by-forced-merger-plan.

Jolly, Jasper. "Mining Giant Glencore Flew Cash Bribes to Africa Via Private Jet." *The Guardian*. November 2, 2022. https://www.theguardian.com/business/ 2022/nov/02/mining-giant-glencore-flew-cash-bribes-to-africa-via-private- jet-uk-court-hears.

Kahneman, Daniel, Jack L. Knetsch, and Richard H. Thaler. "Experimental Tests of the Endowment Effect and the Coase Theorem." *Journal of Political Economy* 98, no. 6 (1990): 1325–48.

Kamleitner, Bernadette, and Berna Erki. "Payment Method and Perceptions of Ownership." *Marketing Letters* 24, no. 1 (2013): 57–69.

Kapner, Suzanne. "The Rise of Stealth Shopping: How Americans Are Hiding Big Purchases from Their Partners." *Wall Street Journal* (2024): A1. https://www .wsj.com/personal-finance/stealth-shoppers-hide-purchases-fashion-11745267.

Kary, Tiffany. "Cashless ATMs Have Grown into a $7 Billion Marijuana Loophole." Bloomberg. April 1, 2022. https://www.bloomberg.com/news/articles/2022-04-01/ legal-weed-dispensaries-embrace-debit-card-workaround.

Kelly, John. "The Handwriting Is on the Wall: Fountain Pens Are Back." *Washington Post.* June 10, 2019. https://www.washingtonpost.com/local/the-handwriting-is-on-the-wall-fountain-pens-are-back/2019/06/10/aa8d3b38-8b92-11e9-b08e-cfd89bd36d4e_story.html.

Keynes, John Maynard. *The General Theory of Employment, Interest and Money.* Harcourt, Brace, 1936.

"Key Points from Coutts' Dossier on Nigel Farage." *Sky News.* July 28, 2023. https://news.sky.com/story/key-points-from-coutts-dossier-on-nigel-farage-12924078.

Kidwell, David. "Bagman Says He Handed over $557,000 in Cash Bribes at Lunches." *Chicago Tribune.* January 13, 2016. https://www.chicagotribune.com/suburbs/lake-county-news-sun/ct-red-light-cameras-trial-met-0114-20160113-story.html.

Kinosian, Sarah, and Nelson Renteria. "Short on Cash, El Salvador Doubles Down on Bitcoin Dream." Reuters. February 2, 2024. https://www.reuters.com/technology/short-cash-el-salvador-doubles-down-bitcoin-dream-2024-02-02.

Kugel, Seth. "Help! A Gas Station Charged Me $1,500 and My Bank Won't Believe It's Fraud; Tripped Up." *New York Times.* June 6, 2024, Travel.

Laboure, Marion "The Future of Payments: Series 2: Part II." Deutsche Bank Research. February 202, p. 9. https://www.dbresearch.de/PROD/RPS_DE-PROD/PROD0000000000516270/The_Future_of_Payments:_Series_2_-_Part_II__When_d.PDF.

Lacker, Jeffrey. "Payment System Disruptions and the Federal Reserve Following September 11, 2001." *Journal of Monetary Economics* 51, no. 5 (2004): 935–65. https://doi.org/10.1016/j.jmoneco.2004.04.005.

Lahiri, Amartya. "The Great Indian Demonetization." *Journal of Economic Perspectives* 34, no. 1 (2020): 55–74. https://doi.org/10.1257/jep.34.1.55.

Lauer, Josh. "Plastic Surveillance: Payment Cards and the History of Transactional Data, 1888 to Present." *Big Data & Society* 7, no. 1 (2020). https://doi.org/10.1177/2053951720907632.

Leonhardt, Megan. "'Nigerian Prince' Email Scams Still Rake in over $700,000 a Year—Here's How to Protect Yourself." CNBC. April 18, 2019. https://www.cnbc.com/2019/04/18/nigerian-prince-scams-still-rake-in-over-700000-dollars-a-year.html.

Li, Selena. "Explainer: China Unionpay, Russia's Potential Payments Backstop." Reuters. April 21, 2022. https://www.reuters.com/business/finance/china-unionpay-russias-potential-payments-backstop-2022-04-21.

Lieber, Ron. "Tips to Keep Your Bank from Closing Your Account." *New York Times.* November 28, 2023, Section B, p. 1.

Lieber, Ron, and Tara Siegel Bernard. "Payment Data Could Become Evidence of Abortion, Now Illegal in Some States." *New York Times*. June 29, 2022. https://www.nytimes.com/2022/06/29/business/payment-data-abortion-evidence.html.

Lieber, Ron, and Tara Siegel Bernard. "Dumped by a Bank: Why Accounts Suddenly Close." *New York Times*. November 5, 2023, Section BU, p. 1.

Lombard, Amy. "The Rise of Stealth Shopping." *Wall Street Journal*. July 16, 2024.

Mastercard. "2022–2023 U.S. Region Interchange Programs and Rates." 2022. https://www.mastercard.us/content/dam/public/mastercardcom/na/us/en/documents/merchant-rates-2022-2023-apr22-2022.pdf.

McCoy, Terrence. "Isis Just Stole $425 Million, Iraqi Governor Says, and Became the 'World's Richest Terrorist Group.'" *Washington Post*. June 12, 2014. https://www.washingtonpost.com/news/morning-mix/wp/2014/06/12/isis-just-stole-425-million-and-became-the-worlds-richest-terrorist-group.

McNally, Tracey. "2010 Census Enumeration at Transitory Locations Quality Profile." June 2012. https://www.census.gov/content/dam/Census/library/publications/2012/dec/2010_cpex_209.pdf.

Michaels, Dave, and Inti Pacheco. "FTC Eyes Firms' Use of Data to Personalize Pricing." *Wall Street Journal*. July 24, 2024. https://www.wsj.com/business/ftc-to-examine-if-companies-raise-prices-using-consumer-surveillance-d7921be1.

Miyake, Fusa, Kentaro Nagaya, Kimiaki Masuda, and Toshio Nakamura. "A Signature of Cosmic-Ray Increase in Ad 774-775 from Tree Rings in Japan." *Nature* 486, no. 7402 (2012): 240-42.

Mohammed, Rafi. "How Retailers Use Personalized Prices to Test What You're Willing to Pay." *Harvard Business Review* (October 20, 2017). https://hbr.org/2017/10/how-retailers-use-personalized-prices-to-test-what-youre-willing-to-pay.

de Montjoye, Yves-Alexandre, Laura Radaelli, Vivek Kumar Singh, and Alex Sandy Pentland. "Unique in the Shopping Mall: On the Reidentifiability of Credit Card Metadata." *Science* 347, no. 6221 (2015): 536–39.

Morse, Susan Cleary, Stewart Karlinsky, and Joseph Bankman. "Cash Businesses and Tax Evasion." *Stanford Law & Policy Review* 20, no. 1 (2009): 37–67. https://law.stanford.edu/publications/cash-businesses-and-tax-evasion.

Myer, Greg. "In an Ongoing Race, Ukraine Tries to Repair Faster Than Russia Bombs." *Morning Edition*. December 6, 2022.

Natasha Frost, Mitra Taj, and Eric Nagourney. "Tsunami Claims 2 Lives in Peru; World Awaits News from Tonga." *New York Times*. January 17, 2022. A. https://www.nytimes.com/2022/01/16/world/asia/tonga-tsunami-peru.html.

National Bank of Ukraine. "About E-Hryvnia, the Digital Currency of the National Bank of Ukraine." 2021. https://bank.gov.ua/en/payments/e-hryvnia.

National Reserve Bank of Tonga. "Financial Services Demand Side Survey Tonga." 2016. www.reservebank.to/index.php/financials/financial-access/dss.html.

National Reserve Bank of Tonga. "The Official Launching of the National Reserve Bank of Tonga's Domestic Electronic Payment System." 2022. http://www.reservebank.to/data/documents/Media/PR/2022/NRBT_PR_DEPSLaunched_ENG.pdf.

Neate, Rupert. "Payment in Gold Bullion Banned under New Law to Combat Tax Evasion." *The Guardian*. August 7, 2017. https://www.theguardian.com/politics/2017/aug/07/payment-in-gold-bullion-banned-under-new-law-to-combat-tax-evasion.

Needleman, Sarah, and Sarah Donaldson. "Kids Don't Want Cash Anymore—They Want 'Robux'." *Wall Street Journal*. December 4, 2022. https://www.wsj.com/articles/robux-kids-virtual-currency-metaverse-cryptocurrency-11669929636.

Nelson, Jacqueline. "Corruption and Cognac: China's Crackdown Hits Luxury." *The Globe and Mail*. August 20, 2014. https://www.theglobeandmail.com/report-on-business/international-business/corruption-and-cognac-chinas-crackdown-hits-luxury/article20146104.

"New Reality Check: The Paycheck to Paycheck Report." Pymnts.com. August/September 2022. https://www.pymnts.com/wp-content/uploads/2022/08/PYMNTS-New-Reality-Check-August-September-2022.pdf.

Newman, Eric. "Counterfeit Continental Currency Goes to War." *The Numismatist* 1 (January 1957): 5–16.

Newman, Eric. "The Successful British Counterfeiting of American Paper Money During the American Revolution." *British Numismatic Journal* (1958). https://www.britnumsoc.org/publications/Digital%20BNJ/pdfs/1958_BNJ_29_18.pdf.

Ngcobo, S. Sandile, Thokozile Masipa, and Mahlape Sello. *Report of the Section 89 Independent Panel* (Vol. 1: Parliament of the Republic of South Africa). November 30, 2022. https://www.parliament.gov.za/storage/app/media/Links/2022/november/30-11-2022/33659%20SECTION%2089%20INDEPENDENT%20PANEL%20Volume%201.pdf.

Nilson. "Card Fraud Worldwide." December 2021. https://nilsonreport.com/newsletters/1232/.

NOAA. "Billion-Dollar Weather and Climate Disasters." National Centers for Environmental Information. 2024. https://www.ncei.noaa.gov/access/billions/.

North Bay/North Coast Broadband Consortium. "Telecommunications Outage Report: Northern California Firestorm 2017." April 2018. https://www .tellusventure.com/downloads/safety/nbncbc_report_2017_firestorm_tele-com_outages_10may2018.pdf.

Nouchi, Rui, Yasuyuki Taki, Hikaru Takeuchi, Takayuki Nozawa, Atsushi Sekiguchi, and Ryuta Kawashima. "Reading Aloud and Solving Simple Arithmetic Calculation Intervention (Learning Therapy) Improves Inhibition, Verbal Episodic Memory, Focus Attention and Processing Speed in Healthy Elderly People: Evidence from a Randomized Controlled Trial." *Frontiers in Human Neuroscience* 10 (2016). https://www.frontiersin.org/articles/10.3389/fnhum.2016.00217/full.

Office of Cybersecurity, Energy Security, and Emergency Response. "*Electric Disturbance Events (Oe-417) Annual Summaries.*" U.S. Department of Energy. 2024. https://www.oe.netl.doe.gov/oe417_annual_summary.aspx.

Office of Management and Budget. "Historical Tables, Table 4.1 – Outlays by Agency: 1962–2027." 2024. https://www.whitehouse.gov/omb/budget/historical-tables/.

Okunogbe, Oyebola, and Victor Pouliquen. "Technology, Taxation, and Corruption: Evidence from the Introduction of Electronic Tax Filing." *American Economic Journal: Economic Policy* 14, no. 1 (2022): 341–72. https://doi.org/10.1257/pol.20200123.

"An Old Swindle Revived." *New York Times.* March 20, 1898. https://timesma-chine.nytimes.com/timesmachine/1898/03/20/issue.html.

Olson, Carly. "Ukraine Bans Some Russian Music and Books." *New York Times.* June 19, 2022. https://www.nytimes.com/2022/06/19/world/europe/ukraine-bans-russian-music-books.html.

Ozili, Peterson K. "Using eNaira CBDC to Solve Economic Problems in Nigeria: Revolutionizing Financial Services and Markets Through FinTech and Blockchain." May 13, 2023. https://ssrn.com/abstract=4447036.

Park, Joowon, Clarence Lee, and Manoj Thomas. "Why Do Cashless Payments Increase Unhealthy Consumption? The Decision-Risk Inattention Hypothesis." *Journal of the Association for Consumer Research* 6, no. 1 (2021): 21–32.

PayPal. "Annual Report/10-K." 2023. https://investor.pypl.com/financials/annual-reports/default.aspx.

Porter, Richard, and Ruth Judson. "The Location of U.S. Currency: How Much Is Abroad?" *Federal Reserve Bulletin* 82, no. 10 (1996): 883–903.

Prasad, Eswar. "Cash Will Soon Be Obsolete. Will America Be Ready?" *New York Times.* July 22, 2021. https://www.nytimes.com/2021/07/22/opinion/cash-digital-currency-central-bank.html.

Prelec, Drazen, and George Loewenstein. "The Red and the Black: Mental Accounting of Savings and Debt." *Marketing Science* 17, no. 1 (1998): 4–28. http://www.jstor.org.ezproxy.bu.edu/stable/193194.

Prelec, Drazen, and Duncan Simester. "Always Leave Home Without It: A Further Investigation of the Credit-Card Effect on Willingness to Pay." *Marketing Letters* 12, no. 1 (2001): 5–12. http://www.jstor.org.ezproxy.bu.edu/stable/40216581.

Pressler, Jessica. "The Hustlers at Scores." *New York Magazine.* December 27, 2015. https://www.thecut.com/2015/12/hustlers-the-real-story-behind-the-movie.html.

Princewill, Nimi. "Phone and Internet Shutdown in Nigerian State Enters Sixth Day as Security Forces Target Kidnappers." CNN. September 9, 2021. https://www.cnn.com/2021/09/09/africa/phone-services-suspended-zamfara-intl/index.html.

Qian, Nancy, and Jaya Wen. "The Impact of Xi Jinping's Anti-Corruption Campaign on Luxury Imports in China." *Kellogg School of Business Working Paper.* 2015.

Quaden, Guy. "Costs, Advantages and Drawbacks of the Various Means of Payment." *Economic Review*, National Bank of Belgium (June 2006): 41–47. https://ideas.repec.org/a/nbb/ecrart/y2006mjuneiip41-47.html.

Raczkowski, Konrad, and Bogdan Mróz. "Tax Gap in the Global Economy." *Journal of Money Laundering Control* 21 (2018): 545–54. https://doi.org/10.1108/JMLC-12-2017-0072.

Raszewski, Eliana. "Argentina Revives 'Soy Dollar' FX Rate until Year-End to Boost Reserves." Reuters. November 25, 2022. https://www.reuters.com/article/grains-argentina-soy-fx/argentina-revives-soy-dollar-fx-rate-until-year-end-to-boost-reserves-idUSKBN2SF1GB.

Reuters. "The Long Power Restoration Process in Puerto Rico." October 30, 2017. https://www.reuters.com/article/usa-puertorico-power-timeline/timeline-the-long-power-restoration-process-in-puerto-rico-idINL2N1N51KV/.

Reuters. "Tonga and Its Volcanic Eruption." January 18, 2022. https://www.reuters.com/business/environment/tonga-its-volcanic-eruption-2022-01-18/.

Rhodes, Karl. "The Counterfeiting Weapon." *Richmond Federal Reserve: Region Focus*, First Quarter. 2012. https://www.richmondfed.org/-/media/RichmondFedOrg/publications/research/econ_focus/2012/q1/pdf/economic_history.pdf.

Richtel, Matt. "Egypt Cuts Off Most Internet and Cell Service." *New York Times*. January 29, 2011. https://www.nytimes.com/2011/01/29/technology/internet/29cutoff.html.

Richter, Wolf. "Hey Greece: Tax Fraud Is a National Sport in Germany Too." *Business Insider*. April 1, 2012. https://www.businessinsider.com/final-spasm-greco-teutonic-tax-wrestling-2012-3.

Rick, S. I. "Tightwads and Spendthrifts: An Interdisciplinary Review." *Financial Planning Review* 1, no. 1–2 (2018): e1010. https://doi.org/10.1002/cfp2.1010.

Rogoff, Kenneth. "Costs and Benefits to Phasing out Paper Currency." In *NBER Macroeconomics Annual 2014*. NBER Macroeconomics Annual series, no. 29. Chicago: University of Chicago Press, 2014, 445–56.

Rogoff, Kenneth. *The Curse of Cash*. Princeton University Press, 2016.

Rogoff, Kenneth, and James McAndrews. "Should We Move to a Mostly Cashless Society?" *Wall Street Journal*. September 24, 2017. https://www.wsj.com/articles/should-we-move-to-a-mostly-cashless-society-1506305220.

Rose, Jonathan. "Understanding the Speed and Size of Bank Runs in Historical Comparison." *Economic Synopses* 12. Federal Reserve Bank of St. Louis. 2023. https://doi.org/10.20955/es.2023.12.

Ross, Tom, and Neal Lott. "A Climatology of 1980–2003 Extreme Weather and Climate Events." National Climatic Data Center. 2003. https://www.ncdc.noaa.gov/monitoring-content/billions/docs/lott-and-ross-2003.pdf.

Rossi, Peter E., Robert E. McCulloch, and Greg M. Allenby. "The Value of Purchase History Data in Target Marketing." *Marketing Science* 15, no. 4 (1996): 321–40. http://www.jstor.org.ezproxy.bu.edu/stable/184168.

Rothbard, Murray. *History of Money and Banking in the United States: The Colonial Era to World War II*. Ludwig von Mises Institute, 2002.

Rowland, Michelle. "Press Conference: Ban on Use of Credit Cards for Online Wagering." April 28, 2023. https://minister.infrastructure.gov.au/rowland/interview/press-conference-ban-use-credit-cards-online-wagering.

Sammut-Bonnici, Tanya, and Derek F. Channon. "Pricing Strategy." In *Wiley Encyclopedia of Management*, Cary Cooper, ed. Wiley, 2014. https://www.um.edu.mt/library/oar/bitstream/123456789/21817/1/sammut-bonnici%20pricing%20strategy.pdf.

Sanger, David. "Ignoring Sanctions, Russia Renews Broad Cybersurveillance Operation." *New York Times*. October 25, 2021. https://www.nytimes.com/2021/10/25/us/politics/russia-cybersurveillance-biden.html.

Saxe, Geoffrey. "The Mathematics of Child Street Vendors." *Child Development* 59, no. 5 (1988): 1415–25. https://doi.org/10.2307/1130503.

Schmacker, Renke, and Sinne Smed. "Sin Taxes and Self-Control." *American Economic Journal: Economic Policy* 15, no. 3 (2023): 1–34. https://doi.org/10.1257/pol.20200479.

Schneider, Friedrich. "Restricting or Abolishing Cash: An Effective Instrument for Fighting the Shadow Economy, Crime and Terrorism?" International Cash Conference 2017. Island of Mainau, Germany. 2017. https://www.econstor.eu/bitstream/10419/162914/1/Schneider.pdf.

Schuh, Scott, Oz Shy, and Joanna Stavins. "Who Gains and Who Loses from Credit Card Payments? Theory and Calibrations." *Boston Federal Reserve Research Department Public Policy Discussion Papers* 10-3 (2010). https://www.boston-fed.org/publications/public-policy-discussion-paper/2010/who-gains-and-who-loses-from-credit-card-payments-theory-and-calibrations.aspx.

Shachmurove, Yochanan. "The Premium in Black Foreign Exchange Markets: Evidence from Developing Economies." *Journal of Policy Modeling* 21, no. 1 (1999): 1–39.

Siegel Bernard, Tara, and Lieber Ron. "No Answers When Banks Cut You Off." *New York Times.* April 8, 2023, Section B, p. 1.

Simmons, Matty. "The First Credit Card Ever." *Saturday Evening Post.* April 2016. https://www.saturdayeveningpost.com/2016/04/day-cash-died.

Slater, Cliff. "General Motors and the Demise of Streetcars." *Transportation Quarterly* (1997): 45–66. https://babel.hathitrust.org/cgi/pt?id=mdp.39015047411684&view=1up&seq=368.

Smatrakalev, Georgi. "Is Tax Evasion Our National Sport? The Bulgarian Case." In *The Ethics of Tax Evasion: Perspectives in Theory and Practice*, ed. Robert W. McGee. Springer, 2012, 371–85.

Smith, Adam, and Richard Katz. "US Billion-Dollar Weather and Climate Disasters: Data Sources, Trends, Accuracy and Biases." *Natural Hazards* 67, no. 2 (2013): 387–410. https://doi.org/10.1007/s11069-013-0566-5.

Soman, Dilip. "The Effect of Payment Transparency on Consumption: Quasi-Experiments from the Field." *Marketing Letters* 14, no. 3 (2003): 173–83. http://www.jstor.org.ezproxy.bu.edu/stable/40216497.

St. Clair, David. "Los Angeles Public Transit in the 1930s: The All-Bus Proposal. "*International Journal of Business, Humanities and Technology* 10, no. 3 (2020). 10.30845/ijbht.v10n3p1.

State of Hawaii. "Update on Price Freeze for Commodity Sales, Landlord-Tenant Guidance for the Island of Maui." September 25, 2023. https://cca.hawaii.gov/blog/7thproclamationpricefreezelt/.

State of Wisconsin. "Credit / Debit Card Processing for Online Applications," 2010. https://doa.wi.gov/budget/SCO/creditdebit%20flowchart.pdf.

Supreme Court of the United States. *Supreme Court of the United States Opinion 16-1454 Ohio v. American Express Co.* June 25, 2018. https://www.supreme-court.gov/opinions/17pdf/16-1454_5h26.pdf.

Sutton, Willie, and Edward Linn. *Where the Money Was.* Viking Press, 1976.

Swedish Civil Contingencies Agency. "If Crisis or War Comes." 2022. https://rib.msb.se/filer/pdf/30307.pdf.

Tait, Robert. "'Isis' Half-a-Billion-Dollar Bank Heist Makes It World's Richest Terror Group." *The Telegraph.* June 14, 2014. https://www.telegraph.co.uk/news/worldnews/middleeast/iraq/10899995/ISIS-half-a-billion-dollar-bank-heist-makes-it-worlds-richest-terror-group.html.

Taylor, Jack. *Corporation Income Tax Brackets and Rates, 1909-2002.* Internal Revenue Service, Statistics of Income, 2003. https://www.irs.gov/pub/irs-soi/02corate.pdf.

Thaler, Richard H. "Toward a Positive Theory of Consumer Choice." *Journal of Economic Behavior & Organization* 1 (1980): 39–60. http://dx.doi.org/10.1016/0167-2681(80)90051-7.

Thomas, Manoj, Kalpesh Kaushik Desai, and Satheeshkumar Seenivasan. "How Credit Card Payments Increase Unhealthy Food Purchases: Visceral Regulation of Vices." *Journal of Consumer Research* 38, no. 1 (2011): 126–39.

Tobias, Ben. "Is Attacking Ukraine's Power Grid a War Crime?" *BBC News.* December 1, 2022. https://www.bbc.com/news/world-europe-63754808.

Toder, Eric. "Reducing the Tax Gap: The Illusion of Pain-Free Deficit Reduction." Urban Institute and Urban-Brookings Tax Policy Center. July 3, 2007. https://www.urban.org/research/publication/reducing-tax-gap-illusion-pain-free-deficit-reduction.

Tong, Scott. "China's National Sport: Tax Evasion?" APM Marketplace. April 9, 2010. https://www.marketplace.org/2010/04/09/chinas-national-sport-tax-evasion.

Transparency International. "Corruption Perceptions Index 2022," 2023. https://images.transparencycdn.org/images/Report_CPI2022_English.pdf.

Treasury Inspector General for Tax Administration. "The Internal Revenue Service's Bank Secrecy Act Program Has Minimal Impact on Compliance."

September 24, 2018. https://www.tigta.gov/reports/audit/internal-revenue-services-bank-secrecy-act-program-has-minimal-impact-compliance.

Turco, Marco, Sonia Jerez, Sofia Augusto, Patricia Tarín-Carrasco, Nuno Ratola, Pedro Jiménez-Guerrero, and Ricardo M. Trigo. "Climate Drivers of the 2017 Devastating Fires in Portugal." *Scientific Reports* 9, no. 1 (2019): 13886–88.

Turkish Statistical Institute. "Consumer Price Index, January 2023." February 3, 2023. https://data.tuik.gov.tr/Bulten/Index?p=consumer-price-index-january-2023-49655&dil=2.

UK Finance. "UK Payment Markets Summary 2022." July 16, 2024. https://www.ukfinance.org.uk/system/files/2022-08/UKF%20Payment%20Markets%20Summary%202022.pdf.

U.K. Gambling Commission. "Gambling on Credit Cards to Be Banned from April 2020." January 14, 2020. https://www.gamblingcommission.gov.uk/news/article/gambling-on-credit-cards-to-be-banned-from-april-2020.

United Nations. "Report and Recommendations Made by the Panel of Commissioners Concerning Part One of the Second Instalment of Individual Claims for Damages Above US$100,000 (Category "D" Claims)." Compensation Commission Governing Council. 1998. https://digitallibrary.un.org/record/265103.

United Nations. "Estimating Illicit Financial Flows Resulting from Drug Trafficking and Other Transnational Organized Crimes." Office on Drugs and Crime. October 2011. https://www.unodc.org/documents/data-and-analysis/Studies/Illicit_financial_flows_2011_web.pdf.

United Nations. "Population Facts, Department of Economic and Social Affairs, No. 2019/4." September 2019. https://www.un.org/development/desa/pd/sites/www.un.org.development.desa.pd/files/files/documents/2020/Feb/un_2019_factsheet4.pdf.

United Nations. "World Drug Report 2021" (Vol. Sales No. E.21.XI.8). Office on Drugs and Crime. 2021. https://www.unodc.org/unodc/en/data-and-analysis/wdr-2021_booklet-3.html.

US Senate. "Facilitating Fraud: How Consumers Defrauded on Zelle Are Left High and Dry by the Banks That Created It." Office of Elizabeth Warren. October 2022. https://www.warren.senate.gov/imo/media/doc/ZELLE%20REPORT%20OCTOBER%202022.pdf.

Urban, Carly, and Olivia Valdes. "Why Is Measured Financial Literacy Declining and What Does It Mean? Maybe We Just "Don't Know." *Insights: Financial Capability* (2022): 13. https://finrafoundation.org/sites/finrafoundation/files/Why-Is-Measured-Financial-Literacy-Declining.pdf.

Uretsky, Elanah. *Occupational Hazards: Sex, Business, and HIV in Post-Mao China*. Stanford University Press, 2016.

USDA Forest Service. *The Great Fire of 1910*. Author, 2013. https://www.fs.usda.gov/Internet/FSE_DOCUMENTS/stelprdb5444731.pdf.

U.S. Energy Information Administration. *Electric Power Monthly*. Author, 2024.

Valentino-DeVries, Jennifer, Jeremy Singer-Vine, and Soltani Ashkan. "Websites Vary Prices, Deals Based on Users' Information." *Wall Street Journal*. December 24, 2012.

Vanderford, Richard. "AI Experts Warn of Potential Cyberwar Facing Banking Sector." *Wall Street Journal*. March 22, 2022. https://www.wsj.com/articles/ai-experts-warn-of-potential-cyberwar-facing-banking-sector-11647941402.

Vieira, Paul. "What Is the Freedom Convoy?" *Wall Street Journal*. February 16, 2022. https://www.wsj.com/articles/freedom-convoy-canada-trucker-protest-what-11644441237.

Vigna, Paul. "What to Know About the Hidden Costs of Digital Currency." *Wall Street Journal*. December 18, 2021. https://www.wsj.com/articles/crypto-and-its-many-fees-what-to-know-about-the-hidden-costs-of-digital-currency-11639825202.

Visa. *The Visa System: Rates, Fees and Rules*. Author, 2024. https://usa.visa.com/support/small-business/regulations-fees.html.

Vrushi, Jon. *Global Corruption Barometer: Asia 2020*. Transparency International, 2020. https://images.transparencycdn.org/images/GCB_Asia_2020_Report_Web_final.pdf.

Wahlquist, Calla, and Donna Lu. "Zaporizhzhia Nuclear Power Plant: Everything You Need to Know." *The Guardian*. March 4, 2022. https://www.theguardian.com/world/2022/mar/04/zaporizhzhia-nuclear-power-plant-everything-you-need-to-know.

Walker, Joseph. "Cuban's Pharmacy Seen as Medicare Cost-Saver." *Wall Street Journal*. June 21, 2022.

Wallace, David, "Solar Storm Knocks out Farmers' High-Tech Tractors – An Electrical Engineer Explains How a Larger Storm Could Take Down the Power Grid and the Internet." *The Conversation*. March 18, 2022. https://theconversation.com/solar-storm-knocks-out-farmers-high-tech-tractors-an-electrical-engineer-explains-how-a-larger-storm-could-take-down-the-power-grid-and-the-internet-177982.

Waller, Governor Christopher J. "CBDC: A Solution in Search of a Problem?" August 5, 2021. https://www.federalreserve.gov/newsevents/speech/waller20210805a.htm.

Wallerstein, Eric. "How a Hack Shook Wall Street's Multitrillion-Dollar Foundations." *Wall Street Journal*. November 19, 2023. https://www.wsj.com/finance/regulation/how-a-hack-shook-wall-streets-multitrillion-dollar-foundations-6a574bd7.

Waters, Maxine. "Chairwoman Maxine Waters' Statement on Status of Stablecoin Legislation." July 27, 2022. https://democrats-financialservices.house.gov/news/documentsingle.aspx?DocumentID=409710.

Webster, Karen. "Seven Years Later, Only 6% of People with iPhones in the US Use Apple Pay in-Store When They Can." September 7, 2021. https://www.pymnts.com/apple-pay-tracker/2021/7-years-later-6pct-people-with-iphones-in-us-use-apple-pay-in-store.

Wetzel, Corryn. "Solar Storm Knocks 40 SpaceX Satellites out of Orbit." *Smithsonian Magazine*, February 14, 2022. https://www.smithsonianmag.com/smart-news/solar-storm-knocks-40-spacex-satellites-out-of-orbit-180979566/.

White, Lindsey, and David Hayes. "Hurricane Maria: 1 Year on, Puerto Rican Bankers Recall a 'Desperate Time'." *S&P Global*. October 16, 2018. https://www.spglobal.com/marketintelligence/en/news-insights/latest-news-headlines/hurricane-maria-1-year-on-puerto-rican-bankers-recall-a-desperate-time-46927776.

Williams, Sean. "How Apple Pay Could Become Consumers' Worst Nightmare." *NASDAQ*, September 26, 2014. https://www.nasdaq.com/articles/how-apple-pay-could-become-consumers-worst-nightmare-2014-09-26.

Willingham, Daniel. "Ask the Cognitive Scientist: Do Manipulatives Help Students Learn?" *American Educator* (Fall 2017). https://www.aft.org/ae/fall2017/willingham.

Wolfe, Rachel. "Tipping at Self-Checkout Has Customers Crying 'Emotional Blackmail'." *Wall Street Journal*. May 8, 2023. https://www.wsj.com/articles/tipping-self-checkout-restaurants-airports-c3e09f7.

World Bank. "World Development Report 2016: Digital Dividends." 2016. https://documents1.worldbank.org/curated/en/896971468194972881/pdf/102725-PUB-Replacement-PUBLIC.pdf.

World Meteorological Organization. "Weather-Related Disasters Increase over Past 50 Years, Causing More Damage but Fewer Deaths." August 31, 2021a. https://public.wmo.int/media/news/weather-related-disasters-increase-over-past-50-years-causing-more-damage-fewer-deaths.

World Meteorological Organization. *WMO Atlas of Mortality and Economic Losses from Weather, Climate and Water Extremes (1970–2019)*. Geneva, 2021b. https://library.wmo.int/index.php?lvl=notice_display&id=21930.

World Trade Organization. "International Tourism to Reach Pre-Pandemic Levels in 2024." *World Tourism Barometer* 22, no. 1 (2024). https://www.e-unwto.org/doi/epdf/10.18111/wtobarometereng.2024.22.1.1.

Zagorsky, Jay. "Do Individuals Know How Much They Are Worth?" *Financial Counseling and Planning*, 11, no. 1 (2000).

Zagorsky, Jay. "Bitcoin Is Now 'Legal Tender' in El Salvador – Here's What That Means." *The Conversation*. September 2, 2021. https://theconversation.com/bitcoin-is-now-legal-tender-in-el-salvador-heres-what-that-means-167099.

Zagorsky, Jay. "Americans Leave a Huge Chunk of Change at Airport Security Checkpoints — Here's What It Means for the Debate over Getting Rid of Pennies." *The Conversation*. May 20, 2024a. https://theconversation.com/americans-leave-a-huge-chunk-of-change-at-airport-security-checkpoints-heres-what-it-means-for-the-debate-over-getting-rid-of-pennies-229958.

Zagorsky, Jay. "Target Just Became the Latest Us Retailer to Stop Accepting Payment by Checks. Why Have So Many Stores Given up on Them? *The Conversation*. July 16, 2024b. https://theconversation.com/target-just-became-the-latest-us-retailer-to-stop-accepting-payment-by-checks-why-have-so-many-stores-given-up-on-them-234616.

Zami, Muhammad Tahmid. "Bangladesh's Internet Shutdown Isolates Citizens, Disrupts Business." Reuters. July 26, 2024. https://www.reuters.com/world/asia-pacific/bangladeshs-internet-shutdown-isolates-citizens-disrupts-business-2024-07-26.

Zelalem, Zecharias. "Six Million Silenced: A Two-Year Internet Outage in Ethiopia." Reuters. September 28, 2022. https://www.reuters.com/article/ethiopia-internet-shutdown-idAFL8N2ZM09X.

Zellermayer, Ofer. "The Pain of Paying." PhD thesis, Carnegie Mellon. 1996. https://www.researchgate.net/publication/280711796_The_Pain_of_Paying.

Zraick, Karen. "Sweetgreen Scraps Its Cashless Policy as Criticism Grows." *New York Times*. April 25, 2019. https://www.nytimes.com/2019/04/25/business/cashless-stores-sweetgreen-amazon-go.html.

INDEX

Page numbers followed by *f* and *t* refer to figures and tables, respectively.